NEW YORK REVIEW BOOKS
CLASSICS

A VISIT TO DON OTAVIO

SYBILLE BEDFORD (1911–2006) was born Sybille von Schoenebeck in Charlottenburg, Germany, to an aristocratic German father and a partly Jewish, Hamburg-born mother. Raised variously in Germany, Italy, France, and England, she lived with her mother and Italian stepfather after her father's death when she was seven, and was educated privately. Encouraged by Aldous Huxley, Bedford began writing fiction at the age of sixteen and went on to publish four novels, all influenced by her itinerant childhood among the European aristocracy: *A Legacy* (an NYRB Classic), *Jigsaw* (short-listed for the 1989 Booker Prize), and *A Favourite of the Gods* and *A Compass Error* (forthcoming from NYRB in a single volume in 2017). She married Walter Bedford in 1935 and lived briefly in America during World War II, before returning to England. She was a prolific travel writer, the author of a two-volume biography of her friend Huxley, and a legal journalist, covering nearly one hundred trials. In 1981 she was awarded the Order of the British Empire.

BRUCE CHATWIN (1940–1989) was born in Sheffield, England. He was appointed a director of Sotheby's at age twenty-five, but left to study archaeology at the University of Edinburgh and soon began a career as a travel writer for *The Sunday Times Magazine*. His 1977 book *In Patagonia* is considered a classic in the field of travel writing, and his 1988 novel, *Utz*, was short-listed for the Man Booker Prize.

A VISIT TO DON OTAVIO
A Mexican Journey

SYBILLE BEDFORD

Introduction by
BRUCE CHATWIN

NEW YORK REVIEW BOOKS

New York

A VISIT TO DON OTAVIO
A Mexican Journey

SYBILLE BEDFORD

Introduction by
BRUCE CHATWIN

NEW YORK REVIEW BOOKS

New York

THIS IS A NEW YORK REVIEW BOOK
PUBLISHED BY THE NEW YORK REVIEW OF BOOKS
435 Hudson Street, New York, NY 10014
www.nyrb.com

First published in Great Britain in 1953 as *The Sudden View: A Mexican Journey*
by Victor Gollancz Ltd, London. Reprinted, with slight revisions, in 1960 as *A
Visit to Don Otavio* by William Collins Sons & Co. Ltd, London.

Library of Congress Cataloging-in-Publication Data
Names: Bedford, Sybille, 1911–2006.
Title: A visit to Don Otavio : a Mexican journey / by Sybille Bedford ;
  introduction by Bruce Chatwin.
Other titles: Sudden view
Description: New York : New York Review Books, 2016. | Series: New York
  Review Books classics | Autobiographical. | Originaly published: London :
  Gollancz, 1953. | Description based on print version record and CIP data
  provided by publisher; resource not viewed.
Identifiers: LCCN 2015038517 (print) | LCCN 2015037857 (ebook) | ISBN
  9781590179703 (epub) | ISBN 9781590179697 (alkaline paper)
Subjects: LCSH: Mexico—Description and travel. | Bedford, Sybille,
  1911–2006—Travel—Mexico.
Classification: LCC F1215 (print) | LCC F1215 .B4 2016 (ebook) | DDC
  917.204—dc23
LC record available at http://lccn.loc.gov/2015038517

ISBN 978-1-59017-969-7
Available as an electronic book; ISBN 978-1-59017-970-3

Printed in the United States of America on acid-free paper.
10 9 8 7 6 5 4 3 2 1

Contents

Introduction   ix

PART ONE
In Search of a Journey

I   New York to Nuevo Laredo   3
II   Mesa del Norte – Mesa Central – Valle de
      Mexico   23
III   Mexico City: First Clash   34
IV   Mexico City: Climates and a Dinner   45
V   Mexico City: The Baedeker Round   52
VI   Coyacán: Tea and Advice   62
VII   Mexico City: The Past and the Present   70
VIII Cuernavaca   75
IX   Morelia – Pazcuaro – A Hold-Up   87
X   Money and the Tarrascan Indians   109
XI   Guadalajara   118

PART TWO
Don Otavio

I   San Pedro Tlayacán   131
II   A Well-Run House   141
III   Tea with Mr Middleton   148
IV   Le Diner en Musique   155
V   Mrs Rawlston's First Appearance   162
VI   Bridge with Mrs Rawlston   168

VII Don Enriquez Unfolds a Plan   178
VIII Doublecrossings   204
IX   A Family and a Fortune   212
X   A Party   217
XI   Mazatlán: An Ordeal   221

PART THREE
Travels

I   Guanajuato or Sic Transit   239
II   Querétaro: A Modest Inn   247
III The Emperor Maximilian at Querétaro   254
IV   Cuernavaca – Acapulco – Taxco   278
V   Oaxaca: Mitla and Monte Albán   288
VI   Oaxaca: Some Agreeable People   292
VII Puebla: A General and a Ship   299
VIII Tuscueca: The Last of the Journeys   311

PART FOUR
The End of a Visit

I   Return to San Pedro   327
II   Clouds   333
III A Trip in the Jungle: Mr Middleton Wins 336
IV   Local Medicine   350
V   The Best of All Possible Worlds   354

INTRODUCTION

AMONG THE many mysteries of twentieth-century publishing is the fact that Sybille Bedford's *A Visit to Don Otavio* could ever have gone out of print. For when the history of modern prose in English comes to be written, Mrs Bedford will have to appear in any list of its most dazzling practitioners. 'Travel books' (that meaningless category!) did admittedly go through a slump in the 1960s, while many pretentious and unreadable novels remained in print. But then this is no more a travelogue than Turgenev's *Sportsman's Sketches* is a book about shooting woodcock. It is a novel in the best sense – the sense of something 'new and fresh' – and, as such, it belongs among her three more or less autobiographical novels that begin with *A Legacy*. It is a story of release from the claustrophobia of living in wartime New York; it tackles that most intractable of subjects, Mexico (where so many literary reputations have come to grief); and ends up with the portrait of one unforgettable Mexican, Don Otavio de X y X y X.

'Of course it's a novel,' Mrs Bedford once said to me. 'I wanted to make something light and poetic . . . I didn't take a single note when I was in Mexico . . . If you clutter yourself with notes it all goes away. I did, of course, send postcards to friends, and when I started writing, I called them in.'

She is a most lively and articulate woman, resolutely blind to the commonplace, whose three inseparable passions are writing, friendship, and the finest claret. She was born in Germany some years before the First War, yet seems to have been born on the move. Her mother was a compulsive wanderer of bohemian temperament and varied nationality. Her father was a south German baron, the 'friend of all the best chefs in London and Paris', who, when she was six, taught her how not to overcook his *haricots verts* and how to recognize a great vintage: 'It would never have occurred to my father that a child of six would not have a palate.'

He died a year later – whereupon she was bundled off to her mother in Italy, and then shipped off to England 'for so-called education which did not take place'. Later, as a young girl adrift in the south of France, she steeped herself in Baudelaire, Stendhal, Flaubert – and read none of the great English classics. Aldous Huxley first encouraged her to write and, under his influence, she wrote (but never published) 'three portentous novels of ideas'. When the war came, she escaped from France to North America; and when the war was over, she travelled south to Mexico: 'I had a great longing to move, to hear another language, eat new food; to be in a country with a long nasty history in the past and as little present history as possible. Surely there was scope in the Americas, the New World that had touched the imagination of the Elizabethans?'

There is no point in trying to summarize the trials, sights, tastes, and delicious surprises of Mrs Bedford's 'Wonder Voyage', nor to comment on the uncluttered lucidity of her style. It is simply a book of marvels, to be read again and again and again. She never stoops to satire. She is never facetious, never pontificates, never makes use of the cheap ironic asides that are the stock-in-trade of the travelling writer. Even when expounding the murky chronicles of

Mexico – whether of Montezuma and Cortés, the Emperor Maximilian and Benito Juárez, or the more recent Marxist revolutionaries – she never moralizes or scores a political point. What she does convey – here and in all her novels – is that everything is problematic; and that the human condition consists of millions and millions of people being tossed up and down the earth, trying vainly to connect but somehow being prevented from doing so.

– BRUCE CHATWIN

A VISIT TO DON OTAVIO

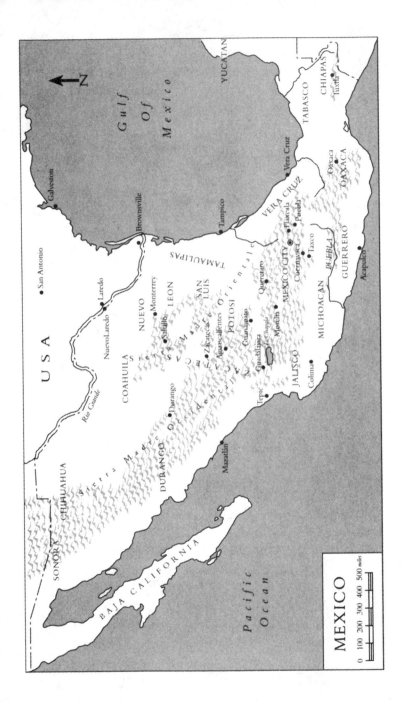

To
Esther Murphy Arthur
and to
Allanah Harper

Part One

IN SEARCH OF A JOURNEY

Chapter One
NEW YORK TO
NUEVO LAREDO

O le pauvre amoureux des pays chimériques!

T HE UPPER part of Grand Central Station is large and splendid like the Baths of Caracalla.

'Your rooms are on Isabel la Catolica,' said Guillermo.

'How kind of you,' said I.

'Pensión Hernandez.'

'What is it like?'

'The manager is very unkind. He would not let me have my clothes when I was arrested. But you will have no trouble.'

'Whatever next,' said I.

'One cannot tell,' said Guillermo. His mother was a Mexican lady; his father, so Guillermo says, had been a Scotchman. Guillermo looked like an alley cat, not sleek; survival only seemed to be his forte. 'Friends will look after you.'

'What friends?'

'Friends. Very sweet and useful.' His louche fly's eyes swept the floor. 'Don't mention my name at the Pensión.'

'I suppose not.'

'Much better so,' said Guillermo.

After some years in the United States where a seat at a successful movie has to be booked six weeks in advance and hotel reservations are a matter of patience and cunning settled at the last minute by luck, one never expected to move freely again. You couldn't get into the Reforma at Mexico City for love or money, they told one at the American Express. One did not wish to get into the Reforma, one explained. Well, the Ritz was just as hard. At that point one gave up. Hence Guillermo, hence the Pensión Hernandez. Guillermo was lonely and serviceable and always rushed in to do the things one wanted in a way one did not want them done.

'Shall we have a little drink?' he said.

We were sitting in the station bar, waiting. There was a great deal of time. The bags were in the hands of porters and suddenly, after the rush of days, there was nothing more to do. We were receiving. That is people were dropping in to see us off and to buy us and each other drinks. People we had not seen for years. Arrival and Departure are the two great pivots of American social intercourse. You arrive. You present your credentials. You are instantly surrounded by some large, unfocused hopefulness. You may be famous; you may be handsome, or witty, or rich; you may even be amiable. What counts is that you are *new*. In Europe where human relations like clothes are supposed to last, one's got to be wearable. In France one has to be interesting, in Italy pleasant, in England one has to fit. Here, where intercourse between man and man is without degrees, *sans lendemain*, where foreign visitors are consumers' goods, it is a matter of turnover. You are taken up, taken out, shown around, introduced, given parties for, and bang, before you can say American Resident, it's farewell parties and steamer baskets. Your cheeks are kissed, your back is slapped, your hand is pressed; you are sent bottles and presents and flowers – you are Sailing. The great empty wheel of hospitality has come full circle.

These last days have atmosphere and intensity, there is a quantitative increase of everything, more parties, more people, drinks. And for all their slapdash bonhomie these agitations are not meaningless. The warmth, the sudden intimacies, the emotion, are not false, they are ritual. To Americans, sailing is a symbol. Of travel past and potential, of their peril and their safety, of isolation and flight. They stay and are safe; they too may go and prove themselves free. The dangerous, the coveted, the despised and admired continent of Europe lies only a few days across the sea. One's sailing drives it home. Farewells are vicarious magic: Americans still believe in *l'adieu suprême des mouchoirs.*

Between arrival and departure — if one is tactless enough to stay — there is a social no-man's-land in which one is left to make one's friends and lead one's life. The country is large and so is the choice. One's life and friends are rarely among the hospitable figures of the first whirling weeks. Some vanish, and, if one runs into them, are too kind to ask, 'You still around?' Instead they say, 'Call me some time.' 'Indeed I will,' one says, and that is that until another year. Others recede to fixtures, the unseen faces in the middle distance one meets through the winters at the same New York parties. One calls them by their Christian names, one hands each other drinks, but there is no impact.

When at last one leaves, one undergoes a social resurrection. Invitations and steamer baskets come rolling in as though one were the Sitwells and had only stayed five weeks. A partial resurrection in my case because leaving by land is not the game, and Mexico cuts little ice: the same continent, or almost.

The bar was air-cooled. Which means that first one feels cool, then one feels cold, then one begins to shiver. Then one feels warm again and rather clammy; then the air begins to taste of steel knives, one's ears begin to hum, it becomes hard to breathe; then one breaks into a cold sweat and then it is time to leave.

We emerged into the Hall of Mosaics. It was steaming like a Chinese laundry, the heat hit us on the head like a club. Summer in the large American cities is an evil thing. It is negative, relentless and dead. It is very hot. The heat, radiated by concrete and steel, is synthetic, involuntarily man-made, another unplanned by-product of the industrial revolution. This urban heat grows nothing; it does not warm, it only torments. It hardly seems to come from the sky. It has none of the charm and strength of the sun in a hot country. It is neither part of nature nor of life, and life is not adapted to it and nature recedes. In spirit and in fact, in architecture and habits, the eastern seaboard of the United States remains harshly northern, a cold country scourged by heat.

Through the day a grey lid presses upon the city of New York. At sunset there is no respite. Night is an airless shaft; in the dark the temperature still rises; heat is emanating invisible from everywhere, from underfoot, from above, from the dull furnaces of saturated stone and metal. The hottest point is reached in the very kernel of the night: each separate inhabitant lies alone, for human contact is not to be endured, on a mattress enclosed in a black hole of Calcutta till dawn goes up like a soiled curtain on the unrefreshed in littered streets and rooms.

This kind of suffering is quite pointless. It does not harden the physique, it just wears it out. Yet it goes on. Clerks dream of deep cold lakes, of a camp in the Adirondacks, a fishing shack in Maine where, the myth goes, you have to sleep under a blanket. But nobody does anything about it. Nobody knows what to do about it. There are already too many sheep in the pen.

We went underground, where the trains were champing in grey, concrete tunnels. Guillermo was still with us. Though not travelling, he carried a brown canvas bag. A porter tried to take it, Guillermo resisted. The bag clinked. He peered inside.

'I should have brought some paper,' he said.

I peered too. Half covered by a bath mat, there were some tooth-glasses, a quantity of hangers, loose mothballs, a metal teapot, bulbs and a roll of blotting paper.

'*Guillermo?*'

'From your apartment,' he said. 'Do not worry, my dear, your landlord cannot want these.'

Guillermo runs a rabbit warren of rooms in a condemned brownstone house in the East Thirties. This must be how he furnishes them.

The river-bound Island of Manhattan is not a junction but a cul-de-sac. Leaving New York by train is a somewhat crab-wise affair. We are bound south-west, but have to tunnel out due north. At 96th, one emerges into the upper air. The St Louis Express bowls along a kind of ramp above street level like any elevated railway. Harlem. 125th Street Station, that absurd small stop under corrugated iron near the housetops. The upper Hundreds. Low brick houses, washing in the casements, men in undershirts sweating out the long evening in rooms. Children on the pavements below hopping in and out of chalk circles in those old, old games. 205th Street. A man shaving by an open window. If one were on a boat, one would now be going down the Hudson. There would be the boat noises and the river noises. Perhaps the *Queen Elizabeth* would be in. One would sail past wharves and docks and warehouses and read the names of liners going to Rio and to China. One would smell the ocean and one would want the World. Then one would turn the Battery and there would be the famous skyline, just lighting up. It would be the New York of the splendid contours, not the New York of the sordid details, and one would probably be in tears.

As it was, one felt rather smug. And private. E. and I had managed to get a compartment to ourselves. They are only about a dollar more than a berth in the dormitory, but hard to come by. Off at last. I got out a pint of gin, a thermos with ice cubes, some Angostura and from a leather case the Woolworth glasses that had long replaced the silver-bound, cut-glass mugs with which our elders travelled about a better world, and made two large pink gins.

'Did someone tip the boy from Bellows?' said E.

'I didn't. Did you return the book to Mr Holliday?'

'I forgot. How awful.'

'There is nothing we can do about it now.' What respite, what freedom! We were in someone's anonymous and by assumption capable hands, the Great Eastern and Missouri Railroad's. There'd be four nights of it and almost four days. Four hours upright on a seat are a bore; eight damned long, twelve frightful. A difference in degree is a difference in kind: four days on a train are an armistice with life. And there is always food. I had packed a hamper and a cardboard box. Whenever I can I bring my own provisions; it keeps one independent and agreeably employed, it is cheaper and usually much better. I had got us some tins of tunny fish, a jar of smoked roe, a hunk of salami and a hunk of provolone; some rye bread, and some black bread in cellophane that keeps. That first night we had fresh food. A chicken, roasted that afternoon at a friend's house, still gently warm; a few slices of that American wonder, Virginia ham; marble-sized, dark red tomatoes from the market stands on Second Avenue; watercress, a flute of bread, a square of cream cheese, a bag of cherries and a bottle of pink wine. It was called Lancer's Sparkling Rosé, and one ought not be put off by the name. The wine is Portuguese and delicious. A shining, limpid wine, full almost, not growing thin and mean on one in the way of many rosés. It has the further charm of being bottled in an earthenware jug, so that once cooled it stays nicely chilled for hours. I drew the cork with my French Zigzag. The neatest sound on earth.

'Have an olive,' I said.

With a silver clasp-knife I halved the tomatoes. A thread of oil from a phial, two crushed leaves of basil. 'Have you seen the pepper?'

I took the wooden mill from its case. It was filled with truffle-black grains of Tellichery. I snuffed them. That pepper mill must be the last straw. The gods could not smile on it. A friend once told me about a dachshund who used to be led about the streets of Paris on a red leash. He wore a trim red coat and in the coat was a pocket and out of the pocket peeped a handkerchief with the dachshund's initials. It proved more than canine flesh and blood could stand. He was set upon by a dog without a collar and bitten through the neck. I often felt for that dachshund.

The journey was decided at the last moment. I was not at all prepared for Mexico. I never expected to go to Mexico. I had spent some years in the United States and was about to return to England. I had a great longing to move, to hear another language, eat new food; to be in a country with a long nasty history in the past and as little present history as possible. I longed in short to travel. Surely there was scope in the Americas, the New World that had touched the imagination of the Elizabethans. Canada? One did not think of Canada. The Argentine was too new and Brazil too far. Guatemala too modern, San Salvador too limited. Honduras too British. I chose Peru.

It filled the bill and had for me the most delirious associations. Saint Rose of Lima. Peruvian architecture: rich façades, glowing and crumbling, the colour of biscuits soaked in Romanée-Conti. These must have been illustrations, but to which book? Massine in his prime, dancing the Peruvian in Gaietés Parisiennes. He came on in black ringlets and white satin breeches bearing a parrot cage in one hand and in the other a carpet-bag with the word PERU embroidered on it in beads, and everybody went mad with joy. There was also a character I identified myself with for years: 'You may not know me under this humble disguise but I am Don Alonzo d'Alcantarra, the son of Don Pedro. One day my knock shall be heard at the gates of Lima and warn the noble youth of Peru that Don Alonzo has returned to the city of his fathers!' I had come upon this stirring masterpiece at the age of seven and for some reason, I forget whether it was grown-up intervention or missing pages, I was not able to finish it. Meanwhile Don Alonzo 'practised absolute immobility of his facial muscles to conceal his noble purpose from the world', and so did I. I took this to mean not moving anything in one's face at all, and used to sit for what seemed a long time trying not to bat an eyelid. It was very difficult and I did not succeed.

Oh yes, Peru, decidedly Peru. I set out to tour the travel agencies with energy. They showed little, but proffered what turned out to be an extremely expensive air ticket to Lima. I could not afford it. There were no boats to Chile for the next six months. Then I sported with the idea of going to Uruguay. A friend from Montevideo who loved Italy had talked and left a sense of opera and red plush, late hours and delicious food, an impression that this city bore the burden of urbanity with something of the casual grace of Rome. The friend also talked of a freighter. The freighter did not materialize. I was not tempted by Mexico then, if anything vaguely put off by the artiness of the travel literature. At the point of total discouragement, E. M. A. joined me in my pursuit of shopping for a country. Her ardour was tempered. E.'s life is history and politics; she used to appear on Radio Forums described as Traveller and Commentator. She detests travelling, or rather she has neither aptitude nor tolerance for the mechanism of actual travel in progress.

'Perhaps I ought to see something of my native continent,' she said; 'although, frankly, I never felt the slightest desire to see Latin America.'

An agency, at which I had my name down, offered train reservations to Mexico City for the end of the week. We took them.

That afternoon I went down to the Public Library on 42nd Street, and returned with the diary of Madame Calderon, Fanny Inglis, the Scotchwoman who married the first Spanish Ambassador to Mexico and spent two amazed years in that country in the 1830s. Later, Madame Calderon became governess to one of the various children of Queen Isabella. She stood up to the court of Madrid for some twenty years, followed an Infanta into exile and at the return of the Bourbons to Spain, was created, like that other royal governess, Mme de Maintenon, a marchioness. She died in the

Palace at Madrid at the age of eighty-one of a cold she had caught at a dinner party. Her Mexican diary is of the same stuff. The full title is *Life in Mexico, A Residence Of Two Years In That Country*, by Madame Calderon de la Barca. It came out in England in 1843, was prefaced by Prescott himself, became a best-seller at once, and was praised in the *Edinburgh Review*. I read *Life in Mexico* until dawn and have not thought of Peru since.

In the plains of Indiana, nature certainly has it. We have been going through the wheat fields for hours; miles upon miles of fat, yellow alien corn visibly ripening under a wide-awake sky. A spread of cruel wealth. Of human life and habitation there are few signs, no farm houses, no animals by the roadside.

What part does man play in the farming of these fields? Does he work the earth or does he operate it? Is he peasant, mechanic, or businessman? Perhaps here is the scene of his last defeat: eating tinned vegetables in a frame house, setting out in a tractor to cultivate his one-crop harvest mortgaged to the banks, he has been undone by a monstrous mating of nature with the machine.

Corrective: if the fields of Canada, the Middle West, the Argentine and the Ukraine were run like so many farms in the Home Counties, we'd all starve. Oh, double-faced truth, oh, Malthus, oh, compromise – there *are* too many sheep in the pen.

The beggar to Talleyrand, '*Monseigneur, il faut que je mange.*' Talleyrand to the beggar, '*Je n'en vois pas la nécessité.*' Ah, that is Talleyrand's word against the beggar's.

★

E., who is gregarious, has gone to the club car ostensibly in search of coffee. I am lying on the lower berth, my paraphernalia littered about me, trying to forget that we shall have to change trains at St Louis later in the afternoon. Patience cards, writing board, mineral water, brandy flask, books. *Terry's Guide to Mexico*; Miss Compton-Burnett's *Elders and Betters*; *Howards End*; *Decline and Fall*; *Horizon* and the *Partisan Review*; Hugo's *Spanish*; *The Unquiet Grave*; two detective stories, one of them an Agatha Christie and, what rarity, unread. I know that I am comfortable, at peace with myself. I know that this is a victory or an outrage. Am I enjoying this moment? I know of it, perhaps that is enough.

Still, the fields of Indiana stretch. The past is everywhere; the fragile present already the past. Paul Pennyfeather strolls through injustice like Candide; the tragedies of Ivy Compton-Burnett throw Sophoclean light on the workings of men, women and fate; Palinurus has his hand on our feeble pulse, and Mr Forster's connecting seems the last answer. They have all touched truth.

E. has come back from the club car, very cross. It appears that this state is dry in a particularly thorough-going manner. Not only that you cannot get a drink on the train, you cannot even order what is called a set-up, soda water and ice being suspected of one use only. E. was told to wait until we have crossed the state line. It is all very confusing. Oklahoma and Kansas are bone dry, that is everybody drinks like fishes. In Vermont you are rationed to two bottles of hard liquor a month. In Pennsylvania you cannot get a drink on Sunday; in Texas you may only drink at home, in Georgia only beer and light wines, in Ohio what and as much as you like but you have to buy it at the Post Office. Arizona and Nevada are wet but it is a criminal offence to give a drink to a Red Indian. In New York you cannot publicly consume anything on a Sunday morning but may have it sent up to an hotel bedroom. And nowhere, anywhere, in the Union can you buy, coax or order a drop on Election Day.

The Mississippi – to what child, what youth, is the word not rich in exotic longings? A river world of travel and far mornings . . .

'Comme je descendais des Fleuves impassibles,
Je ne me sentis plus guidé par les haleurs:
Des peaux-rouges criards les avaient pris pour cibles,
Les ayant cloués nus aux poteaux de couleurs.

. . . .

Les Fleuves m'ont laissé descendre où je voulais . . .'

And now, here, through the windows of our closed carriage, inexorably apart, we see the broad, slow stream, flowing, tranquil, between willowed banks through a country of remote and heroic beauty. Untouched, the great, sad landscape floats by the train in silence; grave, darkly green, pastoral on a majestic scale, piercing the heart with melancholy, with separateness and foreboding. A way we shall never be. Will this June day not close? Oh, the heavy, drawn-out loneliness of the American evening.

An elderly man comes shuffling down the aisle. He steadies himself at our table. 'Have a shot, sister,' he holds up a quart of Bourbon, 'you look as if you need it.'

'Thanks,' I say, 'I do,' and reach for the bottle with the ubiquitous, the inevitable nightly gesture of the country.

We are now on the through train to Mexico City. It is called the Sunshine Special, and is a slowish, shabby sort of train. We no longer have a compartment, only a section of a sleeping car, which means a lower and an upper bunk in one of those faintly comic dormitories known from the films, where men and women undress and sleep, buttoned inside curtained recesses. In day time bed, draperies and partitions are somehow doubled back and tucked away in a cumbersome, ingenious manner, and the car takes on the aspect of a tram with tables. The arrangement is as old as the American railroads. The distances made it necessary to devise an inexpensive way for every person on the train to lay his head during the many nights. It is not bad at all. The air is cool and neutral, and although there are some forty people to a car, one is anonymously semi-private the way one would be on a large bus.

We felt like hot food that night and went to the dining car which turned out to be an apartment decorated with machine-carved Spanish Renaissance woodwork of astonishing gloom and ugliness. Dinner, which you are supposed to order like a deaf-mute, by scribbling your unattainable wishes on a pad of paper, was a nondescript travesty of food served with the quite imaginative disregard of what goes with what that seems to be the tradition of the American table d'hôte. The one starch and vegetable of the day is supposed to be eaten as an accompaniment to any of the main dishes on the menu. So if it is cauliflower and French-fried potatoes, cauliflower and French fried potatoes will appear on your plate whether you are having the Broiled Halibut Steak, the Corned-beef Hash, the Omelette or the Lamb Chops. I have seen – not eaten – such inspired misalliances as tinned asparagus tips and spaghetti curled around a fried mackerel. This is not a traveller's tale.

Last night somewhere in the depths of Arkansas, the machine broke down. Something went wrong with the air-cooling. It stopped, and as there is no way of letting in the outer air, the temperature in the car quietly rose to what we were later told was 110° Fahrenheit. When I woke I thought I was in the inside of a haystack, and of course delirious. Such a scene. Faces peering from behind curtains, calling for ladders and explanations; purple faces on the verge of apoplexy, livid faces gasping for air; babies squalling, men in underclothes struggling in upper bunks, angelic Negro porters helping ladies in kimonos down the aisle.

One woman went on sleeping through it all. 'Lady, lady,' a porter crooned to her, 'you's better wake up, lady, or you find you'self with a lily in you' hand.'

At last they had us all settled in an ice-cold day coach, with our clothes and belongings piled about us. We would probably catch pneumonia, for the moment we had escaped death. Meanwhile dawn was breaking, somebody suggested a drink of Coca-Cola braced with sal volatile. This was a new one on me. It certainly does you a power of good. The worst sufferers were the mothers, the formulas had curdled in their bottles and the little ones howled. No dining car until Texarcana. I offered to heat whatever needed heating over my spirit lamp.

'Just look at that,' said a mother, 'she can boil water whenever she wants to.'

One sagging executive treated another sagging executive to a disquisition on *our* rolling stock. E. joined them.

'Replacements—'

'Steel—'

'Priorities—'

'Commitments—'

'ERP—'

There is time for reflection in the galleys of Spain.

Dominion over his environment was supposed to be a hallmark of man. Now, that dominion is almost wholly vicarious, derived from the past ingenuity of others. In urban and industrial communities it is never direct, physical or spontaneous. Our implements are at twelve removes and we may all live to live inside so many thermos flasks. It may be well to remember how to use a pair of sticks and a stone.

They have promised us a new sleeping car at San Antonio.

We are late. There is a lot of shunting going on and everybody is tired. Texas since cockcrow. It's the size of France, the British Isles, the Netherlands, Spain and Portugal combined, as one was taught. Or was it France, the British Isles and Italy? It certainly seems too vast to be true. And flat. And empty. But rich, as I was told at least six separate times today. Oil, beef, grain. E. tells me that after seceding from Mexico, the Lone Star Republic sent a deputation to

Queen Victoria offering Texas to the Crown. Palmerston refused.

The new car has been coupled on. The conductor has allotted the sections and we are off again. It seems, however, that we are to sit up for the Customs at Laredo. Apparently we cannot be inspected by the Immigration in our bunks. We are hours late and nobody seems to know when we shall get to the border. We are passing by a straggle of frame houses, each house has a veranda with a crumpled man sitting in a rocking chair looking as exhausted as we feel.

Spires are piercing the shallow horizon. A cathedral? It turns out to be oil wells.

Another dinner in the dining car, which failed to cheer. It is midnight. Still no border. Only Texas.

The US Immigration has just been. Two men in shirtsleeves, informal, friendly.

They began by asking US citizens where they were born. Americans need no passports for coming and going by the continental borders of the States.

'Birmingham, Alabama, mister.'

'Terra Haute, Indiana.'

'Las Vegas, Nevada.'

'Walla Walla, Washington.'

'Little Temperance, Iowa.'

Those whose accents were too peculiar or who were what is called foreign-born produced birth certificates or driving licences. Nobody was deliberately made uncomfortable. The officials created no atmosphere beyond that of their employment.

They have sealed the train.

After another wait, the pointless frontier dithering where everybody's leisure is consulted except the passengers', we crossed the International Bridge over the Rio Grande. We are now technically in Mexico. It is two in the morning, and again nothing is happening.

We've been ordered into the dining car for the Mexican Passport Control. If the American authorities did not wish to see us in bed, the Mexicans cannot bear to see us seated. We form a queue. And there one stands in tedium and fatigue punctuated by waves of anxiety. Tablecloths and cutlery have been whisked away, the dining car has taken on the aspect of a court martial. The atmosphere is hostile. The officials are in military uniform. There are armed guards. Two over-belted and buckled officers with their caps on sit behind a table. At last everybody's turn comes. The officers make a point of speaking no English. Each separate, identical tourist card – the Mexican travel permit one acquires as a matter of course with one's ticket – is stared at. Now and then a finger comes down on the figure of somebody's birth date. But nothing frightful happens, could happen as one has been trying to tell oneself all the time; this is supposed to be a casual border, good neighbours all, with paths smoothed for the advertised-at tourist.

Back in the sleeping car, we are told to get off the train for the Customs inspection. Yes, with all our hand luggage. Overcoats too, and sponge bags. A gang of porters appears to drag these articles down for us. There is, we find, a special exorbitant tariff for these nocturnal services. So out we step into the subtropical night. Once more the heat is appalling. We are kept hanging around a squalid station for two hours while Red Indian Pygmies, male and female, dig into our bags in the manner of so many terriers burrowing down a hole.

The passengers are beginning to feel the strain. Many of them are elderly or with small children and most of them believed they were travelling for pleasure. They had been coaxed into this by the literature of the travel bureaux: a smiling Mexican in a cartwheel hat holding up a piece of pottery; a smiling brown boy in the surf at Acapulco holding up a speared fish; a smiling woman in a *rebozo* holding up a *rebozo*. At Nuevo Laredo there is not a smile to the square league. The American railroad men across the river at Laredo despise the Greasers; the Mexicans at Nuevo Laredo loathe the Gringos. The passengers, shoved about and resentful, remember what they used to say at school about people who were coloured and smaller than themselves. The Mexicans do not understand the passengers at all – great, enormous women most of them, going about on trains without hats or escorts, so rude too, what can they be doing it for? Not vows, surely, being all heretics. No one trusts anyone a millimetre.

That Customs inspection is a malevolent rigmarole. One fails to see its practical point. The peso is considered hard currency and Mexico has no money restrictions. Cigarettes, spirits, French scent, textiles, tea and coffee are all much cheaper in Mexico than in the United States, so no one would bother to bring them in as contraband. Everybody has registered their visible cameras. Indeed, it is revealed that few of these hopeful spinsters have brought much besides the print dresses, the one warm tailored suit and the raincoat prescribed by *Terry's Guide*, which most sensibly admonishes one to travel light, and it seems futile to suspect them of smuggling sewing machines, harvesters and electric washtubs. All they are bent on is spending their dollars on a huge loot of native arts and crafts, and bringing them home in original Mexican baskets. To subject the luggage of these benefactresses to those thorough and callous indiscretions can have no other purpose than using power and inflicting discomfort on the temporarily powerless by the temporarily powerful.

British passport officials sometimes bring to bear the pressure of their better clothes and accents on the elderly refugee fumbling in her handbag for that letter of invitation from the lady at Great Marlborough. Here, the passportees are borne down upon by the underpaid, the brutish and the ignorant. One might be in the Balkans or the East. For the individual there is more danger, more degradation, more delay, but also more *hope* – there is always the bribe. There is also no hope at all. Among Anglo-Saxon officials the decencies are at times replaced by loyalties; here, the decencies civic or human do not exist. There is corruption as a matter of course, cynicism without thought, ill-will as a first reaction, life and pain held cheap, and the invincible ignorance of man of man.

For E. and me the tussle of the night is not over. Returning to our section, we find the beds made up and two people asleep in them. It transpires that the Mexican personnel is not going to honour the change of cars made by the Americans at San Antonio. But what are we to do? Where are we to be? There are still some thirty hours to go to Mexico City.

Rubbed the wrong way, the conductor shrugs. We rush out on to the platform and demand to see the stationmaster. E. stamps her American foot, 'Third-rate country . . . Didn't want to come in the first place . . . The President of the Missouri Pacific shall hear of this. Mrs R . . .' Everybody looks quite blank. The train is about to leave. Not unnaturally, we are reluctant to be left at Nuevo Laredo and allow ourselves to be pushed into a third-class Mexican day coach. We stumble forward into a rank box. The door closes behind, and in the breaking light of dawn we find ourselves among huddled figures in a kind of tropical Newgate.

Chapter Two

MESA DEL NORTE – MESA CENTRAL – VALLE DE MEXICO

Regardez, après tout, c'est une pauvre terre

I T IS high morning. We wake to a fawn-coloured desert of sun-baked clay and stone. This is indeed a clean slate, a bare new world constructed of sparse ingredients – here and there a tall cactus like a candle, adobe huts homogeneous like molehills, and always one man walking, alone, along a ridge with a donkey.

We are headed south and we are climbing. Slowly, slowly the train winds upwards to the plateau of the Sierra Madre. Presently there are some signs of Mexican life, a promiscuity of children, pigs and lean dogs grubbing about the huts in the dust. How do they exist? There does not seem to be a thing growing they could possibly eat.

E. and I had been released early this morning. The turnkey appeared, beckoned, led us up the train and to a couple of upper berths in a sleeping car. Ours not to reason why. He held the ladder, we climbed into our bunks and sank into sleep. Now we find ourselves among a carful of fair boys and girls in trim shorts and crisp summer dresses. It is a private car chartered by a New Orleans school for a holiday. A cavalry officer from Monterrey and two overdressed Mexican ladies have also been pushed into their privacy. These handsome, mannerly Southerners and their chaperons are taking it like angels.

*

The first stop is a town called Saltillo. It is the capital of one of those lonely vast territories stretching from the US frontier roughly to the Tropic of Cancer: the states of Coahuila, Chihuahua, Baja California, Sonora and Durango, which are the limbo and ante-room to Mexico. Between them, the population is rather less than that of the city of Birmingham, which means that there is just about one person to every barren square mile. It is hot, stony, dry country, almost without rivers or rain, part desert, part mountain, part mining district. Innocent of art and architecture, yet innocent also of the amenities, these states are a kind of natural poor relations to the Western American ones across the border, and a reminder that a very large portion of the earth's surface is, if not uninhabitable, unattractive to inhabit. Some are born there, no one goes to Sahuaripa or Santa María del Oro except to drill a shaft, lay a railway or quell a rebellion.

We all get out on to a long dusty platform covered with Indios selling things to eat – men and women squatting on the ground over minute charcoal braziers stirring some dark stew in earthenware pots, boys with structures of pancakes on their heads, children dragging clusters of mangoes and bananas. There is no noise. Everything is proffered silently if at close quarters. Wherever I turn there is a brown hand holding up a single round white cheese on a leaf.

Since 1810 and Secession from Spain, Mexico has had a dozen full-blown constitutions and a larger number of Declarations of Independence and Reform. Many of the constitutions were modelled after that of the United States. In their time, some were called liberal, some radical, some centralizing. All were wonders of theoretical perfection; all followed

as well as initiated a great deal of bloodshed. The Constitutional Assembly would sit in a besieged mountain town while
two rebel generals advanced on it from the north; another
general of yet uncertain allegiance would be advancing from
the coast; there would be a Counter-President at Vera Cruz
and a revolt in Mexico City. There would be a Constitutional
Party and a Reform Party, an Agrarian Party and a Liberal
Party, there would be Church interests and Landowners'
interests and Creole interests, and the interests of foreign
capital. Some of these interests combined, others did not.
There would be an elected President whose election was
illegal, a constitutionally elected President who was murdered
after election, and a President by pronunciamento. One
would not be recognized by the American administration,
another not supported by British oil interests, a third would
be fought by the French. Between actual sieges and pitched
battles, liberators, reformers and upholders of the Faith rushed
about the countryside with armed bands, burning crops and
villages and murdering everyone in sight. Meanwhile the
people got more poor and more confused, and in turn more
angry, fatalistic, murderous or cowed. This millennium continued for a hundred and twenty years, from Hidalgo's revolt
against Spanish rule until Calles' suppression of the Spring
Revolution of 1929. Sometimes a general would be more
victorious than usual and have a chance to look round and
create order; sometimes more people would be involved in
the actual killing, sometimes less. BUT THERE WAS NEVER
ANY PEACE. The unhappy country only enjoyed two breathing spaces: the US–Mexican War of 1848 in which it was
defeated and lost half its territory, and the forty years'
despotism of the Diaz Dictatorship.

(Once more Providence spared Mexico. In the war of

1914, Germany drafted a secret note proposing an alliance against the United States, offering in return the restitution of what could hardly be called the Mexican Alsace-Lorraine, the states of Texas, Arizona, New Mexico, California, Utah and Nevada. In a moment of abstraction, Dr Albrecht, a member of the German Embassy, left the dispatch case with the draft in a carriage of the Third Avenue Elevated Railway of New York City. The contents were published in the *N. Y. World*. Mexico remained neutral.)

All through the pleasant lazy day, the slow southward climb; and, gradually, with it, the country unfolds, ingredients multiply. There are trees now, rain-washed, and fields; young corn growing in small patches on the slopes; and a line and another line of mountains, delicate on the horizon.

This is the state with the name of a saint, San Luís Potosí. Already there are glimpses, too fragmentary, of churches and ruins. We are still sealed in our air-cooling, but on the platforms between coaches one can stand and breathe the warm live air of summer. At any moment now we shall be passing, unrecorded, the Tropic of Cancer. It is here that we enter the *Tierra Templada*, the mild lands, and it is here that the known Mexico begins, the Mexico of the wonderful climate, the Mexico of history and archaeology, the traveller's Mexico. Here, between the Twenty-second Parallel and the Isthmus of Tehuantepec, between the Pacific and the Gulf, on the Mesa, in the two Sierras, down on the hot strips of coast and the flats of Yucatan: everything happened – the Aztecs and the Conquest, the Silver Rush and Colonial Spain, the Inquisition and the War of Independence, the Nineteenth Century of Revolutions and Hacienda Life, of the Church

Rampant and the Church at Bay; General Santa Anna, always treacherous, always defeated, rattling his wooden leg for office, and Juarez tough with Robespierrean obstinacy and virtue; the shadowy reign of Maximilian and the harsh, prosperous reign of Diaz; Civil War, Banditry, Partition of the Land, President Calles and President Cardenas, the Oil-rush and the March of US Time.

Here it is then, the heartland of Mexico, the oldest country in the New World, where Montezuma lived in flowered splendour among the lily-ponds and volcanoes of Tenochtitlán; where an arbitrary, finicking and inhuman set of concepts was frozen into some of the world's most terrifying piles of stone; where Cortés walked a year into the unknown, the blank unmeasured ranges of no return, with a bravery inconceivable in an age of doubt; where the silver was discovered that built the Armada, and the Spanish viceroys and judges sat stiff with gold and dignities, wifeless, among the wealth and waste and procrastination of New Spain; where the law's delay meant four years' wait for a letter from Madrid, where the plaster images of angels wore Aztec feathers, where bishops burnt mathematical data in public places and priests started a Boston Tea Party because they might not breed silkworms; where highwaymen shared their spoils with cabinet ministers, where a Stendhalian Indian second lieutenant had himself crowned Emperor at the age of twenty-four, and Creole ladies went to Mass covered in diamonds leading pet leopards; where nuns lived and died for eighty years in secret cupboards, where squires were knifed in silence at high noon, and women in crinolines sat at banquet among the flies at Vera Cruz to welcome the Austrian Archduke who had come to pit the liberalism of enlightened princes against powers he neither understood nor suspected while the messengers of treason sped already along the uncertain roads; where at the haciendas the family sat down to dinner thirty every day but the chairs had to be brought in from the bedrooms, where the peon's yearly wage was paid in small copper coin and the haciendado lost his crop in louis d'or in a week at Monte; where the monuments to the devouring sun are indestructible, where baroque façades are writ in sandstone, and the markets are full of tourists and beads.

Everything happened, and little was changed. There was the confusion, glitter and violence of shifting power but the birth and death rates remained unchecked. Indians, always other Indians, move and move about the unending hills with great loads upon their backs, sit and stare in the market place, hour into hour, then cluster into one of their sudden pilgrimages and slowly swarm over the countryside in a massed crawl in search of a new face of the Mother of God.

Someone has come in to say that we shall be in Mexico City some time tomorrow morning and not very late after all. Everybody is getting restless. I have laid out a patience on a table kindly cleared for me by the rightful occupants. Two boys are dithering by the sides of my seat. They are terribly polite.

'Please, ma'am, what kind of cards are these?'

They are very small patience cards that used to be made in Vienna before the war, and I dare say are made there again.

'Have you ever seen such cute cards, Jeff? Aren't they cute? Come and look at these cute cards, Fleecy-May. Miss Carter, ma'am, come and look at these cards, have you ever seen such cute cards, Miss Carter, ma'am?'

'Now, Braxton, you must not disturb the lady.'

'What kind of solitaire is this, ma'am?'

'Miss Milligan.' It is almost my favourite patience and it hardly ever comes out. It needs much concentration.

'My Grandpa does one just like that.'

'Oh the Jack, ma'am! The Jack of Diamonds on the Black Ten.'

'The Jack doesn't go on the Ten, dope, the Jack goes on the Queen. Doesn't the Jack go on the Queen, ma'am?'

'Braxton Bragg Jones, will you leave the lady alone,' says Miss Carter.

'Oh, not at all,' I say, 'it's perfectly all right. Please.'

It does not come out. I could still use the privilege of waiving, but Braxton Bragg and Jefferson are beginning to get bored with Miss Milligan. I am shamed into starting something quick and simple with a spectacular lay-out.

As the train moves through the evening, the country grows more and more lovely, open and enriched. There are oxen in the fields, mulberry trees make garlands on the slopes, villages and churches stand out pink and gold in an extraordinarily limpid light as though the windows of our carriage were cut in crystal.

I start a conversation — so good for one's Spanish — with the officer from Monterrey. Our exchange of the civilities takes this form.

'Where do you come from?' I am asked.

'America.'

'This is America.'

'From North America.'

'This is North America.'

'From the United States.'

'These are the United States, *Estados Unidos Mexicanos.*'

'I see. Oh dear. Then the Señora here,' I point to E., 'is what? Not an American? Not a North American? What is she?'

'*Yanqui. La Señora es Yanqui.*'

'But only North Americans are called Yankees . . . I mean only Americans from the North of the United States . . . I mean only North Americans from the States . . . North Americans from the North . . . I mean only Yankees from the Northern States are called Yankees.'

'*¿Por favor?*'

In happier days it used to be one's custom to read about a country before one went there. One made out a library list, consulted learned friends, then buckled down through the winter evenings. This time I did nothing of the sort. Yet there is a kind of jumbled residue; I find that at one time and another, here and there, I must have read a certain amount about Mexico. The kind of books that come one's way through the years, nothing systematic or, except for Madame Calderon, recent. Prescott's *Conquest* when I was quite young, and by no means all of it. Cortés' letters. Volumes on Maximilian and Carlota, none of them really good and all of them fascinating. Travel miscellany of the French Occupation always called something like *LE SIÈGE DE PUEBLA, Souvenir d'une Campagne ou Cing Ans au Mexique par un Officier de Marine en Retraite, Chevalier de la Légion d'Honneur, Attaché à l'État-Major du Maréchal Bazaine.* Excruciating volumes where sometimes a mad, enchanting detail of farm kitchen or highway robbery pierced through the purple lull of pre-impressionist descriptions *où jallissaient les cimes majestueuses et enneigées du vénérable Popocatepetl.*

The writer who first made people of my generation aware of Mexico as a contemporary reality was D. H. Lawrence in his letters, *Mornings in Mexico* and *The Plumed Serpent. Mornings in Mexico* had a lyrical quality, spontaneous, warmed, like a long stroll in the sun. *The Plumed Serpent* was full of fear and violence, and Lawrence loudly kept the reader's nose to the grindstone: he *had* to loathe the crowds in the Bull Ring, he *had* to be awed by the native ritual. Perhaps the reality, for better or for worse, was Lawrence's rather than Mexico's. There were two realities actually. The *Mornings* were written down in the south at Oaxaca, in the Zapotec country; *The Plumed Serpent* in the west at Chapala, by a lake. I never liked *The Plumed Serpent.* It seemed portentous without good reason. *Something* was being constantly expostulated and one never knew quite what, though at times one was forced into accepting it at its created face value. And Lawrence's mysterious Indians, those repositories of power, wisdom and evil, remained after chapters and chapters of protesting very mysterious Indians indeed.

Nor were those stacks of *littérature engagée* particularly enlightening. One read one book and became convinced that the Mexican Indians lived outside the grip of economic cycles in a wise man's paradise of handicrafts; one read another and was left with the impression that they were the conscious pioneers of an awakening working class. There were villains – the Mexican Diet, so lowering; Drink; Oil; the Church; the Persecution of the Church; President Cardenas, so like Stalin and that Man in the White House. Panacea – Partition of the Land; Irrigation; Confiscation of Foreign Holdings; the Church; the Closing of the Church; President Cardenas, so like Lenin and F. D. R.

The thirties were the wrong time to be much stirred by the Diaz controversy: Good Don Porfirio or the Despot? One knew that he had been a practical man in a vulgar era, a champion of order and a business promoter in a land of sloth and anarchy, who jailed his opponents, cooked his elections and had no truck with the liberty of the press. It did seem rather mild and remote and old-fashioned; Diaz had been dead a long time and it was all very much in another country. Now I constantly hear his name on the train.

There is an air of expectancy in our coach, a feeling of the last night on board. The boys and girls are singing. The mistresses try to hush them but look awfully pleased themselves. The porter, however, is already banging up the beds. Everybody protests and it does no good. Pillow fights are in the air. I escape to the dining car for some beer. One of the mistresses – what is called a nice type of woman – has escaped too.

'What is it really like?' I ask her.

'Mexico? You will see marvels,' she said with a look of illumination.

Prompted by some excitement, I wake and decide to get up at seven which is not my habit. I struggle into some clothes inside my buttoned tent and go to the dining car where the windows are down at last and the air is flowing in clean and sharp, fresh with morning. And there under an intense light sky lies a shining plain succulent with sugar cane and corn among the cacti, a bright rich tropical country miraculously laved: green, green, green, the Valley of Mexico.

Chapter Three
MEXICO CITY: FIRST CLASH

A day or so must elapse before I can satisfy my curiosity by going out, while the necessary arrangements are making concerning carriages and horses, or mules, servants etc. . . . for there is no walking, which in Mexico is considered wholly unfashionable . . . nor is it difficult to forsee, even from once passing through the streets, that only the more solid-built English carriages will stand the wear and tear of a Mexican life, and the comparatively flimsy coaches which roll over the well-paved streets of New York will not endure for any length of time.

MADAME CALDERON DE LA BARCA

THE FIRST impact of Mexico City is physical, immensely physical. Sun, Altitude, Movement, Smells, Noise. And it is inescapable. There is no taking refuge in one more insulating shell, no use sitting in the hotel bedroom fumbling with guidebooks: it is here, one is in it. A dazzling live sun beats in through a window; geranium-scented whitewashed cool comes from the patio; eardrums are fluttering, dizziness fills the head as one is bending over a suitcase, one *is* eight thousand feet above the sea and the air one breathes is charged with lightness. So dazed, tempted, buoyed, one wanders out and like the stranger at the party who was handed a very large glass of champagne at the door, one floats along the streets in uncertain bliss, swept into rapids of doing, hooting, selling. Everything is agitated, crowded, spilling over; the pavements are narrow and covered with fruit. As one picks one's way over mangoes and avocado pears, one is tumbled into the gutter by a water-carrier, avoids a Buick saloon and a basin of live charcoal, skips up again scaring a tethered chicken, shies from an exposed deformity and bumps into a Red Indian gentleman in a tight black suit. Now a parrot shrieks at one from an upper window, lottery tickets flutter in one's face, one's foot is trodden on by a goat and one's skirt clutched at by a baby with the face of an idol. A person long confined to the consistent North may well imagine himself returned to one of the large Mediterranean ports, Naples perhaps: there are the people at once lounging and pressing, there is that oozing into the streets of business and domesticity; the show of motor traffic zigzagged by walking beasts; the lumps of country life, peasants and donkey carts, jars and straw, pushing their way along the pavements; there are the over-flowing trams, the size and blaze of the Vermouth advertise-ments, the inky office clothes, the rich open food shops strung with great hams and cheeses, and the shoddy store with the mean bedroom suite; the ragged children, the carved fronts of palaces and the seven gimcrack skyscrapers. Nothing is lacking: monster cafés, Carpet Turks, the plate-glass window of the aeroplane agency, funeral wreaths for sale at every corner and that unconvincing air of urban modernity. One looks, one snuffs, one breathes – familiar, haunting, long-missed, memories and present merge, and for a happy quarter of an hour one is plunged into the loved element of lost travels. Then Something Else creeps in. Something Else was always here. These were not the looks, not the gestures. Where is the openness of Italy, that ready bosom? This summer does not have the Southern warmth, that round hug as from a fellow creature. Here, a vertical sun aims at one's head like a dagger – how well the Aztecs read its nature – while the layers of the air remain inviolate like mountain streams, cool, fine, flowing, as though refreshed by some bubbling spring. Europe is six thousand miles across the seas and this glacier city in a tropical latitude has never, never been touched by the Mediterranean. In a minor, a comfortable, loopholed, mitigated way, one faces what Cortés faced in the absolute five hundred years ago: the unknown.

Well what does one do? Where does one begin, where does one turn to first? Here we are in the capital of this immense country and we know nothing of either. We don't know anybody. We hardly know the language. We have an idea of what there is to see, but we do not know where anything is from where, nor how to get there. We do not have much money to spend, and we have much too much luggage. Winter clothes and clothes for the tropics, town clothes and country clothes and the bottom of our bags are falling out with books. We have a few letters of introduction. They are not promising. From vague friends to their vague friends, Europeans with uncertain addresses who are supposed to have gone to Mexico before the war. Guillermo had pressed a letter into my hand at the station; a German name covered most of the envelope. 'Great friends,' he had said, 'they have had such trouble with their papers.' E. had been told to put her name down at the American Embassy. Nobody seemed to know any Mexicans. No one had written to people running a mine or a sugar place; or heard of some local sage, a Norman Douglas of the Latin Americas, who knew everything, the people and the stories, plants and old brawls, how to keep the bores at bay and where to get good wine.

God be praised we have a roof over our heads and it is not the roof of the Pensión Hernandez. The spirit that made us fall in with Guillermo's suggestion has waned, already there is a south-wind change. A man on the train told us about a small hotel, Mexican-run, in front of a park. To this we drove from the station, and found a Colonial palace with a weather-beaten pink façade. Of course there were rooms. We have a whole suiteful of them. Bedrooms and sitting room and dressing room, and a kind of pantry with a sink, a bathroom and a trunk closet and a cupboard with a skylight. Everything clean as clean and chock-full of imitation Spanish furniture, straight-backed tapestry chairs, twisty iron lamps with weak bulbs. There is a balcony on to the square and a terrace on to the patio. The patio has a pleasant Moorish shape; it is whitewashed, full of flowers, with a fountain in the middle and goldfish in the fountain, and all of it for thirty shillings a day.

The first step obviously is luncheon. Time, too, we were off the streets. That sun! E.'s face is a most peculiar colour. One had been warned to take it easy. One had been warned not to drink the water, to keep one's head covered, to have typhoid injections, beware of chilli, stay in after dark, never to touch ice, eat lettuce, butter, shellfish, goat cheese, cream, uncooked fruit . . . We turned into a restaurant. I had a small deposit of past tourist Spanish to draw on; it did not flow, but it was equal to ordering the *comida corrida*, the table d'hôte luncheon. Every table is occupied with what in an Anglo-Saxon country would be a party but here seems just the family. Complexions are either café-au-lait, nourished chestnut, glowing copper, or milky mauve and dirty yellow. Everybody looks either quite exquisite or too monstrous to be true, without any transitional age between flowering

37

ephebe and oozing hippopotamus. The male ephebes are dressed in extreme, skin-tight versions of California sports clothes, shiny, gabardiny, belted slack-suits in ice-cream colours, pistachio and rich chocolate; their elders are compressed in the darkest, dingiest kind of ready-made business outfits, and ladies of all proportions draped in lengths of sleazy material in the more decorative solid colours, blood-orange, emerald, chrome yellow, azure. There is a wait of twenty-five minutes, then a succession of courses is deposited before us in a breathless rush. We dip our spoons into the soup, a delicious cream of vegetable that would have done honour to a private house in the French provinces before the war of 1870, when two small platefuls of rice symmetrically embellished with peas and pimento appear at our elbows.

'*Y aquí la sopa seca.*' The dry soup.

We are still trying to enjoy the wet one, when the eggs are there: two flat, round, brown omelettes.

Nothing is whisked away before it is finished, only more and more courses are put in front of us in two waxing semicircles of cooling dishes. Two spiny fishes covered in tomato sauce. Two platefuls of beef stew with spices. Two bowlfuls of vegetable marrow swimming in fresh cream. Two thin beefsteaks like the soles of children's shoes. Two platters of lettuce and radishes in an artistic pattern. Two platefuls of bird bones, lean drumstick and pointed wing smeared with some brown substance. Two platefuls of mashed black beans; two saucers with fruit stewed in treacle. A basket of rolls, all slightly sweet; and a stack of tortillas, limp, cold, pallid pancakes made of maize and mortar. We eat heartily of everything. Everything tastes good, nearly everything is good. Only the chicken has given its best to a long and strenuous life and the stock pot, and the stewed fruit is too sticky for anyone above the age of six. The eggs, the stew, the vegetables, the salad, rice and beans are very good indeed. Nothing remotely equals the quality of the soup. We are drinking a bottled beer, called Carta Blanca, and find it excellent. At an early stage of the meal we had been asked whether we desired chocolate or coffee at the end of it, and accordingly a large cupful was placed at once at the end of the line with another basket of frankly sugared rolls. This *pan dulce* and the coffee are included in the lunch. The bill for the two of us, beer and all, comes to nine pesos, that is something under ten shillings.

It is four o'clock and the sun has not budged from its central position in the sky. We do not fool with hats and shade, but return to the hotel by cab. I close the shutters, lie down, and when I wake I do not know where I am nor where I was just now. I hardly know who I am. These pieces of escaped knowledge seem immediately paramount; hardly awake I struggle to fill the blanks as though it were for air. When identity is cleared, I cannot put a finger on my time, this is when? At last the place, too, clicks into place. It must have taken half a minute, a minute, to catch up with my supposed reality. It seemed much longer. One sleeps like this perhaps two or three times in a life and one never forgets these moments of coming to. That intense pang of regret. For what? The boundless promise of that unfilled space before memory rushed in? Or for the so hermetically forgotten region before waking, for the where-we-were in that sleep which we cannot know but which left such a taste of happiness? This time reaction is reversed, opportunity lies before not behind, adjustment is a joy. I am at the edge of Mexico – I rush to the window. It must have been raining. It has. This is the rainy season, and it does every afternoon from

May till October. The square looks washed, water glistens on leaves and the sky is still wildly dramatic like an El Greco landscape. Half the male citizenry is unbuttoning their American mackintoshes and shaking the water out of the brims of their sombreros; the other half is huddling in soaked white cotton pyjamas, their chins and shoulders wrapped in those thin, gaudy horse blankets known as *sarapes* in the arts and crafts. It is no longer hot, only mild like a spring evening. Two hours ago we were in August, now it is April.

I take a look at a plan and set out. I cross the Alameda, a rather glum squareful of vegetation cherished as a park. It was started, like so much else in Mexico, in honour of some anniversary of Independence, and its plant life seems to be all rubber trees. I come out into Avenida Juarez ablare with jukebox, movie theatre, haberdashery and soft-drink parlour. Our street, Avenida Hidalgo, was handsome if run-down – a length of slummy *palacios* with oddments of Aztec masonry encrusted in their sixteenth-century façades, and no shops but a line of flower stalls selling funeral *pièces montées*, huge wreaths and crosses worked with beads, filigree and mother-of-pearl skulls. The wrong side of the Alameda, we are later told. The right side looks like the Strand.

I walk on and am stunned by the sight of as amazing a structure as I could ever hope to see. It is the National Theatre and was obviously built by Diaz and in the early nineteen-hundreds. I had best leave the description of this masterpiece of eclecticism to *Terry*:

'El Teatro Naciónál, an imposing composite structure of shimmering marble, precious woods, bronze, stained glass and minor enrichments, stands on the E. end of the Alameda ... It ... cost upwards of 35 million pesos. The original plans, the work of the

40

Italian Adamo Boari (who designed the nearby Central Post Office) called for a National Theatre superior to any on the continent . . . The Palacio presents a strikingly harmonious blend of various architectural styles . . . When about half completed the enormously heavy structure began slowly to sink into the spongy subsoil. It has sunk nearly five feet below the original level.'

This sounds an optimistic note. But no, the Teatro Nacionál is no iceberg, there are still some three hundred feet to sink.

When I reach the centre it is quite suddenly night. On Avenida Francesco Madero − a murdered president − the shops are bright with neons. Wells Fargo, where I had hoped to collect some letters, keep American hours and are closed. Everything else is open and bustling. After the three-hour lunch, the siesta and the rains, a new lease of business begins at about eight. The food shops are as good as they look. Great sacks of coffee in the bean, York hams and Parma hams, Gorgonzolas, olive oil.

'May I buy all the ham I want?' I feel compelled to ask.

'How many hams, Señora?'

I have no intention of leaving this entrancing shop. It is as clean as it is lavish, and they are so polite . . . One might be at Fortnum's. Only this is more expansive: that warm smell of roasting coffee and fresh bread. And the wines! Rows and rows of claret, pretty names and sonorous names of *Deuxième Crus*, Château Gruaud-Larose-Sarget, Château Pichon-Longueville, Château Ducru-Beaucaillou, alas all are expensive. A tray of small hot pasties is brought in, *mille feuilles* bubbling with butter.

'*¿Qué hay en el interiór?*'

'Anchovy, cheese, chicken.'

I have some done up to take back to E. There is French brandy, Scotch whisky, Campari Bitter, none of them really ruinous, but none of them cheap. Decidedly, the local produce. I get a quart of Bacardi rum, the best, darkest kind. Five pesos. A peso is almost exactly a shilling. And a bottle of Mexican brandy. The name of this unknown quantity is appropriate, *Cinco Equis*, Five X's. It costs nine pesos and has three stars. We shall see.

As I leave the shop, a small child relieves me of my parcels. She does it with dignity, hinting that it is not so much her wish to earn a tip, as that it is not suitable for me to go about the streets with bottles done up in brown paper and half a dozen meat pasties dangling from my fingers by a string. I do not like being fetched and carried for by persons older or smaller than myself, but I realize that here I must submit to so comfortable a custom. There are more shops like the first, and thanks to my companion I am now free to enjoy them all. I buy a bottle of tequila (two pesos a quart and every pint guaranteed to give DTs), succumb to Campari, but resist Spanish Pernod. After these additions I have a suite. But it is always the first child who receives the parcels from my hands and distributes them among the other tots. We have some stilted conversation. A young man is sitting on the pavement outside a branch of His Master's Voice with six avocado pears for sale. He shifts them before him in a pattern and as they are moved about in the dusk the avocados look like trained mice. I buy his stock. He has nothing to wrap it up in, so my head child commandeers three passing babies with two empty hands each. The notion of having acquired half a dozen avocado pears for threepence makes me slightly light-headed. I do not buy the two puppies from the man who came rushing out of a church, but I buy a pineapple, a heap of papayas, a straw hat, some plums, some sweets for the porters (squeamishness about plain money to children), some hot chestnuts and some flowers: two armloads of tuberoses, and they too cost next to nothing. As we trail back through the business streets, Bolivar and Cinco del Mayo, and the pitch black Alameda, I feel like the Pied Piper. In the lobby, the children accept their fruit drops and pennies with self-possession. They thank me and express wishes for my well-being in this world and the next, *que Dios la proteja, que la vaya bien*, hand their parcels to a rather older hotel child and depart like well-bred guests at an Edwardian dinner party without haste or lingering.

I had the impression that the desk clerk was obscurely distressed by my purchases. Sure enough, ten minutes later we are visited by the housekeeper. She looks Spanish, one of those neat, middle-aged, efficient Latin women who are so much better at their linen cupboards than one can ever hope to be at anything. She does not come to the point. Does Mexico please us?

Oh, indeed.

'Yes, it is pretty.' We were not displeased by the rains?

We reassure her.

The hotel is also to our taste?

We try to say how pleased we are.

Yet those flowers. We did not like their flowers?

The vases were already filled with lilac and narcissus. Mexican hotels, that is Mexican-run hotels in Mexico, put flowers in their guest rooms with the towels and the bottle of drinking water. Fresh flowers every day, all year round. I try to explain that we had not been aware of this charming practice. We are not believed. The housekeeper leaves in a confusion of mutual apologies. Then the boy comes in from behind the door and bears away the lilac and narcissi. Next day, a great sheaf of tuberoses appears in my bedroom, and all during our stay there are fresh tuberoses every morning. I love them, and I am delighted.

Chapter Four

MEXICO CITY:
CLIMATES AND A DINNER

Glaciers, soleils d'argent, flots nacreux, cieux de braises . . .

THERE ARE three climatic zones in Mexico, one hot, one
cold, one temperate. The *Tierras Calientes, Fría* and
Templada. The Hot Zone is very hot, the Cold not as cold as
it sounds; the Temperate is celestial perfection.

It is also the most inhabited portion of the Republic – the
best part of the *Mesa Central* lies in *Tierra Templada*. Yet this
plateau is not a temperate place at all: the mildness is luxuriant
and dynamic, the temperance the product of the clash
between two intemperances. It is a tropical region anoma-
lously cool, combining the geographical extremes of Switz-
erland and Central Africa, high as Mont Blanc, equatorial as
the Sahara. At sea level, the Mexican latitudes would be
desert and jungle; in the north, the Mexican heights would
be alpine wastes. Joined, these excesses of parallel and altitude
created a perennial Simla better than Simla. As a matter of
recorded fact, the annual mean temperatures of the *Tierra
Templada* vary between 66° and 73° Fahrenheit. The average
rainfall is some 80 inches a year and concentrated within four
months, June to October. In terms of human experience this
means: it is always warm; it is never hot; it is never cold. It
only rains in season and when it does it pours at fixed and
regular hours, and afterwards the air again is dry and light,
leaves and fields shine, there is no damp, no mud, no dripping,
only a great new freshness.

45

Grey days are unknown. Except for a few minutes of dramatic preparation for the actual burst, the sky is always clear. There is little difference in the weather between July and February; it may get rather warm in the late spring and there are chilly evenings when the wind is blowing from the coast, yet a person with a change of clothes suitable for an exceptionally fine English June, a blanket and a hut made of waterproof leaves and bamboo canes would be comfortable day and night from one end of the year to the other. Ownership of a mud cottage and some pine cones for a fire around Christmas would assure a sybaritic existence. This opens, and shuts, economic vistas. A promoter from Germany, Gruening tells us in his wonderfully detailed *History of Mexico*, arrived some time in the nineteenth century full of business projects, and departed so disgusted that he wrote a long and angry volume on the natives' cursed lack of wants, their *verdammte Beduerfnigslosigkeit*. He should see them now, poor man, sipping their Coca-Colas.

The second zone is at sea level and frankly tropical. Hundreds of miles of jungle, beach and silted port on the Pacific. The Gulf, with Vera Cruz, the oil trade, coffee *fincas* and a certain commercial bustle. The deep south: Chiapas, Tabasco, Campeche – swamps and forests, the Graham Greene country of *The Lawless Roads*; Yucatán and the pre-Columbian ruins. The third zone is not a region but a number of separate points of especial altitude. It is a matter of exposure, on the whole every place above seven thousand feet is considered to be *Terra Fría*.

Thus Mexico City belongs to the cold land. It is, however, a rule unto itself. It has four distinct climates, one for the night – which is bitter – and three for every day. In the morning we are on the coast of New England. It is autumn.

A golden late September; the air is brisk but informed with warmth, luminous with sun. The kind of morning when one cannot bear to be in bed, when numbed insects stir to a new lease and one picks up one's teacup and walks out into the garden. Here the unexpected gift comes every day. Breakfast is laid in the patio: there is fruit, the absurd goldfish are swishing in the fountain and everything smells of geranium; warmth lies gently across one's shoulders; E. has ceased to talk politics, the housekeeper stops to chat, the boy comes running with hot rolls and butter . . . It is good to be alive.

At eleven, the climate becomes continental. It is the height of summer on the top of a mountain. The sun is burning, brilliant, not to be fooled with; the *fond de l'air* cool and flowing like fine water. One feels tremendously exhilarated, charged with energy. This is the time of day when I like to pick my way through the streets, walk slowly across the Cathedral Square under the shade of the brim of my hat. This full noon lasts for several hours. Then comes the cloudburst and through the early evening rain falls with the sound of rain falling in the hot countries all over the world, in Egypt, in Burma . . . Later, it is a spring evening in a large city: mild, tenuous, nostalgic, laid out to be long. It is not long. Darkness descends with a sudden extinguishing sweep like the cover on the canary's cage. Energy ebbs, the heart contracts with fear. This is no time to be out in the streets, this is the hour of return, of the house, the hearth, the familiar ritual. *Alors, il s'est retiré dans son intérieur.*

The hotel room is desolate, the lamp dim. There is nothing then but the panicked dash for the clean, well-lighted places.

There are none. The current is wretched all over the city. The story goes that the last president's brother is still selling power across the border. There are no cafés, no pubs, only bars for men and huge pastry shops. You do not dine before ten, unless you are willing to eat waffles in a pharmacy got up like a mosque at Sanborn's astonishing emporium; the cinemas waste no money on illumination; there is going to be a concert on Friday week . . . Some of the hotel bars are open to women. They are full of tourists and Mexicans emphatically without wives. Besides, this is not a good country to drink in: in daytime one does not want it at all, and at night one wants it too much.

We decide to have dinner at X's, a French restaurant that enjoys a reputation in the hemisphere. We push through the doors. One night in the early nineteen-thirties a friend was good enough to take me to a restaurant in London which in its day had been a very famous restaurant indeed. The list of its patrons was literary and glamorous, the wine and cooking admirable; it had a speakeasy cachet. Our elders and betters had talked and drunk there through the nights of the First War when they were young and notorious; they had dined there in the 'twenties when they were well known and middle-aged. It had had the honours of at least five contemporary novels. Let us call it Spisa's. I had never been there, and I believe it was my twentieth birthday, or the eve of my twentieth birthday. When we got to Spisa's the shutters were down, the dining room was dark and the owner dying. I mean literally dying. Mr S. was on his deathbed and the priest had just been. My friend was a face from better days, so they were much touched to see her at this hour. She was also a Catholic. They took her in to Mr S.'s where she stayed in prayer for some time. I was put into a parlour where an Austrian waiter and an Italian waiter were saying their rosaries. I had no rosary, but the Italian waiter went and found me one. Later they would not let us go but insisted that we have our dinner. They sent out for some chops and lager from the pub in Charlotte Street and made us eat it in the dining room. There was just one lamp lit above our table, otherwise it was quite dark. As we ate people came to us and whispered to my friend in Italian. I could see she had been weeping. Presently we walked home and later became quite unreasonably gay.

As E. and I pushed through X's swing-doors, there was just one lamp lit above one table. The waiters stood huddled in gloom. I sank into self-pity. I know it is futile to indulge in my regret that I came too late upon this earth to enjoy the pleasures of the table at Edwardian house parties, but to think what I missed in my own time – I have never been to the Chapon Fin at Bordeaux, I was too late for Voisin's at Paris, too late for Spisa's, and now too late for X of Mexico City. Then I pulled myself together: a fellow creature was dying; I still had no rosary but I was ready to pay such respects as I could.

A second lamp was lit with small effect above a second table, chairs were pushed back and one of those French menus, large as a poster, was laid before us decorously like a floral tribute. Service as usual? But no, the place was too preposterous: the hush, the darkness, the gloom; no funeral parlour in the USA could stay in business for a week with such an atmosphere. We had yet to learn that this was merely the regular nightly aspect of public eating places all over the Republic.

I must try a Mexican wine. I order a bottle of something called Santo Tomás. When poured out, it looks quite black. I sniff before tasting, so the shock when it comes is not as devastating as it might have been. I yell into the darkness to have the bottle removed.

The head waiter shuffles up gracefully. 'Anything wrong, Señora?'

'Taste it.'

He does. His face stays serene. Sheer self-control.

'There is something very wrong with this bottle. Taste it again.'

'? ? ? *es regular.*'

Regular? Cheap ink dosed with prune juice and industrial alcohol, as harsh on the tongue as a carrot-grater? Regular! What a country, what palates, what digestions. They refuse to change the Santo Tomás for another bottle of Mexican wine – rather disobliging of them I thought then – but insist that we take an imported wine instead. I choose a Spanish claret, one of the Marqués de Riscal's honest *riojas*. It is good, but it costs ten shillings a bottle, which is too much to pay for one's glass or two at dinner in a wine country. Perhaps, it begins to dawn on me, Mexico is not a wine country. It was by nature and in God knows what fashion before the Conquest; then the Spanish dug up the vines, the idea being to import wine from Spain and charge duty. For the same reason they cut down the olive trees and forbade the culture of silkworms. Oil, silk and wine were to New Spain what rum and tea were to Massachusetts and Maryland. After Independence, everybody was too busy murdering each other to plant vineyards and olive groves, and what is being produced now is only a new incentive to murder. Santo Tomás comes from some infernal valley in Baja California where the climate is so unsalubrious that the very grapes breed acid antidotes inside their skins. And what the Indios do not do to those grapes . . . Santo Tomás is the best wine in the Republic. For one thing it contains only a limited amount of syrup, and the vats are always rinsed after being scrubbed with turkey excrement. I learned to swallow my Santo Tomás, with a liberal admixture of water, like a man.

The service at X's is as regular as the lighting and the wine. To sit in the penumbra with nothing but death and Santo Tomás to occupy one's mind is unnerving. My cries rend the shadows for something to eat.

'Where is that Terrine we ordered? It must be ready.'

'It is ready. But the Prawns-and-Rice are not.'

'But we are having the Terrine first.'

'Yes, the Terrine comes first, but the Prawns are not ready.'

'We are not going to eat them at the same time. Please bring us the Terrine now.'

'Señora: we must wait for the Prawns. Then you will eat the Terrine first.'

'I mean first now, not first then.'

'Yes, Señora, first. First in a little while.'

'*Will you please bring the Terrine at once.*'

'At your taste, Señora. I shall run to tell the chef to hurry up the Prawns.'

We wait. Then the Terrine is brought over from the sideboard in the Stygian corner where it had been reposing, and here on its heels are the Prawns, sizzling. So much is clear now, everything is allowed to take its time but once your dinner is on its breathless way, there must be no pause. The custom must have ruined tempers and digestions. It is unfathomable, and it is bedrock.

Chapter Five
MEXICO CITY:
THE BAEDEKER ROUND

There were three masked balls at the theatre, of which we only attended one. We went about ten o'clock to a box on the pit tier, and although a pronunciamento *(a fashionable term here for a revolution) was prognosticated, we found everything very quiet and orderly, and the ball very gay and crowded.*

MADAME CALDERON DE LA BARCA

WE HAVE been to the Pensión Hernandez.

We were walking along Isabel la Catolica, a smart street in the business quarter, when we had to do the equivalent of taking cover, we flattened ourselves against a wall to avoid being crushed by a train of mules carrying boulders; the mules were flattening themselves against us to avoid being barged into by a motor hearse that was avoiding a tram. The tram, tramlike, pursued its way; we fell backwards through a door into a patio. Above our heads, like the finger of providence, was a plate saying *HERNANDEZ Casa de Huéspedes*.

One is sometimes less intrigued by the future than by what the past might have held. 'Let us go in,' I said; 'there may be letters.'

The pensión was on the third floor. An old Indian, barefoot and very clean, conveyed without uttering a single word that he was entirely at a loss as to who we were and what we had come for. He edged us into a sombre parlour. In the exact centre of this apartment stood a large, brand-new sewing machine. It was covered, like a concert grand, with a tapestried runner representing several phases of the life of Geneviva of Brabant in port-wine colours. On the runner was a vase with a neatly rounded bouquet made of artificial flowers and barbed wire. The remainder of the parlour was stocked like a cross between the votive chapel at Lourdes and a cupboard of Queen Victoria's presents. Everything was spotless. We spent a long time looking at water stoops, statues of the Virgin clothed in doll's dresses, bronze stags and leaning towers, and absolutely nothing happened. Then we opened the door. The Indian had gone. We began to walk downstairs. Something compelled us to look up. An exquisite apparition wrapped in a foulard dressing gown, looking as though it had been kept pinned in the glass case for rather a number of years, was leaning over the banisters.

We started. It spoke.

'You are the friends of Guillermo's,' it stated in Central European English.

We edged two steps down.

A second apparition from a butterfly collection appeared behind the first. 'I was shaving.'

'I adore New York,' said the first.

'I thought it was bailiffs,' said the second.

'Guillermo wrote to look you up,' said the first.

We put a foot on the landing.

'Do you know Bubi von der Witzleben?' said the second.

'They should go to Taxco,' said the first.

We had turned the landing. There was the door. We bolted.

The mules had passed. There was only an old man milking a goat into an empty tin of Campbell's Cream of Tomato, and a taxi. We took the taxi.

★

Concert at the Teatro Nacionál. Virtuosi from the USA. The National Orchestra. Brief Bach. Brahms. A contemporary suite, not brief at all, thumping with fiesta motives, failing to do for Mexico what Ravel does for Spain. The public is cosmopolitan provincial, like an afternoon audience at the Casino in Nice. At midnight, more stanzas of the national anthem are played than is usual elsewhere at such occasions. Then we disperse from the stuffy foyer into a remote and silent night, bitter as a night in the desert. On the pavement hundreds of Indios are curled in sleep.

The city has many open squares in which markets are continuously held and the general buying and selling proceeds . . . There are barber shops where you may have your hair washed and cut. There are other shops where you may obtain food and drink. There are street porters such as there are in Spain to carry packages. There is a great quantity of wood, charcoal braziers made of clay, mats of all sorts, some for beds and others more finely woven for seats, still others for furnishing halls and private apartments. All kinds of vegetables may be found there, in particular onions, leeks, garlic, cresses, watercress, borage, sorrel, artichokes, and golden thistles. There are many different sorts of fruit, including cherries and plums. They sell honey obtained from bees . . . All kinds of cotton threads in various colours may be bought in skeins . . . A great deal of chinaware is sold, including earthenware jars of all sizes for holding liquids, pitchers, pots, tiles and an infinite variety of earthenware all made of very special clay and almost all decorated and painted in some way. Maize is sold both as grain and in the form of bread . . . Pasties are made from game and fish pies may be seen on sale and there are large quantities of fresh and salt fish both in their natural states and cooked ready for eating. Eggs from fowls, geese, and all others may be had, and likewise omelettes ready made.

The last paragraph was written in 1520. It is part of a letter by Cortés to the Emperor Charles V on the Aztec capital as he found it on his first entry as a guest of Montezuma's. The description still serves.

When I join E., I find her at a table with a stranger and some bacardies.

'S., S.,' she cries across the room, 'this kind lady from Ponkah City wishes to know whether she should visit the Pyramid of the Moon?'

We end up all three eating the rather rustic luncheon – rice and pork, chickpeas and goat, and such portions – the Ritz serves for seven pesos in a tight, gilded back parlour.

Ribera's frescoes in Cortés' Palace are hard, flat and huge. The figures are flat, static and huge; the colours flat and drab. They are as narrative as the illustrations to the rhyme sheet, but without innocence. They have a dead serious overemphasis that results not in power but in boredom. The subject is a pageant of Mexican history culminating in the Apotheosis of the Revolution, a kind of Dialectical Last Judgement, one of the many remarkable features of which is the five times life size figure of the wife of Carlos Marx standing almost haloed, among the elect with the tool-bearing worker and the sheaf-laden peasant, while the Señora Doña María-Carmen Romero Rubio Diaz hovers on the other side in murky shadow with bankers and the members of the upper clergy.

★

'Can you make me a pair of these sandals?'

'No, Señora.'

'I mean, can you make me a pair of these sandals?'

'No, Señora.'

'But you do make sandals? '

'Yes, Señora.'

'Then why can't you make me a pair? '

'I made sandals yesterday.'

'That's no reason.'

'It is, Señora. I have got all I need.'

'All you need? You're not going to retire on yesterday's sandals? '

'Who knows, Señora? I have all I need now.'

The note of fear again.

The rains were late today and I was caught by them and darkness, alone and far from the shop-lit streets of the centre. One was aware of the presence of silent people sitting in doorways. Nothing happened, but I was seized by such a sense of desolation that several times I broke into a run. Once I thought that I had lost my way. I made the hotel and E. in the state of a person reaching shelter from a panic. It was half-past eight in the evening.

Homage to D. H. L.

'We have had a letter from Anthony,' said E. 'It is his vacation. He's going to join us.'

'How nice.'

'He's coming out to Mexico City by air.'

'We must wait for him.'

'Of course, we must.'
'Of course.'

It appears that we have been called upon by Rosencrantz and Guildenstern.

'Do make some sense out of the porter,' said E.

The porter said there were two gentlemen and these were their names.

We find their cards in our rooms upstairs.

Freiherr Karl-Heinz-Horst von Rautenburg zu Landeck
Baron Guenther von der Wildenau-Schlichtleben

'Golly,' said I. 'Pensión Hernandez.'
'The long louche arm of Guillermo,' said E.
'What do they want?'
'We shall see,' said E.

Already a week in Mexico City. One entire day we were gated by the housekeeper. Not exactly polling day, but some kind of recount of a previous election we gathered, perhaps incorrectly, from the papers.

'Yes, yes, an *eleccioncita*, a tiny election. It is of no matter,' said the housekeeper.

But why should we not go out? Was it not safe?

'Yes, safe. Very safe. Safe as safe. Only a little shooting. Quite safe. *But it is better to stay in.*'

On the day the massive front door of the hotel stayed barred and bolted. The hotel has no restaurant, nevertheless from dawn to dusk our detention was enlivened by a succession of trays – sandwich trays and cold meat trays, fruit and cake trays, tea trays, trays with covered dishes and chafing dishes, trays piled with tiered triple boilers balancing casseroles, until one could no longer tell snack from meal. We were never charged for these treats. We did not hear any shooting. Next morning the housekeeper told us that there had been a few dead, one hundred, two hundred? Just a small election.

Other days pass in a rhythm of going out and exhausted return to the cool, flower-scented peace of the patio. Outside everything is just a bit too near, too loud, too much. One is always pressed upon, there is always something to dodge – the beggars, the insane traffic, the sun, pineapples cascading off a stall.

The Baedeker round is quickly done.

Palace and cathedral are vast Spanish Colonial edifices conceived in ambition and the high if interested purposes of the Counter-Reformation, and built with rather more than the usual deal of delay through low funds, change of policy and volcanic tremor. The Paséo de la Reforma, Maximilian and Carlota's Champs-Élysées, casts a dank Victorian pall, dispiritedly *dépaysé* with its unbending line of tropical trees mercilessly clipped *à la française*. The gallery has its Rubens (a religious subject), its Murillo, 'what', I am quoting *Terry*, 'is believed by many to be a genuine Titian', cracked and darkened portraits of Spanish gentlemen with heads like Spanish gentlemen painted by El Greco, many battle-pieces and room upon roomful of Schools. The Museum has the Aztec Calendar Stone, an assortment of sacrificial stones of all sizes and a large collection of imp-faced deities, but pre-Columbian sculpture can be seen bigger and better in Oaxaca and at the British Museum.

Yes, the showpieces on the itinerary are numbered and on

the whole disappointing. But how much there is to see. Everywhere. No need, no point, to plan and rush, only to stand, to stroll and stare; to connect. Not great beauty, not the perfect proportions, the slow-grown, well-grown balance (you will never be further from Greece), not the long-tended masterpiece of thought and form, the tight French gem, but the haphazard, the absurd, the overblown, the savage, the gruesome. The fantastic detail and the frightening vista; the exotically elegant; the vast, the far, the legendarily ancient.

Everywhere. In the thoroughfare where the baby mule is born; by the fountain in the cool courtyard of the Spanish merchant's house where the Churrigueresque façade is gently weather-worn like a half-wiped slate; in the Street of the False Door of Saint-Andrew where two lovely, epicene young workmen are weaving a custom-made cage of soft twigs for a waiting parrot; in the lobby of the Ritz where of a Sunday morning Creole businessmen sit, heavily powdered, missals on their laps, discussing fat deals.

The Church of the Assumption of María Santísima, the Cathedral of Mexico City, the Archiepiscopal See of the Distrito Federál, the Holy Metropolitan Church of Mexico, the Patriarchal Basilica of the Americas, *l'Iglesia Mayor*, the First Christian Church on American Soil, is dense from sunrise to nightfall with a religious rabble, the vagrant camp-followers of holy shrines, prostrate, agape, chanting, swaying, scraping on their knees, hugging images with oriental intensity – mindless, far gone, possessed, separate and at one, unarrestable, frightening to the pitch of panic.

*

The city is full of bookshops, large recent establishments stocked with cheap, well-turned-out paper editions of *David Copperfield*, *Le Père Goriot*, *The Mill on the Floss*, *Point Counter Point*. The showcases are stuffed with the translated editions of Stephan Zweig, Emily Brontë and Professor Sigmund Freud. Who buys them? One quarter of the people cannot read. Another quarter can only read laboriously. Every grown-up, who can, is supposed by law to teach his letters to one illiterate grown-up a year. The question is often what letters. The current language is Spanish, but there are still two million Mexicans who speak only one of sixty different pre-Columbian tribal dialects. In the state of Sonora, they do not even use Arabic or Roman numerals, but a system they invented on their own.

I bought a Manual of Conversation. In the section headed *Useful Words and Phrases*, I find on page one:

'Are you interested in death, Count?'

'Yes, very much, your Excellency.'

One of the happiest places in this town is a room of early nineteenth-century Creole genre paintings in the Chapulte-pec Museum. These graceful pictures of hummingbird, butterfly and country life (unusual subjects of inspiration in Latin America) are quite unlike anything one has ever seen, luxuriant but domestic, naive and worldly, fresh, faintly absurd, wholly delicious. Young women in striped silk on a veranda mocked by a femur, a muslin dress shimmering through magnolia trees, fruit like flowers and flowers like birds, give intimations of a better world. One can hear the leaf fans rustling through the afternoon, soft sucking of bare feet on patio tiles, ice clinking in punch glasses . . .

But here too, the other note is sounded. There is a picture of a small boy led by a governess through a most peculiar garden of sugar cane and coffee bush, followed by a curly lapdog and an Indian boy carrying his doll, a neatly dressed and bonneted baby skeleton.

There are three active volcanoes in the valley, all within easy lava-throw of the city. Popocatepetl, Iztaccihúatl, Xinantecatl – monsters in name and size, fragile in appearance; Japanese-contoured shapes of pastel blue and porcelain snow, and three thin formal curls of smoke afloat in a limpid sky. There is also an unobtrusive mound, a tiny volcano now quiescent, Peñon, which according to the geologists will one day destroy the city.

In the spaces of the Plaza Mayor, walking over the grave of a pyramid, one is assailed by infinity, seized at the throat by an awful sense of the past stretching and stretching backwards through tunnels of time . . . Can this be Here, can one be in it? One is in a legend, one is walking in Troy.

Chapter Six
COYACÁN: TEA AND ADVICE

Some Mexican visits appear to me to surpass in duration all that one can imagine of a visit, rarely lasting less than one hour, and sometimes extending over the greater part of the day. And gentlemen, at least, arrive at no particular time. If you are going to breakfast, they go also — if to dinner, the same — if you are asleep, they wait till you awaken — if out, they call again. An indifferent sort of man, whose name I did not even hear, arrived yesterday, a little after breakfast, sat still, and walked in to a late dinner with us!

MADAME CALDERON DE LA BARCA

WE WERE asked to tea by some academic friends of friends, Spanish refugees, Mexican residents for some ten years. Their house was at Coyacán, the suburb in which Trotsky lived and was murdered. We set out with little idea of how to get there. Asking one's way is an uncertain business as pleasantness seems to be the guiding principle of one's informants, not truth. Everything is made to appear wonderfully near. Thus, the hotel porter suppressed the second tram, and the women at the terminal a mile of walk on an unpaved road full of mudholes and happy grubbing pigs, and we arrived very late at the C.s'.

The unprepossessing road ended in an alley by a small door in a high unbroken wall. A manservant in a striped coat and no shoes opened from within and we stepped into the colonnaded garden of a Carmelite convent choked with bougainvillaea and large, lush rambling roses. Seven or eight people were waiting for their tea and chocolate in a long domed room lined with books, French windows open to the garden. We were punctiliously introduced, shook hands and apologized for being late.

'You found? You came by taxi, yes?'

E. explained that I had prevented her from doing so.

The company seemed favourably impressed. 'And you walked after tramway? That is good. The tourists are so helpless.'

'Be charitable,' I said, 'call us travellers.'

'But you have not come to live?'

'I think I can bear it for six weeks,' said E.

'About a year,' said I.

We exchanged a look.

'And where do you go?' said our host.

'You must go to the Colonial towns,' said his wife.

'Don't miss Puebla,' said their daughter.

'They can go to Puebla on their way to Oaxaca.'

'I should like to get out into the country,' said I, 'and stay somewhere for a few months; get my bearings, learn Spanish properly and then start travelling. Somewhere near water if possible.'

'You can't go to the seaside before December,' said our host. 'Too hot.'

'They could go to the lakes.'

'They're far.'

'They could get there.'

'I've been told of Lake Pazcuaro,' said I.

'Very lonely.'

We had settled meanwhile to a solid tea around a polished table. 'You see,' said Señora C. with melancholy as I declined a second helping of the third cake, 'this is our last meal. One cannot eat at night in this altitude; not after some time that is. We had to give up dinner.'

And I realized that these people were in exile.

'The children don't feel it so much. My husband and I just have a snack before we go to bed, an omelette, a little beefsteak, a cup of chocolate.'

We remarked on the loveliness of the house.

'Yes,' said Señor C. 'My wife seldom leaves it. She does not like Mexico City.'

It was a European tea party. Czechs and Germans besides our Spanish hosts, a Frenchman. Middle-aged, mildly learned people, mellowed in disillusionment, who had given their political youth to anti-Fascism. There were no Anglo-Saxons, and there were no Mexicans. The conversation was general, the topic for our benefit Mexico.

'You have no car, no? The roads, when there are roads, are good. It's sometimes hard to get petrol.'

'*Here?*'

'Oh, that oil business was much exaggerated. There never was that much to begin with. Then there were seepages and now there's sea water in the wells. Nor has nationalization worked out, whatever one may have hoped. Nor kicking out the foreign engineers. And that's not the whole of it. Of course there is plenty of oil for home consumption and to spare, only distribution happens to be one of the biggest rackets in the country. It's quite an elaborate graft, and sometimes there is a row and then there just is no petrol for weeks.

'Glad to hear you don't want to go by air. Oh, it's safe enough. The pilots are good; better than the planes. When President Truman came in '47, a Mexican pilot took over to fly him over the Sierra Madre. But it is a stupid way of travelling. Don't take a train if you can help it. Whenever there's a road, go by bus. They're slow. But you'll stop at places you'd never get to see otherwise. One thing about this country, don't be in a hurry, don't *think* about time, take things as they come when they come, and *always go first class.*'

'Do the buses have classes?'

'No. There are first-class buses and second-class buses.'

'What's the difference?'

'All the difference. More people, less seats, more stops, larger animals. You just don't go second-class bus.'

'Are there any third-class buses?'

'There *are*.' They looked at each other. '*You* won't come across them.'

'. . . Hotels: as a rule always go to the second-best hotel in the provinces. It'll be Mexican run, and you'll get better value, better manners, more to eat. Don't go to the new places, half the time they forget to put in something like the doors. Don't *ever* expect to read in bed. You will find a bulb in mid-ceiling and the switch by the door.

'Never come straight to a point. Mexican Indians are formalists. Americans offend them by being businesslike or friendly, both are considered *una barbaridad*. Always be *polite.*

'. . . Water: don't touch what comes out of a tap. You needn't always buy bottled water. You can trust the carafes they put in the bedrooms. The water is electrically sterilized, or at least boiled.'

'Do they take the trouble? It would be so easy to cheat.'

'They won't. Crime is a profession here. You either set up as a bandit or you are an honest man. Cheating is outside their habits and characters.'

'Except in Mexico City,' said Señora C.

'Except in Mexico City,' said her husband.

'. . . Food: you said you liked chilli? One does need a touch of good hot pepper sometimes. Eat anything you please. There's too much fuss among foreigners about that. As a matter of fact, you'd be hard put to find fresher food anywhere. Nothing stored, nothing frozen, or lugged across half a continent in freight cars. Everything produced in small quantities near the consumer. Vegetables picked and eggs laid just in time for dinner. Alas, meat is killed in time for dinner too. I shouldn't eat uncooked lettuce though, unless I knew where it came from; certainly not in Mexico City where the market gardens are watered from the city sewer. It's different in the provinces. Everything is.'

They all sighed, and again I was aware of the note of revulsion whenever the city is mentioned.

'It is an evil place,' said Señora C.

'The people's diet is sound enough. *Frijoles* and tortillas. Black beans, hand-ground maize cakes; and chilli pepper. That's what the Aztecs ate and that's what they are eating now. It never changed. It's not the most energy-building diet, but it's complete. Down to all the vitamins. We only found out in the laboratories what they've known by instinct for three thousand years. You see, the Aztecs had no cattle, which meant no milk. The rich ate turkey, eggs and game, and fresh vegetables, but no one had any butter, or butcher's meat, or even pork. All that, with the horses and goats and pack animals, came with the blessings of the Conquest. The Indios haven't really taken to the new food. They say butter turns parrots mute, and they won't eat bread. As it takes four hours to grind the maize for one person's daily tortillas, you can imagine what this means in a household. We need two servants to run this place, and two servants to keep them and themselves in tortillas, and a fifth to tend the baking braziers. She has no teeth, so the others feed her on mashed beans and chilli which are luxury food, but save us, *pobres acedémicos*, a sixth servant.'

I was fascinated and quite shameless.

'If you *really* want to know, we pay our manservant a peso a day. The cook gets a bit more as she comes from Monterrey, which is supposed to have a faint Yankee chic. The tortilla menials are paid in coppers. Oh yes, it's all cheap enough by Western standards. In Mexico everything is cheap and everybody is underpaid.

'Take the electric light. You don't pay for the current you consume, you pay for the number of sockets you have in the house. Of course the system is quite mad. It comes to as much for a ballroom chandelier blazing away all night with hundreds of watts as for the bulb on your attic steps. So far so bad. Now comes the collector, who is so ill-paid that he couldn't exist without bribes, literally not exist. You have just taken a house, he goes into your living room and counts the sockets — ceiling light, standing lamp, side lamps, *unos, dos, tres, cuatros* . . . "Nonsense," he says, "you must put in one point and connect all your lights with extension wires." It saves you four-fifths of the bill, and you split the saving. This is where your troubles begin. The one point is overstressed, your lights fuse, you keep tripping over wires. Then a controller appears and threatens to denounce you for what he quite correctly calls fraud. You bribe him as expected, and at the end of the year you are fined by the company anyhow. If you refuse this arrangement to begin with — we all did — you never get any current at all. Your application's simply not honoured. It gets lost.

'. . . Health: better get yourselves revaccinated against

smallpox. Yes, there *is* a lot of typhoid and dysentry. In fact, one-fifth of the people die of some kind of intestinal infection. The rest die of malaria, bronchitis, whooping cough and the measles. They all die young and fast. There is no heart disease, they don't live old enough. Oh, they've got a sort of wiry strength – you've seen them with those pianos on their backs – but they get tired quickly, no staying power, they just slip out of life. There's not much of a dividing line. They don't prepare against death any more than they prepare against the next dry season. Although they do have a high opinion of Paradise.

'Doctors are not bad on the whole. Good surgeons. The trouble is that they won't set up practice outside the larger towns. The Government tried to make them. Passed a law that a man couldn't take his degree unless he signed up to work seven years in an Indian village. But you know what *laws* are here. Too many of them as it is. Even old Don Porfirio used to complain about them.'

'Diaz?' said I.

'The old devil could be quite sensible at times. Don't look shocked. It takes ten years in Mexico to make a Catalonian Anarchist put in a good word for Diaz.

'The Indios don't go to doctors much anyway. It's not that they prefer the witches, they're afraid of snubbing them. Nursing's poor too, with so many of the nuns still gone. When the Sisters were allowed back a few years ago, the people knelt in the streets and kissed their skirts. Lay skirts, of course. Nuns and priests still may not wear their habits in public.'

'What do you really think of the expulsion of the clergy?' said E.

There was a weary pause. 'You might say that we are not

exactly pro-clerical. The Mexican Church used to be quite fantastically corrupt. But the Reform Laws – a hundred years of them – soon made so much bitterness and misery . . . Such violence, such brutality, such excesses on all sides. They put half the country and half the world against Juarez, they helped to make that Habsburg foolery possible; they kept the Revolutions going for an extra decade. After six or seven years of war and eighty years of persecutions, one doesn't think so much about the original rights and wrongs. One accepts the Concordat. Such as it is.

'Some of the priests are hogs, others are good men. One used to talk about the Church keeping people in ignorance. Well, they *are* ignorant. I'm not so sure now that our brand of universal education wouldn't merely add another kind of ignorance. Mexico has the most up-to-date humanitarian legislation imaginable, but even when it doesn't stay on paper, it seems to have no impact on any known Indio's life. Perhaps only the priests could be a power against bestiality . . . This is not a Western country. They are not the heirs of the French Revolution. Here, one lives to learn the futility of the principle of equality.'

We stay for supper, and presently the C.s' daughter offers to drive us back. From that graceful house we tumble into a pitch-black lane and feel our way to the Model A Ford waiting at the end. It is mild; the road leads through an avenue of tamarinds, frogs are croaking in the streets of Coyacán, but the night is without beauty.

Chapter Seven
MEXICO CITY:
THE PAST AND THE PRESENT

All, all of a piece throughout
Thy chase had a beast in view,
Thy wars brought nothing about,
Thy lovers were all untrue.

WHO BUILT the city? What is the history of this jumble of main street and chunks intact from an almost legendary past, this rather tremendous place, so squalid, so splendid, that bears the megalomaniac imprint of three civilizations?

Many hundred years ago, the Valley of Mexico, an oval seven thousand feet above the seas, walled and sheltered by porphyry and immense volcanic rock, was a valley of great lakes and flowering tropical forests. Here on fifty islands and the shore of Lake Taxcuoco rose the city. Waterways fronted by low-roofed palaces of pink stone, plazas at anchor, floating gardens: Tenochtitlán, waterbound, canal-crossed, bridge-linked, ablaze with flowers . . . And amid the soft magic, a huge temple, a pyramid, squat, vast, solid, dedicated to some deity of war, piled without help of pack animal or metal tool, stone to stone for ever.

For three centuries, back entrances were lapped by water; canoes glided to market upon canals pompous with lilies, shaded by roof-grown trees, and the royal barges sailed the lake between the mainland and the Summer Palace.

★

Then the Spaniards came and changed everything. They couldn't have been more thorough. After four years the city is destroyed and rebuilt, the lakes drained, the waterways filled in, the canals dry, the forests decimated. The countryside begins to look like the bare hills of Castile. Naturally the climate changes too, and the soil. The new terra firma turns into swamp. There are floods, landslides . . . Nine thousand Spaniards die of the fevers. Native deaths are not recorded. Only that martian temple, the pyramid, escaped. Too solid for the old world's most accomplished efforts at destruction, it resisted demolition for some years; then by its own weight sank out of sight into the boggy ground. There it lies, intact below the main square, waiting for archaeologist or messiah. The Spanish built a cathedral on top of it and dedicated it to the Assumption of the Virgin Mary, some four hundred years before the recent promulgation of that dogma. Opposite, on the site of Montezuma's town house (razed), they began a Renaissance mansion, first Cortés' residence, then in turn Gubernatorial, Viceregal, National, Imperial and Presidential Palace.

The fabulous past is over. From now on the history of the city is that of any sixteenth-century outpost. Ecclesiastical and administrative magnificence, throne-room and *audiencia*, space and façade, the prestige building exacted by empire and Counter-Reformation. Good sound Roman masonry, as contemporarily practised at Segovia and Tarragona, but applied to *tezontle* the local soft volcanic stone, and to adobe the native clay. Colonial products of a good period: Renaissance, Plateresque, Baroque, Churrigueresque . . .

The city grows, the population increases – more people living, cooking, dying at close quarters. There are no drains.

As the names of the Viceroys grow longer, the administrative machine becomes creaky; from Garcia Guerra to Diego Osorio de Escobar y Llamas, to Antonio Sebastian de Toledo Molina y Salazar, to Diego Lopez Pacheco Cabrera y Bobadilla Duque de Escalona y Marques de Villena. By 1750, Spain is in full decline and Mexico a city of a hundred thousand inhabitants.

These are the years of the rat, the open sewers, of garbage rotting in the unpaved streets, of the cut-purse and the cutthroat, of cholera and fire unchecked. Madrid is considered the filthiest town in Europe; Mexico City is the death trap of the New World. There were five major inundations since the Conquest, each followed by an epidemic. The cellars are never dry. Once the city was under water for six years and abandoned to the lower orders. At the end of the eighteenth century there is some attempt at reform. Charles III in Spain, Viceroy Conde de Revillagigedo over here. A number of things are done: Revillagigedo regulates the water supply, founds a police force and hangs a number of bandits. But it is late in the day of the Spanish Empire. Charles III dies, Charles IV abdicates, Ferdinand VI (he who called thinking *una funesta mania*) is deposed by Napoleon. Thirty years after Revillagigedo, New Spain is gone. Viva Mexico.

During the next half-century much happens, but there is no natural growth. The War for Independence; Secession; the Kingdom of Annuac; the First Empire; the First Republic; Civil War; war with the United States; another republic; the Reform War; semi-war with England and Spain, war with France; military occupation; the Second Empire; civil war; another republic . . . sieges, triumphal entries, two coronations and the last *auto-da-fé* in the Plaza Mayor — the city stays suspended like a young man's education during a long war. Thus, the fruits of the industrial revolution and the appurtenances of nineteenth-century urban existence reach it late and piecemeal as exotic gifts in the baggage of travellers and occupiers. Like other hostess presents, they are chiefly for the convenience of the guest. Madame Calderon de la Barca brings a portable bathtub, the Empress Carlota one of different design; gentlemen from Bavaria start a brewery; the Americans bide the time for their own century and General Taylor arrives to sign the Peace of Guadalupe Hidalgo, which ceded two-thirds of Mexican territory to the United States, bringing nothing.

In the eighties this trickle of the amenities becomes a flow: plumbing, trams, French fashions, residential suburbs, a racecourse, gaslight — *le confort moderne* is arriving thick and fast. But it is unconnected. In 1876 General Porfirio Diaz had entered the city, was proclaimed Provisional President and made himself dictator for forty years. He managed — at a price — to establish internal peace, resume somewhat dilapidated foreign relations, and set out to attract foreign capital. It is the heyday of the satrap, the politico, the gauleiter, of the pampered investor and the quick foreign fortune; of summary executions — unreported — in a faraway province, discreet exile, the very large bribe, the shop front. Every man has his price, and no man his value. The rate of interest rises to forty per cent and is only surpassed by the death rate. Railways are built over swamp and precipice; opera houses, villas and spas, and roads to spas. For the first time since the murder of Montezuma, the public aspect of the city is clean, safe and comfortable. For whom? Mexico has a bad name for political instability. Without confidence no credit, without credit no expansion. The smug Edwardian cover pulled over a semi-barbarous country by a business-minded ex-soldier is a window dressing, not for home consumption. *There are no home consumers*. Indians, fed on home-ground corn, clothed by home-spun cotton, housed by palm leaf and bamboo, worked on plantations for food and hut, worked in mines for less than subsistence, make no consumer class. As in the good old days of the Conquest, the products of Mexico are wrested from field and mine by more or less forced labour and shipped across the seas.

At Diaz' fall in 1910, Mexico City has three hundred thousand inhabitants and all the attributes of that period's capitals from railway terminal to gasworks. Then there are another twenty-five years of revolution and civil war, and another ritardando: *Maderistas, Rurales, Encomenderos, Peninsulares, Iconoclastes* and *Christo Reyes*; Villa, Huerta, Obregon, Calles and Cardenas. Then settled government once more, and economic wooing, this time of the USA. The latest lap is taken in a leap: cinema theatres, motor buses, petrol stations; jukeboxes, Coca-Cola machines, one million people and tall gimcrack houses full of tiny rooms. But there is still that Indian sitting on the kerb selling a string of onions and one cabbage, still that fortuitous air as though the city were not a town but a sample bag, a travesty of modern urbanism, a cautionary tale perhaps: the caricature that gives the show away.

Chapter Eight
CUERNAVACA

. . . but that was in another country

A T THE end of our second week I am beset by discouragement. It is the weariness peculiar to travellers. A slight shift in focus, and the proposed enchantment is seen as our planned and burdened crawl about the earth. Moving appears both futile and difficult, the apparatus of travel petty. I feel crushed by the fret and tedium of preparations, the vanity of wanting to see new places and the doubts of ever getting anywhere at all.

E., who has left arrangements to me, pretends to be unaware that none are forthcoming. She is holding her breath like a child unnoticed in the wrong room. She does not mind much where she is at the moment – one must exist somewhere – only the past can be patterned into reality; but she dreads the unknown and the setting out for it.

East. South. West. North-west. The tropics, the ruins, the lakes? Which? The roads into Mexico are long and do not converge; once embarked, one must advance or retract.

Then E., on the principle that a move in time saves nine, proposed a day's outing to Cuernavaca.

'I would like to see the Emperor Maximilian's Summer Palace,' she said; 'the one his valet called *das Lust-Schloss*. And remember we ought to wait for Anthony.'

Cuernavaca is a great weekend place some seventy miles from the city, down in the *Tierra Templada*. I do not like to go anywhere for the day – it is always too long and too short, involves hanging about and a wilted return at an unsuitable hour – but I am willing to take E.'s sample journey. She further disclosed that the nice young man who had lost all her mail recommended the conducted tour organized by his travel agency. You just paid thirty pesos per head and that included luncheon, transport (in individual limousines) and a guide. I dislike this kind of travelling more than any private struggle, but in my present mood I might have acquiesced had I not found out that the agency left the worst part of the struggle to ourselves. Those individual limousines were public conveyances plying hourly between Mexico and Cuernavaca, available to any citizen capable of getting himself to the distant outskirt from which such services are apt to start. At these purlieus, the agency expected one to appear unguided at nine. They would not pick us up. All day, through a megaphone, they would tell us where to look, but the step that costs we were to take on our own. No.

We took a taxi at half-past ten, bought our tickets, found two seats in a waiting car and a few minutes after eleven were out of town screeching up a mountain road. As we were threading in and out of hairpin turns and corkscrew curves, the succulent greenery of the Valley of Mexico changed to spindly pines; peaks rose, precipices yawned before our front wheels, snow appeared in the near distance and the view became as spectacular as it is natural to such roads.

E. put down her book. 'Quite remarkable,' she said.

'One likes to be warned,' I said, 'I understood Cuernavaca was a place people ran down to for lunch. Where is it going to end?'

I was flung against my other neighbour, a man with an

attaché case, dressed in wintry brown. I addressed him. 'Is Cuernavaca not below Mexico City?'

'It is low.'

'Then what is this?' Another summit had sprung up above a curve.

'At your orders, the Three Marias.'

'What are the Three Marias?'

'These.'

Later, I learned from *Terry* that they were the three peaks by the La Cima Pass which is indeed one of the highest passes in the Republic; and still later from experience, that before running down to anywhere in this country one must first run up some six or seven thousand feet. The descents are more alarming than the climbs. We hurtled towards Cuernavaca down unparapeted slopes with the speed and angle, if not the precision, of a scenic railway – cacti flashed past like telegraph poles, the sun was brilliant, the air like laughing gas, below an enchanting valley, and the lack of brakes became part of a general allegro accelerando.

The town is not as lovely as the countryside; but it is small and the country is all about it. The plaza looks improvised. There are some booths about to be put up or pulled down; perhaps they are always there. As a resort the place seems unconvincing; for a cathedral town, unsettled. We look into San Francisco, walk down the long, sober nave and, through a side door, come out under the crumbling arcades of a formal, long-neglected garden laid out by a public-spirited eighteenth-century French speculator. We go into the Municipal Palace and see Ribera's frescoes in the loggia. We buy some postcards and at half-past two sit down to lunch under the awning of a restaurant in the square. In all these places we encounter what would have been our conducted tour.

We have some gin – Gordon's under licence – and fresh lime juice. The food when it comes is pleasant and monotonous, and there is perhaps not quite as much of it as there would be in a less-frequented place. The tour gets the same – I watch – minus a dish of fried black beans I asked for. We talk over our coffee in the shade. It is warmer than in Mexico City though the sun is much less violent, and I become aware that I am feeling extremely well.

By four o'clock the tour left. 'We may as well tote up,' I said. 'We've done what they've done, and we've got our return tickets.'

'Do we count the taxi?'

'No. We would have had to pay for that anyhow. Same as tips and drinks. I make it exactly twenty-seven pesos between us. Less than half.'

'Money in our pockets,' said E. 'We must celebrate our victory over this great travel institution.'

'We ought to start for Maximilian's Summer Palace.'

'It was only a shooting lodge,' said E. 'There will be nothing to see.'

'You said you wanted to go,' said I.

'My dear, these things had always best be done in the imagination.'

'It isn't far.'

'You must go. You love a walk. I shall be very comfortable here with my reflections. And may I ask you to be so very kind as to order me another cup of coffee in your excellent Spanish?'

★

78

The road is a country road. The maize stands tall and green. Everywhere there are springs, and the sound of clear running water is magical. Indians pass and call *Adiós*,

> ' . . and the clouds are lightly curled
> Round their golden houses, girdled with the gleaming world.'

I walk on, empty of thought, content.

The Emperor's Lodge is an unconcerned shell in a field. So this is where, in that official incognito so dear to royalty, he dawdled during the lulls in the tragedy. He loved Cuernavaca. Someone passes on a donkey, and I ask to make sure.

'*Si, si, es la casa de Masimiliano.*'

It is Maximilian's house. Now? Yesterday? Eighty years ago? It is improbable anyhow.

'And have you also come from the other side of the sea, *del otro lado del mar*, to look for Maximilian?'

Perhaps I saw it there. On the other side of the sea, Manet's fragment of the execution of the Emperor Maximilian. In grey, softness and damp, among Ophelia in the reeds and La Grande Jatte, soldiers in sombre blue stood at the extreme edge of a canvas, rifles held at right angles, butts pressing into shoulders, rigid, waiting. One need not know what was happening or to whom; one was frozen. I never looked at that painting without a shiver. *Al otro lado del mar.* Here, there is nothing to connect with that grim story. Summer landscapes tell no tales.

In the Plaza, the sun is almost down. I find E. refreshed and full of Maximilian and Carlota. We talk. E.'s memory is prodigious. There is little she does not remember about their sensational and complicated history. Why is it so fascinating? Surely the ingredients are too romantic to be borne – the spider of the Tuileries, Creole glamour, the doom of the House of Habsburg; young princes, sudden rise, fabulous parts and an exotic crown; early death, execution, madness. It is not respectable, and no first-rate writer has touched it with a bargepole. Historically treated, it bogs down in a maze of long-winded, short-sighted political intrigue of undisentang-able intricacy. The threads lead everywhere. They concerned everyone. There was not an event in the 1850s and '60s that did not help to shape the Mexican Empire; not a power, a faction, a person in a privileged position, an interest vested or on the make, that did not have a finger and a stake in that particular pie. Ambitious mothers, a soured brother, a prudent father-in-law and indifferent cousins; Austrian policy in Italy, French policy in Austria, the vacancy of the throne of Greece, Bonaparte insecurity and Coburg consolidation, the Mexican debt in England and the Mexican debt in Spain, the fear of Bismarck in many quarters and the American Civil War. Pio Nono, Napoleon III, the Emperor Francis-Joseph. The Archduchess Sophie of Austria, the Empress Eugénie, Louis-Philippe's widow Queen Marie-Amélie who shrieked on her deathbed, '*Les pauvres enfants, ils seront assassinés!*' Lincoln, Don Pedro of Brazil, white Mexicans in Paris; French militarism and French radicalism; King Leopold of the Belgians, Victor Hugo and the shades of l'Aiglon.

Few of these persons were dunces. A number of them were astute, at least three were brilliant. The men knew their statecraft and their world. All calculated; some meant well. Not one of them knew the first thing about Mexico.

On the face of it, the facts must have looked something like this. It is around 1860. Mexico had been in chaos for fifty years. Juarez was President, but could only maintain himself by the help of arms, some of them US arms. Nevertheless, he went on with nationalist and anti-clerical reforms. Church lands were confiscated and he repudiated foreign debts. France, England and Spain decided on a punitive expedition to recover some of the money owed them. The Spanish double-crossed the French by arriving first and landing before anybody else. The English did not land at all. A squadron lay off Vera Cruz, and a little later withdrew. So, after some time, did the Spanish. The French stayed on and, after an exceedingly hard campaign of almost two years, took Puebla. This, on the one hand, meant about as much or as little as the taking of Kiev. '*Un million d'hommes? Sire, chez nous c'est l'affaire d'une nuit d'hiver.*' In Mexico too, losses count low, and there is always another range of mountains. Fighting went on for three more years and could have gone on for ever if the French had not at last withdrawn their troops. On the other hand, Puebla meant the open road to the capital, which in fact was entered a few days later. At that moment it looked like a triumph for France; the way seemed clear for larger ambitions. Mexico was then still believed to be immensely rich. The United States was too locked in civil war to implement the Monroe Doctrine; there was nothing repulsive in overseas expansion to nineteenth-century Europe. Louis XV lost Canada, Napoleon I sold Louisiana, Louis-Napoleon and Eugénie were tempted to conquer Mexico. The idea of a Catholic dynasty and a stable government in Mexico – and incidentally at the southern borders of the United States – backed by a continental power, appealed as advantageous and creditable to a number of persons and institutions. In the then not unlikely event of the South winning the Civil War, the success of such an enterprise would have ensured perpetual semi-colonial status to the Americas.* In any case Lombard Street would recover its bonds, the Apostolic Church an unfaithful daughter and, it was hoped, her lands. The Mexican émigrés in Paris were excited by what could not even be called a restoration. The atmosphere of fatuous unreality waxed high. The Empress Eugénie told the American Ambassador, '*Je vous assure que si le Mexique n'était pas si loin et mon fils encore un enfant, je souhaiterais qu'il se mette à la tête de l'armée française, pour écrire avec l'épée une des plus belles pages de l'histoire de ce siècle!*' The pages of history written by the sword: what extreme of false values, what insolence, what hot air. Meanwhile not a word of the French conscripts who were dying of fever at Vera Cruz and of wounds in the Sierra Madre; not a thought of the possible wishes of the people of Mexico, which as a matter of fact would have been difficult to ascertain.

The next step was to find an available Catholic prince who would not tread on too many susceptibilities. A Spanish Bourbon would have been too much like attempting to set up the House of Hanover at Washington; an Orleans was not acceptable to the Bonapartes, a Wittelsbach had just cut a small figure in Greece. The Archduke Maximilian of Habsburg was the favourite from the start. After Solferino, Napoleon III had a great deal to make up to Austria. Maximilian's wife, Charlotte, was the daughter of King Leopold I of the Belgians; her elevation to a throne fell in

---

* Is it too far-fetched to conjecture that in this case there would indeed have been no United States capable of intervening in the last two wars, but that, what with France successful in Mexico and Eugénie's ambitions assuaged, Bismarck might have found it harder to bring about his 'third necessary war', and without the war of 1870, there might well have been no wars of 1914 and 1939? A case of *La Guerre de Troie n'aurait pas en lieu.*

with Coburg family expansion, and Leopold could be counted on to write to Queen Victoria. There was also that old rumour that Maximilian was not the son of his legitimate father, the Archduke Francis-Charles, but a bastard of the Duke of Reichstadt's and thus a grandson of Napoleon I. The story was by no means proved, but the kind of thing that appealed to the Empress Eugénie. So Napoleon III offered the crown of Mexico, a crown that was neither his to offer nor had ever existed except as a viceregal jewel in the crown of Spain, to the Archduke Maximilian guaranteeing French military and financial support to see Maximilian to his throne.

The press promptly spoke of the Crown of Montezuma. The French public, so often accused of shrewdness in money matters, subscribed its savings to the enterprise. Gutierrez de Estrada, one of the Mexican intermediaries, referred to the hour of destiny. 'God, the Virgin and all the Saints,' he wrote to Maximilian, 'bear witness that this hour is unique in the history of the world.'

Maximilian, the more amiable brother of the Emperor Francis-Joseph, had been somewhat pushed from pillar to post. One gathers that he was liberal in a sheltered way, high-minded, serious and romantic. He was fond of botanizing; he sketched from nature; he had been to Brazil and loved the tropics. His manners were gentle, and he was liked by his entourage. He was handsome, not very stable, and probably quite weak. His sense of rank was not keen; he had little judgement and often fell in with traitors and charlatans. He was religious without bigotry; he read; he studied; and he never realized that he lived in what was also the age of Darwin and dialectical materialism. He believed in good government and the duties of a monarch; he abhorred despots but was incapable of finding anything anomalous in a perpetual parental relationship between prince and subject. In different circumstances he might have made an excellent officer in the Salvation Army. He had little sense of personal importance, was quite without vindictiveness, and had great personal courage. He pondered much about improvement and he believed that he was meant to do good.

Such a man was not equipped to stand up against a restless wife or deal with Napoleon III. There was not even a place for him in the ossified bureaucracy of his brother's reign. First he tried a hand at reforming the Austrian navy such as it was, then he tried to make a decent Viceroy of Lombardy. The administrative channels of the Habsburg monarchy were like the arteries of a very old person. Every measure of Maximilian's that could be considered in the least new or generous was at once obstructed by the most senile chancelleries in Europe. Maximilian ate his heart out. He did not suspect that the Italians were not so much interested in having a *good* Viceroy as in having no Viceroy at all. The mistake was typical.

When the Napoleonic hour struck, Maximilian was living retired at Miramar on the Adriatic, where he led a dilettante's existence and like Lord Byron played with the idea of emigrating to South America as a private citizen. It must have been impossible for someone of Maximilian's character and upbringing not to have construed the offer as the bugle call of duty as well as destiny. Nevertheless, he put up some objections. Was he really wanted in Mexico? He was told that a plebiscite had been held on that question, and an overwhelming majority returned in his favour. A plebiscite among Indians, most of them illiterate, in a country, then occupied by a foreign army, which to this day has not known anything resembling a free, universal and secret ballot . . . Now, it seems thin. Maximilian accepted. There was much delay over escorts and allowances. Francis-Joseph exacted a renunciation of the Austrian succession from his brother. The Pope was cool. A large painting was done of Maximilian and Charlotte's future landing at Vera Cruz, where they all stand bare-headed in uniforms and Winterhalter dresses on a well-appointed pier, welcomed with bouquets and banners by a deputation in evening clothes. Charlotte changed her name to Carlota, and in '64 they sailed for Mexico on an Austrian destroyer. At Gibraltar, units of the Royal Navy saluted their Mexican colours, that aggressive emblem of a snake perched upon a cactus being devoured by an eagle. The salute was interpreted as a hopeful sign of English collaboration. They were already clutching at straws in the wind.

The rest of the European part of the story is a backing out and washing of hands. Lombard Street did not recover the bonds, nor the Church her lands; no dynasty was established in Mexico, and the government became neither stable nor orderly.

None of these things have the same meaning in Mexico, and it was there that the story began for Maximilian. There was little in nineteenth-century European conceptions that could have helped to prepare him. *Que diable, allait-il chercher dans cette galère?* He never understood what went on. Mexico never understood what he was about. It was in another country. For three years he was up against the quicksand and bedrock of Mexico, then they returned him across the sea on the same destroyer in a shoddy coffin. Again there was much haggling.

The story is fascinating. For all the trappings, it is not a romantic story, but a tragedy of misunderstanding, of the abyss between man and man; pitiful, often squalid, extraordinary only in the baroque detail and the vanity of *everybody's* wishes.

Chapter Nine
MORELIA – PAZCUARO –
A HOLD-UP

. . . ceux-là seuls qui partent
Pour partir; cœurs légers, semblables aux ballons . . .

WE HAVE tasted the countryside: we are off. Two days only after Cuernavaca, and we are on a bus. We have front seats; the luggage has been flung onto the roof; our fellow passengers are decorous Indios with small farm animals on their laps, the coachwork rattles and the driver's dashboard is clinking with holy medals and ex-votos. Tonight, DV, we shall be in a town called Morelia. From there we shall go on to a lake. Meanwhile, we are jolted over hill and dale, through lush fields, mango groves, orchards fat with fruit, and sudden brief villages of mud hut and double-towered church where pigs squeal to safety and a baroque scroll flashes by in the sunlight – on and on, up and down, down and up, with the smells of summer streaming in through the windows, as in some improbably prolonged delicious joke.

When there seems to be no more hope or reason to stop, we stop. In a nameless village. The passengers climb down and disappear into an adobe hut with a Coca-Cola sign. I ask the driver how long we are going to stay.

'To eat.'

'How much time?'

'Time to eat.'

E. is plucking at my sleeve. 'Oh, do come and make the ladies in pince-nez explain what they want.'

Two elderly women in decent black, with scrubbed youthful faces, have remained in their seats. They are trying to ask E. to get them a little broth and some tortillas. One is already fumbling with a snap purse produced from her skirts. I take over and accept the peso note.

'Of course. But from where?'

'Why, the station buffet.'

We try the mud hut. Behind it we find a farmyard with trestle tables pleasantly laid for a collation. We sit down under a wisteria. From a charcoal-burner, everyone is being served, quite efficiently but without hurry, with hot chicken broth, meat stew, vegetables and fruit. Good simple food all, and we devour it with pleasure. First, though, I take two cups of consommé and a stack of tortillas to the women in the bus. They seem able-bodied, so it is odd. Perhaps they cannot afford a meal. We wonder, and there is a guilty sting in the enjoyment of our stop in the sun.

When the bus is about to leave, I turn in the women's cups, and give them their change. They have drunk the broth but saved the tortillas. As they thank me, one explains that their Order does not allow them to enter a public eating place.

Now we understand. They are nuns, travelling in plain clothes according to the law. Not so much as a dog collar is permitted on the streets. Tonight no doubt within some cloistered wall these women will resume their habits. Again we feel a little sorry for them in their false position, their meagre refreshment.

As soon as we are off, the smaller nun pulls a wicker basket from under a seat, lays a snowy linen napkin over their laps and produces a tin which my practised eye recognizes as game pâté. They open it, spread some on their tortillas, and slowly, neatly, genteelly, proceed to eat. When the tin is empty, a dish with a whole roast chicken appears and this, too, they eat deliberately, gently cleaning every bone. The hills of the Sierra Madre rise and fall, barrancas deepen, corn changes to pine and pine to cactus, we crossed the Lerma and we crossed the Tuxpán before they cut the cake and open a jar of peaches. Next come bananas, nuts and dates. The well-mannered company takes no notice, only E. and I like dogs in the dining room watch their every morsel. They finish everything. In between they take long swigs of bottled orangeade. Afterwards, there is a thermos of coffee and an extra in the shape of a box of chocolate mints which does not come out of the hamper but the skirts of the larger nun, who offers the box to the smaller nun with formality. The smaller nun retaliates with a paper bag of sweet biscuits. These, too, they empty reflectively, offering box and bag to each other anew between every helping. They do not utter one word. When the last crumb is delicately licked off a finger, they pull out their rosaries, fold their hands, and close their eyes.

'The Church can sleep and feed at once,' says E. who is beginning to feel the journey.

Night had fallen some time ago, and, again improbably, we stopped. It was raining and we were in the outskirts of a town. A large closed motor car came up to meet the nuns and bore them into the darkness. The passengers melted away, the driver had disappeared, we were left in a mob of unwavering hands and agitated arms.

'!Un quinto! ¡Señora! ¿Un quinto?'
'¿Quieren un cargador?'

'*¡Señoras! Señoras . . .*'
'*¡Una caridad por amor de la Madre de Dios!*'
'*Un quinto . . .*'
'*¿Cargador?*'
'*¡Señora!*'
'*El cargador soy yo.*'
'*Una caridad . . . ¡Señoras!*'
'*Para mí.*'
'*¡Para mí!*'
'*¡Para mí!*'

It has stopped raining. The air is autumnal, almost sharp. Leaves are dripping, and there is a smell of wood smoke. Out of grey, colonnaded streets, I walk into a lighted hall and say, '*¿Tienen habitaciones? Quiero dos cuartos con una cama cada,*' and I am seized by a sense of *déjà vu* so powerful that I stand absorbed and passive trying not to pluck at what strands may rise now from the past. Then the mist of imminence is lifted, and a memory, irrelevant and intact, lies clear.

Avila. There were four of us then, a novelist who was adored by my generation whom he had dazzled and seduced by treading out for them with elegance and erudition a path of disillusionment; his wife who was adored by their friends; and a young woman, an American, with a lovely, secret Etruscan face, whose expression was one of remote broodings and whose thoughts were much concerned with clean milk. We all lived in Provence then, and that autumn, it was the year before the Spanish Civil War, we went to Madrid because we wanted to see the pictures in the Prado and some of us had workmen in the house. It was a time in which one was already uneasy, though not yet frightened. Political concerns were dominant, but by choice rather than for self-preservation. Or at least we thought so. It was also a time in Europe when one could still travel in comfort and have a part of good things without being rich or ruined. Not the good old times before the other war, of fabled hearsay, when one dined off omelette, claret and a roast bird at a French inn for a shilling, and paid one's way across the Continent with sovereigns in the pocket and no passport. But a time when hotels and restaurant meals and a second-class ticket to Florence were still within the means of everyone of moderate means; and a young man who'd got hold of a couple of hundred pounds might have his year in Paris. Well, we left our houses in the morning, lunched in the sun in the port of Marseilles, drove out to the aerodrome and had a fit when we saw the swastika marked on the plane. We refused to go by Luft Hansa. Our tickets said Air France, but there was no Air France service that day. So they put us on a Spanish plane to Barcelona. Something went very wrong indeed. We dropped to about twenty-five feet, and for half an hour hugged the Costa Brava, the cliffiest, craggiest coast in the Mediterranean, while we each in our way composed or failed to compose ourselves for death. Then we landed and were helped out by German airmen in Luft Hansa caps smiling ironic smiles. That night we had dinner upstairs at the café on the Plaza de Cataluña. Someone had just thrown a bomb. A tram was overturned, people injured who were not meant to be, and there was a police cordon.

'Human inability to learn from experience is really too extraordinary,' said the novelist in bell-like tones. 'Everyone knows perfectly well that home-made bombs have never been the slightest bit of use. And they *will* go on throwing them.'

'It's a gesture.'

'My dear. Gestures are *so* adolescent.'

'Well, they are certainly trying to grow up here,' said the young American. 'They're sending children to school, and the women are going to vote next month.'

'Which surely will mean more pro-clerical returns.'

'Why should it? Why do you suppose Spanish women don't know what's good for them?'

'Is it? Do they? Does anybody?'

And so we talked about the Spanish Republic, about Germany, about re-armament. We talked idly, as people who know each other well are apt to do on intense subjects, skirting the fuller impacts. That we all abhorred violence and coercion went without saying, and we did not say it. How to deal with them though? The American, if pressed, might have admitted that she believed in employing them at a reluctant pinch to attain desired ends. I should have called myself, as I would now, a liberal. But a liberal is naturally anti-totalitarian, which puts him at once before a dilemma hard to face, so I was sometimes quite illiberal and often in despair. The novelist saw further than the rest of us but was more aloof like an extremely intelligent person who has read widely of folly, which in fact he was.

That night there was a new note. Benevolent rationalism seemed a little worn: there was a hint that it had had its day, and certainly its bounds, that man was helpless indeed and therefore could be helped and help himself. It was not in any thing definitely said, and I cannot remember words; only when the American at one point said rather exasperatedly, 'Well, if that's no good either, what *would* you do?' and his wife added, 'Yes, darling, what? Do tell us,' the answer was disturbing by an undercurrent of thoughts yet unformed, a sense of tendrils on the move towards the unseen end of the stick, by something we were too shocked to recognize as hope.

For we bristled at once, and sat mute and wary as though we had found ourselves lured to a revivalist meeting. Then the *paella* we had ordered arrived and there was no immediate pursuit. We ate into the mound of saffron rice, drank Manzanilla and talked of this and that, but again and again that evening the conversation led to, hovered, and not quite stopped short at some disquieting threshold. Once or twice, always in that graceful, courteous voice, a short word was dropped from the upsetting vocabulary of the tract. The Self, the All, the One . . . In a good *paella* the rice is quite dry, and grainy; and every single one of the many ingredients is fried, steamed or grilled to its exact appropriate texture. That *paella* was perfect. Fat mussels glistened in their barely opened polished shells; a whiff of charcoal clung to strips of yellow and red pimiento. As one ate, one came upon chunks of lean fried pork sweet as hazelnut, prawns tender inside crunchy shells, small stiff green beans almost raw, and sudden explosive crumbs of hot chorizo sausage. Most of it grew cold on plates. I gave myself as much to the food as I could, first in enjoyment, then tenaciously. This too, it was hinted, would shut one out from that which was not mentioned, as surely as political passion.

'You don't really believe in all this?' the American said, and once more the answer was an intimation. We barged in with Voltaire. In our grievance against a shift from a trusted intellectual position, we quoted from the novelist's own works. We were baffled, and quite cross. Later we walked it out in the Ramblas, and the next morning we flew to Madrid by Air France.

No more cobwebs there. Madrid was lively with the graspable bustle of a capital of provincial size. It was pleasant but we lived apart. The hotel was opposite the Prado and every morning, early, we stepped across into those over-whelming corridors. I was most wrapped up with the Grecos, it was my first visit and I was very young, so I clutched the volume of Meier-Graefe and was duly swept off my feet. I saw that the Velázquez' were sumptuous, I could not see that they were subtle. The others were discovering the astonishing range of Goya, who could sometimes paint like Reynolds and sometimes like Watteau and sometimes like Daumier, who had in turn portrayed the gaieties, the personages and the horrors of the eighteenth century and lived long enough into the nineteenth to outlive Jane Austen eleven years and Beethoven one. We would return to the hotel at three, excited, ready to talk and a little wild with eye-strain – for the days were grey and the light at the Prado bad – and have a long, good, Spanish lunch in the dining room where in the fourth year of the Republic we were still the only respectable women present; then retire to write letters, read Buckle's admirable chapter on Spain in a pocket edition, and the massage advertisements – *gran reacción* guaranteed – in the Madrid papers. Later, at the hour of animation we strolled the evening streets. At ten we went to the theatre. The plays seemed all the same, a murky drawing room, superb acting, a tenuous plot one was never able to follow and an immense amount of talk. We drove to the Escorial and picnicked in the Guadarrama, but our minds were always on next morning and our sleep uneasy with Don Baltazar, lonely in the riding school, garlanded girls tossing harlequin in a hammock, and wafts of flamelike saints in sulphur and emerald, rising towards the ceiling of the Hotel Colón.

Three weeks of it. When it turned November, we spent some days at Toledo and Segovia, still Castilian towns full of melancholy and vigour where we saw imperishable marvels and much rubbish; and one wet evening we arrived at Avila. At the inn, the American had a good look at the beds and discovered that the sheets had been slept in. Horror. The novelist's wife took it up rather and as no bells were answered persuaded her husband to go downstairs to remonstrate. We trooped after him. At the desk he turned and said in his clear voice, 'My dears, how shall I put it?' And that took the wind out of those sails. The American was curled up rigid with the shock of what she had seen, and of no use. So I went out into the town in search of something cleaner. It had stopped raining and there was a smell of wood smoke. Out of walled, nun-grey streets I walked into a lighted hall and said, '¿Tienen habitaciones? Quiero dos cuartos con dos camas cada.'

There were none. Or six rooms would lead out of each other, with a cradle and three extra cots to each. I went from inn to inn, reluctant to leave the streets, open to the sense of being in a spacious and peculiar country that for all the stares and pinches and beggars had kept itself to itself and not been gone through, like Italy and France, with a fine-tooth comb; a closed country, the only one among the Latins that has secrets, and where the screws of logic might be turned to the pitch of the Mad Hatter. When I returned, the sheets had been changed and everyone quietened down, and we all felt a bit absurd in the town of Saint Theresa. In the morning there was another fuss because I thought I had lost a ring in the washbasin, and that was too much and we left for Madrid in a hired motor and soon afterwards returned to France, the land of good sense and the competent, worldly widow where a door had got to be either open or shut and where at first

95

we found everything too obvious and flat to bear, then settled down and forgot.

I have not been to Spain since.

Under next morning's sun, Morelia does not look like Avila and autumnal Castile. All the same it is very Spanish. A town of under fifty thousand, architecturally homogeneous, of long lines of arcades and seventeenth-century façades, compact, grey, handsome, dwindling into mud huts, ending abruptly in unbroken countryside. It is quiet after Mexico City, serene by day and melancholy by night. There is nothing particular to see. From the hotel roof, the view over the plain is enchanting. The inside of the cathedral is decorated to the last square inch in 1890 polychrome. Christ wears a wig of real hair, the Saints' tears are pearly beads, the Martyrs' blood lozenges of crimson wax, and all the images are kissed to a high polish. Before independence, Morelia was called Valladolid, Valladolid of Michoacán. Yes, it is very Spanish, but it is not Spain. Like the Puritans on New England, the Spaniards impressed themselves on Mexico. Both settled in a part of the continent whose climate and countryside were familiar and congenial. Both established their language, their religion and a style of building. However, unlike the Puritans, the Spaniards did not eliminate the Indians. In fact, the Indians have about eliminated them. There are now supposed to be only some forty thousand whites left in a population of three million pure Indians and seventeen million mestizos, and many of these whites are white only by courtesy or the use of face powder.

★

A letter from Anthony announcing his arrival at Mexico City. It seems too bad that we should have lingered there so long and no longer, and he all the way from Baltimore. It cannot be helped now; he will have to catch up with us here.

'So you have come from Mexico,' said the waiter.

'It seems hardly possible,' said I.

'Yes, yes, the porter told me. On the bus.'

'*Did* we get that far? It was a long way,' said E.

'It is a long way to Mexico,' said the waiter.

'Still?' said E. 'How splendidly metaphysical.'

'Long and expensive,' said the waiter.

'Very true,' said E., 'and now I am under the delusion that I have reached it.'

'They say it is unforgettable,' said the waiter; 'one day I shall get to Mexico.'

'I never cared for Kafka, S.,' said E., 'tell that tiresome man to bring the soup.'

'Where did you stay in Mexico?' said the hotel manager.

'We think we are still there,' said I.

'No doubt you kept your rooms on,' said the manager.

'So you have been to Mexico?' said the girl at the café.

'That is what we shall tell our friends at home,' said I.

'But you have really been?'

'I am almost convinced of it now,' said E.

★

'Do you know Mexico?' said the man at the tobacco store.

'Less and less,' said I.

'But you have been there?'

'We believe we *are* there.'

'You are in Morelia,' said the man and spat.

'Morelia is in Mexico.'

'No, no,' said the man, 'Morelia is Morelia, and Mexico is Mexico. Mexico is bigger, but Morelia is more pretty.'

'In the Dark Ages, identical heresies are said to have sprung up simultaneously in different parts of a community,' said E.

'They are foreigners,' said the man to another man.

'*And* perhaps Protestants,' said the other man. 'Everyone knows that the women of Protestants are not allowed to go to school.'

'That is so,' said a woman. 'They do not know much.'

It is true. It has taken us all that time and longer to catch on that Mexico (unless preceded by Viva) means the capital and the capital alone, and that the country as a whole is hardly a concept to the people. It has an official name, Estados Unidos Mexicanos, several sets of administrative initials, and is referred to in political speeches as the Soaring Eagle, the Bleeding Lamb or simply as *La Patria*; in private conversation it is called the Peninsula or the Republic or America, but never, never is the country of the Mexicans (they do call themselves that) called Mexico.

We needed some mending done and the porter told me of a lady who might oblige. I made up a bundle and walked to the address at the end of the town. It was not far. Over the entrance, a bamboo curtain, was a printed notice saying DEATH TO PROTESTANTS. Inside was a single room with a dirt floor, about nine feet by six. It contained a hammock, a straw pallet, a small statue of Our Lady of Guadalupe; a calendar, by courtesy of El Aguila cigars, depicting a bullfighter in full regalia kneeling before a shrine; a Singer sewing machine, a tin trunk, some fresh flowers, a number of children, an Indian woman dressed in black, and two three-legged stools. The woman rose, pulled out the other stool and began conversation. I liked Morelia? It *was* a pretty little town. Civilized. Not like some villages, full of black people. Ignorant. One would not care to live among those.

The children looked charming, some bright, some grave, all handsome. They were well-behaved without seeming in the least suppressed. I told their mother so.

'Oh yes, the dears. Come and give your *mamacita* a kiss, Paco. And you should see the other ones, Señora.'

'How many children have you got, Señora?'

'Eleven, Señora. Six at home, five angels.'

Later I worked round to my bundle of clothes. 'I made out a list of what I want done,' I said.

'I do not read paper,' said the lady. 'I read the clock.'

At nightfall, booths off the plaza light braziers, put out clay pots and set about to cook the town's supper. The life of the very poor is often public; in good climates not unpleasantly so. The middle classes find it cheaper to eat in, the poor are often hard put to get themselves a meal at home. In countries where the gas-ring does not exist, inhabitants of mud hut and tenement have to cook in the street or suffocate with smoke. In working quarters in Rome, one often sees a woman or a boy start a charcoal fire on the pavement. On winter evenings the slums are full of small braziers flaming with twigs and kindling, fanned and watched over until the coal has caught and the embers are carried indoors for the actual cooking. Then the food goes out again – a panful of macaroni, a bowl of minestrone wrapped in a dishcloth, a length of bread, an infant, carried by a family to a wine shop where for the price of a measure of wine they may enjoy light, moderate warmth, a table to themselves and conversation with their fellows. Dinner at Morelia is quieter and more simple. Single Indios wander up to the cook-booths at all hours, carrying neither dish nor spoon. They buy their meal, have it wrapped in a pancake, walk on a few steps, then sit on the kerb, lean against a lamppost, and eat. Later they may push through the low swing-doors into the drinking places or squat in groups bent over some game of luck. The night is packed but the animation is sombre, the business of eating and selling subdued. There is no gaiety. As usual the town lighting is poor. Clustered globes of ineffectual street lamps fail against the night, against white acetylene hissing from the cook shops and the softer glow of coals, and thus the scene is both shadowy and sharp: small pools of light and immense distorted shadows on the walls, the lighting and movement indeed of Goya. Figures are decorous and silent; squalor is transmogrified into the fantastic. There is no singing, no music, human or mechanical, there are only smells. Smells of goat and garlic, smells of acetylene and charcoal, and the sickening smell of tequila – raw alcohol with an underwhiff of festering sweetness as though chrysanthemums had rotted in gin.

After eleven, activity ceases. Lights and fires are put out, booths shut down; here and there on the kerb sits a soldier in arms or a beggar, quite still, a handkerchief tied across his nose and mouth to exclude the night air. Our footsteps sound loud on the pavements, and again I feel as though I had seen the ghost of Spain.

We stayed four days at Morelia, depressed and captivated by the atmosphere. E. said she liked Morelia the way people say they like a grey day or a cemetery. Then we wired Anthony to join us at Lake Pazcuaro, and set off in search of summer quarters in a vehicle so preposterous, so crowded, so lumbering, so smelly, that we decide that the C.s must have been out of their minds to recommend such transport. How *can* it be so frightful?

'Señora, it is regular,' says the driver.

'Not regular for a first-class bus, surely?'

'This is not a first-class bus.'

'But the tickets say it is.'

'There is no first-class bus to Pazcuaro,' says the driver.

'Then why say first-class on the tickets?'

'Because that is the only class there is.'

'They shouldn't say that when there is no first.'

'Yes, yes, *first*. The first class there is.'

A well-grown sow lies heaving in the aisle. My neighbour has a live turkey hen on her lap and the bird simply cannot help it, she must partly sit on my lap too. This is very hot. Also she keeps fluffing out her surprisingly harsh feathers. From time to time, probably to ease her own discomfort, the bird stands up. Supported on six pointed claws, one set of them on my knee, she digs her weight into us and shakes herself. Dust and lice emerge. On my other side, in the aisle, stands a little boy with a rod on which dangles a dead, though no doubt freshly caught, fish. With every lurch of the conveyance, and it is all lurches, the fish, moist but not cool, touches my arm and sometimes my averted cheek. E. has found a seat in the back where, she being of the build of Don Quixote, her knees touch her chin. On one of her feet sits a little old man, obviously very tight. He has a stone crock standing next to him on the floor, which from time to time he lifts to his lips, an operation which pervades the entire vehicle with strong alcoholic vapours. Sometimes he bumps the crock back on to the floor, and sometimes on E.'s free foot. She winces and twitches, but hasn't got the room to extricate herself. He seems a kind old man. He crawls out at the stops and returns with the crown of his hat dripping with muddy water which he takes around to the children on the bus to drink, and when poor E. lets out a small squeak of pain as the crock is once more slammed down on her exposed foot, the old man with an angelic smile lifts it and presses it against her mouth. She takes a polite gulp. It was very strong, she said afterwards, and quite sweet. Then the old fellow scrambled up, tumbled over the sow, hugged the driver and began addressing the air. He was making rather a nuisance of himself. Nobody paid the slightest attention. Then two men got up, seized him, opened the door of the moving bus and with the driver stepping on the gas hurled the old man out into the road. Someone threw the crock after him; everybody craned to get a receding glimpse of a man lying bent double in a pool of blood. Then the whole bus burst into laughter.

At the end of this journey we were deposited in a twilit Indian town. Low roofs of mellow red, propped by elaborate carved beams, hung over steep cobbled streets, and the one-storeyed houses looked very old. They must have been built after the Conquest, but are best described as Medieval Indian.

The town was dusty, poor and silent. There was no wheeled traffic and nobody wore shoes. It was a mile's walk to the lake shore and the inn, and looking back one could see the red, weathered roofs of Pazcuaro spread upon the hillside like a fan. In a way, it was beautiful. The lake, set in an expanse of shrub and stone, was the colour of clay; reedy, forlorn to make one cry. The inn was a frame bungalow. There was a veranda wired with mosquito netting, a barman in a spotty white jacket, a ping-pong table and no guests.

Our room was unswept, there was a rusty shower-bath that dripped and someone's hairpins on the warped chest whose drawers we did not explore. Everything was damp. We spent the evening sitting on the veranda — the barman had said to stay in because of the miasma, and anyway there was nowhere to sit out-of-doors — drinking tequila in speechless gloom. The food tasted of swamps. At last we went to bed. The muslin nets smelled and had holes, insects whirred and our thoughts ran on malaria.

In the morning I walked into the town to send a telegram to Anthony care of American Express, Mexico City, telling him not to join us on Lake Pazcuaro. Now, there are two kinds of countries, the countries in which sending a telegram is nothing — you hand in a shilling or a quarter, and a form, and walk out again — and the countries in which it is hell. They're out of forms, they're out of ink, the pen scratches, you've been waiting at the wrong guichet, your destination does not exist, the post-mistress pretends she cannot read. The worse the postal service, the better the climate, wine and food. Without such compensations, Pazcuaro beats any tele-graph office between the Bosphorus and the Mexique Bay.

I went to enquire about means of escape. A debased character addressed me in English. 'Want guide, miss?'

'No thank you.'

'Want to see museum, many pots-pieces genuine Tarrascan Indian?'

'I want to find out about trains.'

'Want to see genuine Tarrascan featherworks, beautiful pictures all from hummingbird?'

'Is there a train service.'

'You want go excursion on lake? Want to go in Indian canoe to Yuyuáñ?'

'I want a train.'

'Want to go to Tzintzuntzán? No? Want to see waterfall? No? Want to go to Chupicuaro beach? No? Want to see dance of the Fish and the Christians? Very symbolistic.'

I gleaned the following concrete information: that Pazcuaro means Place of Delight in Tarrascan, that there was a train to Uruapan this afternoon and a train to Morelia tomorrow morning.

'What's Uruapan?' said E. when confronted with this choice.

'Oh you remember, that's the place where the baby volcano was born.'

Indeed some years ago, Uruapan had sprung into the kind of prominence enjoyed by Whipsnade or the Brooklyn Zoo at the birth of an elephant. In 1943, a farmer labouring in his field had seen a molehill bubble up in front of his plough and grow to the size of a haystack within the space of minutes. When the farmer returned with the priest, the molehill was the size of a house and spouting red-hot boulders. Within a week, this monster rose to a height of eight hundred feet, buried the land and homes of fifteen thousand people in fire and ashes and was photographed by *Life* magazine. It went on growing under the eyes of geologists who had rushed to its rumbling side from all over the world, war or no war. It was named Paracutín and became the subject of monographs and brochures in many languages. Now it is supposed to have reached its full height – three thousand feet – and very active. The region is devastated but there are many tourists. A professor told the *National Geographic* that '. . . Paracutín is the greatest show on earth. It is, I believe, just as spectacular as Vesuvius ever was, and in its more violent phases it is better.'

'I have not the slightest desire to see the wonders of nature,' said E.

'Of course not, my dear. But what else can we do?'

'*And where* does one sleep under this so-called volcano?'

'I don't know. Perhaps *Terry* . . . Let me find it. ". . . grandiose, awe-inspiring . . . unforgettable . . ."'

'Yes?'

'". . . roads to within twenty miles of the eruptive district may be strewn with volcanic detritus or deep in volcanic ash . . ."'

'*Yes?*'

'". . . best to approach at eventide . . . a wrap . . . heavy shoes are desirable where the sand and lava dust are hot. Rubber overshoes may come in handy. Close-fitting bandanas should be worn to keep the penetrating volcanic dust out of ears and hair . . ."'

'*I will not go to this volcano*,' said E. in the manner of Edmund Burke addressing the House of Commons.

The train back to Morelia was not a success. Even on the timetable it took twice as long as the bus. It was not very crowded, but it was boiling before it started and it did not start for a long time, and afterwards it was very hot. It was filthy. We had second-class seats – the first class there was – and dust rose out of caked plush at our every movement. The doors of the coaches were fastened open, a sensible arrangement as the windows stuck, and at every one of the thirty-seven stops dogs would get on to the train and rush through the carriages in search of leavings from the passengers' provisions. Items in various stages of disgustingness were dragged from under seats by these eager mongrels. If the catch was rewarding, a dog would not get off the train when it started but simply ride on to the next station.

'Let's go to the best hotel this time,' said E., '*if* there is one.'

'There is indeed.'

We were rather out of conceit with the C.s and ready to be guided by *Terry*. 'The management of the Hotel Y is widely known to, and liked by, world travellers. The President and Managing Director, Licentiate Eduardo Laris Rubio, distinguished statesman, internationally known lawyer, diplomat, one of the state's most prominent men, and direct lineal descendant of the Spanish crown families which founded Morelia . . . Lic. Rubio is a leader in jurisprudence, a linguist of ability (speaks scholarly English, Spanish, French and other languages), a writer, and a famous executive.' To one accustomed to the reticences and asterisks of Baedeker and the RAC guides, this was hallucinatory and of course we went.

'You have come from Mexico,' said the porter.

'No. From Pazcuaro,' we said with a glint.

'Not as nice as Mexico, but very nice too,' said the porter. The hotel was quite all right. Corn-flakes appeared at every meal and the staff said OK to our every request. The accomplished licentiate Laris Rubio did not materialize. 'I suppose we ought to wait here for Anthony,' said E.

'Of course we should.'

'How does one get to that other lake of yours?'

'Chapala? By way of Guadalajara.'

'How long does it take?'

'Oh, about eight hours.' I suppressed a few.

'Eight hours in *what*?'

'A nice bus.'

'First-class?'

'First-class.'

'I suppose you wouldn't like to spend the rest of your days in Morelia?'

'I would not.'

'I was afraid so. Then, say, we leave tomorrow? And you *will* send a telegram to Anthony?'

Some thirty miles south of Guadalajara, we stopped by the roadside at dusk and left the bus for some refreshments laid out for us inside a patio, and on coming out again found a mildly operatic outfit fumbling with the luggage ropes: three or four men in fine hats and bandanas tied over their faces on muleback, and a pack-mule.

The driver and conductor shooed us back into the patio. 'Gentlemen, we must wait a little moment,' they addressed us with the disciplined calm of sea captains, 'the bandits have come.'

'What bandits?' said E.

'It is their hour,' said one of the passengers.

'Why doesn't anyone do something about them?'

'Gentlemen: they are armed. Armed with firearms.'

'They do not take much,' said another passenger.

'What is all this?' said E.

'They come down from the mountains at dusk,' was kindly explained to her. 'Bandits do not like to show themselves in broad daylight – there are certain prejudices – and they don't like to come out all that way at night, in the dark, when who knows what criminals and malefactors may be about.'

There was a clatter of hoofs, the conductor said briskly, '*Vamanos*'; we went outside and saw the train of mules cantering off. The luggage ropes had been retied; rather sloppily. Off we went.

'Not in the least Defoe,' said E. 'Trollope.'

At Guadalajara it turned out that a thing or two were missing. From our lot, a large bag and a small box, both brand new, one containing all E.'s clothes, the other some note-books of mine, some photographs and a manuscript without a copy.

'Damn Mark Cross,' said E. 'Never liked new luggage; didn't want to get it in the first place.'

Chapter Ten
MONEY AND THE
TARRASCAN INDIANS

Yesterday, being the festival of San Andres, the Indians were all in
full costume and procession, and we went into the old church to see
them. They were carrying the saint in very fine robes, the women
bearing coloured flags and lighted tapers, and the men playing on
violins, flutes and drums.

MADAME CALDERON DE LA BARCA

THE TARRASCAN INDIANS at Pazcuaro are poor. The
seamstress and the people at the cook-booths in
Morelia are poor; the clerks in New York City who cannot
escape the heat of summer and the elderly people at Chelten-
ham whose investments have dwindled are poor; the major
general who has nothing but his pay might refer to himself as
a poor soldier; the bandits on the Guadalajara highway think
of themselves as making a good living. The descendants of
the Aztecs sleeping on the pavements of Mexico City are
paupers. We speak of poverty as being abject, extreme, dire,
genteel; crippling, unmitigated, relative. It can be all of these
but it is always the last. When we say that someone is
relatively poor, we mean that he is really quite rich; relatively
rich. All wealth is relative; and so is its absence. Poverty is
one of the most relative concepts we have. Absolute poverty
is something else: it *is* either destitution or the voluntary
renunciation of all tangible possessions. The first can only be
a brief and drastic incident, not a pattern of existence, as it
must soon end in alleviation – relative poverty or wealth – or

in death; the second escapes the three most negative concomitants of poverty: anxiety, the threat to fulfilment and the lack of scope.

Poverty has been defined as the lack of means. What means? Means of existence. What kind of existence? Desirable. To whom? Desired by whom, from what vantage ground, for whom? A child? A man? All men? Now? Next year? In five years? Later? In a town? In the country? In *a* country? In the world? In which world?

The answers must lie between two shrugs.

About a quarter of the people in Mexico live on money. Town shopkeepers, army officers, schoolteachers, bus drivers, doctors, miners, post-office and railway employees, clerks, artists and notaries, waiters, domestic servants, lower government officials and beggars. A much smaller number of people has money, makes money, uses money. Holders of concessions, directors of public utilities, hotel managers, middlemen, promoters of new needs and industries and imports, successful lawyers, the few ex-landowners, who were given cash compensation, and officials in the higher graft brackets. The other half, three-quarters in this case, live on the land. Thus Mexico is an agrarian country with no appreciable surplus output and a topsoil stratum of commercial activity. The Tarrascan Indians, in more or less the way of the rest of the country people, live in an economic pattern now obsolete in the West and diluted in the East that was, *mutatis mutandis*, the pattern of agrarian civilization since before Babylon. This pattern is called primitive, but the people who live in it are no more savages than the rural inhabitants of Yorkshire or Normandy. The differences are ones of outlook and domestic objects. The Tarrascan Indians live from hand to mouth, but once more, after a lapse of four hundred years, own the means of production: the land and raw materials. They are not farmers *or* fishermen, shipwrights *or* masons. They grow what they eat and wear, and sometimes a little more. Where there is water, they fish; they are competent to build their own or their neighbour's house and boat and even turn a neat, small dome called a half-orange; they weave cloth, plait straw, knit hammocks, cure hides, make nets and harnesses and cook-pots. Bricks are made of adobe, the clay dug from their land; the thatch comes off the palms, matting off their coconuts, wicker from reeds. There is sugar cane in the fields, tobacco grows in the kitchen garden and coffee in the shrubbery. In lucky regions there is also a vile kind of cactus that can be tapped for a mildly alcoholic liquid which looks like cloudy beer and tastes like buttermilk. They have no capital outlay on seeds, stocking and chemical fertilizers. What they cannot raise or make, they do without. Livestock are hardy and prolific beasts – donkeys, pigs, goats and a species of tough hens. What one man lacks or is not so good at, another one in the community can supply or do in exchange for services or goods. The larger acquisitions, knives, firearms, formal riding clothes, musical instruments, silver ornaments or a cow, can also be made by way of barter. It is all a big round not of taking in each other's washing but of producing each other's food and toys. Schools, when there are schools, are free, and the witch doctor will always accept a chicken. Money is indispensable only for salt, matches, and such personal expenses as drink (for those who cannot grow their own), lottery tickets, baptism, the marriage service, funerals and taxes. As occasions for these arise, a man will sit down and spend a day or two weaving a blanket or turning out a batch of soup-pots, then seize a piglet and a cluster of bananas, bundle everything up and pile it on his wife's back and set off to market. There is no need for a licence or a stall, but the next market place may be miles away and sometimes they will have to walk all night. If their goal is anywhere near a road they will take a second- or third-class bus as far as it will get them. Those bus fares are the only cash items in their budgets that could be put down as overhead. Every time they sell something in the market, a tax-collector of the Republic will peep over their shoulders and then and there grab the amount, and sometimes more, of coppers due. This straight-forward method makes the state look both rapacious and petty, and often unkind, yet in the circumstances – provided that these people ought to pay taxes at all – it is probably the least painful and the most effectual way of administering them.

Salt and matches are dear, being also taxed; but it is easy to manage without by using a bit more chilli, striking a spark or borrowing a live coal. Drink is cheap. A pint of tequila, 90 proof, reliable though decidedly not aged, can be had for a shilling; and doubtless there are concoctions of less standard-ized merit at a lower price. Lottery tickets and the services of the Church are cash. So, many people do not undergo the marriage ceremony and incur debts for a relative's obsequies.

The Church is often blamed for charging for certain of her sacraments, and for charging with such impartiality from the rich and poor. In France, village *curés* rather half starve (and many do) than exact fees from their parishioners. Not so in Mexico. The priests are poor and they have got to live, but the Church, who is not, could make some provision for their living if she chose. This aspect of the Catholic clergy is particularly shocking to those who are accustomed to regard the succour of the poor as an integral part of the duties of the vicar and his wife. Yet the same people will tell one with much smugness that psychoanalysts have to charge large fees — quite against their wills of course — or their patients would have no faith in them; and wasn't it Aimée Semple Mac-Pherson who said that salvation doesn't do them half as much good if they think it's free?

The Tarrascan Indians, then, do not lie awake over the sack and the rent, the next instalment and the possible bonus. They do not plan a future for their children. The lines for that are laid. Whether they eat is not determined by trade slumps, the cost of living or the state of the stock market. What they produce, they consume or their fellows consume and pay for in kind. But they must produce or starve. So eating is determined by a man's health and strength, the quality of his or the village's grant of land and by what he would readily call himself the acts of God — rain or drought, a hailstorm, landslides, a new volcano. The farming is not scientific, and certainly laborious. The climate and valleys are fertile, but there are more mountains than valleys and some of the fields are incredible little acres, almost perpendicular, scratched out of the side of a rock and unworkable with anything but a hand plough. A good downpour or a slide of boulders and the acre is gone. For seven or eight months a year it does not rain at all, and then the rains may not come or wash in torrents down the mountainsides. There is not much rotation, about two-thirds of the land is planted with maize, an exhausting crop at best, so that even in years of no disasters the yields are low by all standards. The Tarrascan Indians might well lie awake after all. They do not. They have an oriental streak; though it is not so much that they submit to fate but are unwilling to concern themselves with anything between the immediate and the eternal. They are Catholic Fatalists.

Is it then a tolerable life? Materially it is insecure, but no more so than most lives, and the worst of insecurity may indeed be apprehension (though it is not for outsiders to discount it on that ground), and it is arguable that it is better for a man to have to pray for rain than scramble for advancement. It is not usually a long life. At the present turn of history, it may be a safer one than ours, but to be ill still means quite likely death. Again, it may be preferable to succumb rapidly to a mortal disease than to be kept breathing for months under oxygen and drugs, but when it comes to dying of appendicitis at thirty-two and of the measles at ten, being lamed for good by a simple ill-set fracture and having to bring nine children into this world in order to keep two in it . . . The work is hard, but neither monotonous nor mechanical, and a man is largely his own master. There is a good deal of leisure. Of course it is back-breaking to dig stones out of a clay soil and walk twelve miles with a hundredweight of mangoes on one's shoulders; but surely it is not as physically and spiritually exhausting as the forty minutes twice a day spent in a crowded underground railway on the way to an office. Against the hours of lugging and hoeing, there are the hours of slow shaping of objects (often hideous), of fishing, of seeing things grow. It is work that can satisfy the body and the smaller flickers of the creative impulse, provide an anchor for the simple mind and not unfertile ruminations for a complex one in middle age. It would drive the modern mind potty with boredom and restlessness. It does not accommodate ambition. It is not, in the Western sense, a comfortable life, and no American workman or English housemaid would put up with a one-ring charcoal stove and no wireless. Indeed, the whole existence would be intolerable to a Westerner today. It is still heaven for any Western child.

Is it a happy life? It is safe to say that it is not a frustrated one. It is ungracious to answer such questions for others. In this encroached and interlocking world one has to ask, and perhaps not stay for the answers. What can I ever know about the Tarrascan Indians? What do they know about themselves? How would they impart it? Would they have started with an account of the economic structure of their lives and the nature of their work? Would they have talked of dances and feast days and rituals, of traditions, dreads and beliefs? Would they have mentioned the lucky grasshopper and the she-ass that cannot be milked under a new moon, the wicked saint who let them down and the lizard who was somebody's grandfather? Would they describe their rhythm of routine and excess, the drinking and knifing that are the joy and commonplace of every holiday? The love for their children? The full and variegated religious life, that happy blend of the more polytheistic aspects of Roman Catholicism with private intimations and the fetishes of an earlier creed, that runs through their days like the bloodstream through the body?

Is it then a good life? If the good life is to live at peace within a pattern and at the same time expand awareness and enlarge the world by letting down the separations between man and man, the unseen and the seen, theirs has at least some of the potentialities. They are not acquisitive; their interest in power is sporadic and slight, their sense of identity undeveloped; they are not much attached to anything, including their own lives. They have a feeling for ritual and form, and their intercourse with the deities appears to be easy and frequent. They have no craving to fill every particle of time with activities and distractions, and they show almost too ready a disposition to waive the prejudice in favour of two times two making four. Thus they have leisure; freedom from possessions and that Western thorn, worry; a framework and a myth. Yet they seem to have made few connections. They are affectionate to animals but it would not occur to them to feed a dog. They love, but lack sympathy and seem as unconscious of their fellows as they are of themselves. Kindliness and decorum are periodically burst by fits of rage and spleen. Any mood or piece of demagogy may turn incitement to murder. If they do not mean to be cruel, their callousness is hair-raising and the result, cruelty. There appears to be something tight-shut about their pattern, a sense of *les jeux sont faits*: they cherish the iron, deaf-mute obstinacy of the ignorant − the baby's always had opium. Our notions of their civilization are blunt; theirs of ours preposterous. They cannot reach out, or be reached through books, and the processes and achievements of Western thought are equally closed to them. The Inquisition dispensed the aboriginal inhabitants of the Americas from conformity to dogma, and thus they never became acquainted with such offshoots of the Aristotelian method as would otherwise have come their way through the theologians. To educated persons from the West this apparent absence of any known form of intellectual life is always disturbing. '*La bêtise n'est pas mon fort.*' Yet the Tarrascan Indians may draw from other sources. Who can tell? Is that implied daily intimacy with another reality only a naive extension of the life they know? The meditations, brooding over slights and wrongs? The raptures day-dreams of beans and women, the contemplation somnolence? Or is there something else? If only they could speak about their hours of listlessness and solitude, and disclose the vacancies or visions of their stares.

Is it the best life they could have? It is the life they know. It has shaped them and they have helped to shape it for centuries. Individuals here and there may make a clean break, communities can only modify their pattern from within, they cannot step out of it. There is no other life, ready-made, waiting for the Tarrascan Indians. There is, of course, room for improvement in their present one. Irrigation, conservation of rainwater, storage of grain in good years against bad, anaesthetics and birth control jump to the mind. How are they to acquire and assimilate these useful things with their prerequisites of foresight, technical training and capital expenditure? They can hardly be dropped, gift-package or loan, into their pattern of existence without disrupting its balance and perhaps its very structure, leaving chaos. The Tarrascan Indians are no wards. Nobody is anybody's ward. It is easy to poke and prod and throw a bit of cheese, but the anthill cannot be added to from outside. The products of a civilization are its own fruits; to graft them as we do, according to the promptings of profit or philanthropy, is like putting the pudding into the soup in order to make the soup less salt. The result is neither soup nor pudding, but a mess. In *Black Mischief*, the Zoukouyous of the Azanian Guards stewed their issue of boots and ate them. Few cultures have so sturdy a digestion.

Chapter Eleven
GUADALAJARA

If I or she should chance to be
Involved in this affair,
He trusts to you to set them free,
Exactly as we were.

A T GUADALAJARA we were met by Anthony. He was wearing a green seersucker suit and a large Mexican hat.

'I've laid on a car for you,' he said.

Later, when we were rolling through long handsome streets in a Studebaker, he said, 'I've been hanging round this bus terminal since noon.'

'When did you get in?' said I.

'11 a.m. On this plane from Mex City.'

'How long did it take you?' said E.

'Couple of hours.'

'Indeed,' said E.

'Did you enjoy yourself?' said I.

'Oh, fine. They didn't serve breakfast though. Lousy little plane.'

'I meant in Mexico City.'

'Oh, that was fine.'

Anthony is a second cousin of E.'s, and one of the best-looking young men I've ever set eyes on. We are all very fond of him.

Later he said, 'That was quite a rat-race you led me. I ought to be mad. I could have saved time and flown out to this Guadalajara straight from Baltimore.' He smiled sweetly.

Anthony is the kind of boy whose radiant looks make him content with the world that gives him such a warm reception, rather than with himself.

We pulled up in front of a large and beautiful sixteenth-century palace. 'Hotel Guzman,' said Anthony. 'Don't worry, it's all fixed up new inside. You've never seen such bathrooms. Solid black marble.'

We all shot up in a small, fast lift. The manager flung open a door and ushered us into a splendid apartment full of divan beds and somebody's clothes.

'Why, that's *my* room,' said Anthony.

'Yes, sir. I had beds for the ladies moved in while you were absent.'

'Now, see here . . .' said Anthony.

E. took over. 'We do not want to be three in a room,' she said gently.

'No room for three? But the gentleman said he was expecting two ladies.'

'Yes, and here we are. But you see we don't want all three to share one room.'

'That is all right, Señora. It is a large room. In Holy Week when there are many travellers we would have a family of seven, nine persons in such a room. And their servants in the bathroom.'

'But this isn't Holy Week.'

'It is not, Señora. In Holy Week there would be a family and servants in every room, now it is only one gentleman and two ladies. It costs more in Holy Week, too.'

'Look here,' I said, 'we have strange habits and we want two, or at least one other room. Have you got them?'

'Yes, yes, many rooms. We are the newest hotel in Guadalajara.'

'Well, can we see them?'

'They are very new, Señora. More new than this room. We are still working on the newness.'

After a good deal more of this, a bed for Anthony was moved into a cupboard leading out of our room. The cupboard had window, but it opened into a corridor. Ours had an open view over red-tiled roof tops and a brilliant nocturnal sky. The night was warmer than it had been in Morelia. We were very hungry.

A cry of distress from E. in the bathroom. 'My dear, I can't make the water run. Do try.'

Indeed: hot tap, cold tap, tub and basin, not a drop. There was a telephone on the wall, I picked it up:

'There doesn't seem to be any water in our bathroom.'

'Of course not, Señora. It has not been laid on. One thing after another. Perhaps next year? Yes, certainly next year. If we do well. You will recommend us?'

Ready first, I proceeded to go downstairs. I walked up the corridor, none too well-lit, then saw, caught myself, and knees buckling reeled a step backward, collapsed against a wall and howled for Anthony.

He came running. 'What's the matter?'

'THERE ARE NO STAIRS.'

'Well, what d'you want stairs for?'

'I was about to go down.'

'What's wrong with the elevator?'

'Oh God, Anthony, don't be so yourself. And don't let's have a Mexican conversation. Go and see . . . No, don't go! Be careful!'

Anthony went a few steps up the corridor. 'Jesus Christ,' he said.

The corridor ended in space. Seventy feet below, at the

bottom of the crater left by flights of marble recently ripped out, lay invisible in a dim pool of light the reception desk, the leather armchairs and the spittoons of the entrance hall. Between, a void. They had begun working on the newness on the top floor. Anthony and I fetched E. from the room and we all went down in the lift.

Anthony was already familiar with a glittering establishment exotically called the Glass of Milk. It had a chromium bar, brand-new murals in a cubist style, and cafeteria furniture. In this cosy setting we first drank sherry, then Spanish claret, then coffee, then white rum. In between – it took a long time to come – we ate a mixed grill, toasted tortillas stuffed with cheese and lettuce, and some avocado pears. It was very crowded. There were tables with sparse American ladies in cotton frocks, and tables with round American ladies in print dresses, and tables and tables with middle-aged men with the more comfortable cast of Spanish features in beautifully cut silk suits.

Anthony said, 'Some friends of yours kept calling me in Mex City. They wanted to know where you'd gone, and could they have your address, and they wanted to take me places.'

'Who were they?'

'Can't remember their names. I didn't care for them too much. I guess they're fairies.'

'Why, Anthony, how old-fashioned you sound,' said E.

'They did take me to this place where we had cocktails and a great big steak.'

'Their names weren't Rosencrantz and Guildenstern?'

'Maybe,' said Anthony. 'Yes, that's it.' Then he said with sudden suspicion, 'Could it?'

'Who paid for the steak and cocktails?'

'Well I did,' said Anthony.

Then we told him about the bandits.

He said, 'Just imagine the poor bastards' faces when they saw all that paper stuff of yours.'

'That is a thought,' said E. 'At least they have my clothes to console themselves with.'

It was after one o'clock when we left the Glass of Milk, and the streets though quiet enough were not oppressed by the exaggerated silence of Morelia and Mexico City at a similar hour. For the first time the night felt what it was, a late summer night in a provincial town. Perhaps it was the presence of Anthony, perhaps it was the rum: Goya was far and Lawrence had been wrong. We went for a long stroll.

Guadalajara is a university town; a junction of the South-Pacific Railway; the capital of Jalisco, the richest of the ex-Hacienda states; the centre of an agricultural region, the hub of the native gin manufacture, the last stronghold of Creole aristocracy and the second largest city in Mexico. It was founded almost immediately after the Conquest and is full of handsome, florid buildings of that epoch in patinaed red *tezontle*. The town shows dignity and powers of assimilation, appearing to be neither in decay nor straining to build itself out of sense and form, and to have escaped so far, but for such thin ends of the wedge as the Glass of Milk, the mongrelization of Mexico City.

We were waked early next morning by Anthony, hair on end, wild-eyed, bursting in.

'There's a man in my room.'

'A man?' E. sat up. 'Anthony, have you become a Victorian lady? Did you look under your bed?'

'He's in my window.'

'What does he want?'

'That's what I've been trying to make out for the last half-hour,' said Anthony. 'He's smiling horribly, and now he's threatened me with an instrument. No, I won't go back. I won't.'

E. and I put on dressing gowns and advanced into the alcove. A very small man in an alpaca suit was leaning into the room. He held up a black leather bag, and his smile was indeed a little fixed. On seeing us, hope gleamed again, and he broke into chatter.

'*Dentista*,' he said, and shook his bag. '*Dentista*, see?'

'As a matter of fact, I don't,' said E.

'Please call back the Señorito. The Señorito took fright. He did not understand. Tell the Señorito it is the dentist. And perhaps Your Excellencies also,' he opened his bag, 'are Americans?'

'And *who*,' said E., 'called you?'

'I call. I am the American dentist.'

'God,' said E., and left the room.

'All is clear, my dears,' I said when I rejoined them, 'whenever Americans arrive at this hotel, the management lets him know. Americans always ask for an American dentist. He is the American dentist, the dentist for Americans.'

Our Consulates took it in their strides.

'I guess you're insured,' said the American Vice-Consul, a friendly young man in a large office in a fine Renaissance mansion.

'I'm not,' said E.

'That's too bad.'

'Should we go to the police?'

'I shouldn't waste my time.'

'You see, we are most anxious to get those papers back.'

'We'll be glad to put a call through for you, Mrs A.,' said the Vice-Consul.

'Where to?'

'That's up to you.'

At the British Consulate, less splendidly installed, they said, 'Unfortunately, these things do happen here. The bus people are supposed to be in on it. I shouldn't stress the point though if I were you.'

'Police?'

'No harm in that.'

'You see, I really want to get those papers back.'

'Well, there's always the Thieves' Market at Mexico City.'

'The Thieves' Market?'

'It's a place where thieves offer goods for sale during a limited time to give the owners a chance. That is to say, goods of more sentimental value that would fetch less elsewhere.'

'Look here,' I said, 'you are not suggesting that I should go all the way back to Mexico City on the chance of finding my manuscript and photographs in the public thieves' market?'

'I am suggesting nothing of the kind. You must make your own decisions.'

E. and I met in great dejection at the Glass of Milk, where Anthony was eating scrambled eggs, grilled ham, hot waffles and avocado pears.

'Tough on you,' he said.

'Succinct as usual, my dear Anthony,' said E.

'Tell you what I'd do. What about those pals of yours in Mex City? I'd call them and ask them to look for your things.'

'Oh, nonsense, Anthony.'

'Let them work on it.'

'No, no. Why should they, anyway?'

'They seem to want to get in good with you. I shouldn't worry about *them*. I'm going to call them right now.'

'And how do you propose to telephone to Mexico City?'

'From the Consulate, of course. *And* the call's on them.'

'*Well*,' said E., delighted, 'as an American taxpayer I should think that I was entitled.'

'Right now,' said Anthony. 'And then we can clear out of this dump tonight and go someplace we can swim.'

And so once more, Guenther von der Wildenau-Schlichtleben and Karl-Heinz-Horst von Rautenburg were put on our track.

We did, however, not leave Guadalajara as quickly as Anthony had hoped. The call to Mexico City did not get through that afternoon, nor the next day. By then E. was quite as keen on it as Anthony himself and very cross and pompous about *Our* Foreign Service. Then it turned out that the Barons had left the Pensión Hernandez under a cloud, and E. and Anthony insisted that the Foreign Service find out their new address. They spent most of their time between the Consulate and the Glass of Milk, working out tactics over Bacardi cocktails. Then E. had to get herself some clothes. Guadalajara has a few good shops and a department store run by a French family. Meanwhile Anthony made friends. He met the American Consul-

General and his wife, a charming and hospitable couple, and soon he was drinking their Bourbon and riding their motor cars. I began to learn Spanish irregular verbs.

tuve	tuvimos
tuviste	tuvisteis
tuvo	tuvieron

puedo
puedes
puede . . .

I should have learned patience from the woman who sat on the pavement opposite the Glass of Milk. She was there every morning and vanished sometime in the night. She neither begged nor had anything to sell and her clothes were decorous. She always sat perfectly still and her expression told one nothing. There are many such persons in the streets.

'What do they think they're doing?' said Anthony.

'Neither,' said E.

'What?' said Anthony.

'Wait for revelation,' said I.

'Apocryphal,' said E.

'Oh,' said Anthony, 'mystics.'

He had also met, in barber shops and bars and without benefit of grammar, some Guadalajarans, male members of the *jeunesse dorée*, the sons of the gentlemen in silk suits at the Glass of Milk. They took him to the French Club and a rodeo, engaged him in versions of gin rummy played for high stakes, and he ceased to wear his Mexican hat.

E. and I were full of curiosity. 'What do you talk about? Do tell us what they're like,' we said.

'They're all right.'

Later he said, 'They talk about sex all day, but they don't seem to know any girls.'

One morning, he said, 'We've had a bust-up. You see there was this night club. It didn't amount to much in the first place. And there were all these whores. It wasn't any fun. I mean who wants to dance with a lot of whores? Some of them just kids. I mean what's the point. So I said to Don Orazio and to Don Joaquím, now if we had some nice girls to take out, haven't you boys got any sisters to introduce to a fellow? Then didn't they get mad. They said their sisters were at the True Cross in England and the Sacred Heart at Seville and my suggestion was an outrage and they guessed I didn't know any better. They were sure my intentions were not dishonourable, but I ought to have realized that as a Protestant I wasn't eligible and where was I brought up. So I said to Don Orazio and to Don Joaquím, in the first place I was an Episcopalian, and not to be such boobies, and all the men in Princeton asked one another's sisters down for the proms; and they said they'd rather die and they expected I believed in divorce too and I was lucky I was their guest. And then they all started jabbering to each other in Spanish.'

'Poor Anthony.'

'I was right, wasn't I? What would you have done?'

'Never ask for a member of the family that isn't on the table,' said E.

'What happened finally,' said I.

'Well, the father of Don Joaquím came in. And he said it was the best joke he had heard in a long while, and I was a Yankee but a good boy, and they all calmed down. So I said, let's forget about it, and what about a round on me. Then they got mad again and acted as though I'd insulted them. Jesus, what a night.'

'Poor Anthony.'

Nevertheless his touchy new friends seemed to love him well enough. And when at last the interest in Rosencrantz and Guildenstern had abated and a letter to them been dispatched to a putative address, and we were able to leave for the Lake of Chapala, we did so in a fine motor lent for the occasion to Anthony, clutching a paper with the address of one of the uncles of Don Joaquím, the son of an ex-governor of the state, whom we understood to be prostrate with joy in anticipation of receiving us on his hacienda expressly erected for that purpose on one of the lake's remoter shores.

Part Two

DON OTAVIO

The 'potamus can never reach
The mango on the mango-tree . . .

Chapter One
SAN PEDRO TLAYACÁN

From the stony Maenalus
Bring your flocks, and live with us;
Here ye shall have greater grace . . .

WIDE FRENCH WINDOWS opened from the domed, whitewashed room on to a sun-splashed loggia above a garden white and red with the blooms of camellia, jasmine and oleander and the fruits of pomegranate, against a shaped luxuriance of dense, dark, waxed leaves; and below the garden lay the lake, dull silver at that hour. At the end of a balustrade, the extravagant stone figure of St Peter, fleeced with moss, raised a broken arm towards the waters. Another figure sprawled ensnared among the creepers where it had fallen a decade or two ago, and from an Italian urn grew a crimson flower like a banner. Three tall, tall, tapering palms swayed lightly on the shore. The air was sweet with tuberose and lime, and dancing like a pointillist canvas with brilliant specks, bee and moth, hummingbird and dragonfly. Birds everywhere: slender birds with pointed scarlet tails, plump birds with yellow breasts and coral beaks, smooth birds with smarmed blue wings; darting birds and soft birds and birds stuck all over with crests and plumes and quills; tight-fitted birds and birds that wore their feathers like a Lully flourish, and striped birds as fantastically got up as cinquecento gondoliers; ibis and heron, dove and quail, egret and wild duck, swallows and cardinals, afloat, in the trees, on the lawn, dipping and skimming, in and out, out and in of a dozen open windows. A white cockatoo shrieked hideously from a shrub and was answered by the house parrot in Spanish. Bead curtains clicked from the kitchen quarters; and below, under the shade of a papaya tree I could see Anthony reclining on a bamboo chaise longue engaged in reading the works of Mr Somerset Maugham.

The room behind me was all space and order and that aired and ample, hard white cleanness of the south that has the quality of lucidity substantiated and forms the limpid element in which the mind and body move at ease. An almost abstract room, rejecting the clutter of personality – a ceiling vaulted by an Indian whose father was taught by a Spaniard taught by a Moor; walls that were walls, and windows that were windows; a red-tiled floor; two or three pieces of Mexican Louis-Seize beautifully waxed, a bed designed in another century and built in this one, a rug of shampooed angora goat and a pair of easy chairs, perennial local products of pigskin and bamboo.

The house was built in the eighteenth century for a family that would spend three months a year, and added on to later without a visible break in style. It is a two-storeyed hacienda, washed apricot, with wings enclosing quadrangles and a long south-western front facing the lake. The ground plan is native, the statuary was brought from Italy; the garden is believed to be English. All is tempered by alternate periods of prosperity and care, absence and neglect.

Presently we shall bathe. E. will call to me, or I shall call to Anthony; we will walk to the end of the garden and slide into the lake without a shock, and with one leaping stroke coolly out of depth splash upon the mild and level water. The lake is immense, an inland-sea with bays set deep into three provinces, freshened by many rivers. A hundred miles of shore, undisgraced by rail or concrete, curve eastward toward Michoacán; and opposite our inlet one can see the outline of green hills upon another coast. Trees dip their branches over the calm waterfront, a donkey drinks stiff-legged and two Indian women stand waist-deep washing each other's hair, while we lie under the palms on coarse sand and crackling birch-bleached weed, Anthony in full repose like an animal that has run, E. and I more restless, teasing a complacent fowl with pebbles and a rhyme in the manner of Edward Lear.

'The fish's come in.' Without lifting head from arms, Anthony has sensed the boat. Now the *comida* will be ready at the house; we shall eat under the thick shade of a west pergola, with the quick, straight, insouciant appetite of these altitudes: rice stewed with vegetables, fried eggs, *blanco*, a kind of small fat sole, very firm, brought up from the cold centre of the lake, avocados and fruit; attended by runners, two stocky Indian boys, Andreas and Domingo, swarthy, eager, tireless and headstrong like a pair of young mules. Something retrieves the meal from chaos:

> *'this eternal spring,*
> *Which here enamels every thing,*
> *And sends the fowls to us in care,*
> *On daily visits through the air; . . .'*

The household and Anthony, who is reverting to some planter ancestry, will sleep the afternoon away. I, enlivened rather by these days of peace, have the choice of many shades to take my book. E. will pace the loggia swinging a small stick, the single upright figure during the slow hours, east west, west east, composing step by step, clause by clause the periods of an exegesis of one of the more incomprehensible personages of seventeenth-century France.

We owe it all to Anthony. He had not been able to enjoy the driving of his automobile for long. Thirty miles out of Guadalajara, at Chapala, the lake began and the road ended. He made an attempt to continue on the rutted trail replacing it, but had to give up. A number of Indians, rigid in their blankets, looked on without comment. We studied the address on Anthony's bit of paper.

'I can hardly pronounce it,' said E.

'Just ask for Don Otavio's place,' said Anthony.

They said, 'A boat will come.'

'Indeed. A boat. *When?*'

'In the little future.'

A child was sent to the shore on lookout, Anthony gazed at his engine, I at my wristwatch, E. flicked the pages of her detective story. The Indians sat well content.

But the boat did not come.

Then a mule cart passed. The Indians stopped it, made the old man who was driving turn round, dump his load, and pile on our bags instead. Anthony and I were helped on to a trunk, a space was cleared for E. on the driver's plank. Somebody stuck flowers into the mule's hat. E. was still sitting in the Cadillac firmly, clutching her book. 'Ask them how far it is,' she said.

'*Es un poquito retirado.*'

'They say it's a little retired.'

Then suddenly we were off. The Indians poked the driver and the beast, and shouted, '*¡Tlayacán, Tlayacán! ¡Que les vaya bien!*' E. bowed from her plank and said politely, 'Boo-ainous dee-as, mooches gratsias, *viva Mexico.*' The mule feigned a second's trot and everything began to shake, sway and rattle in the most concentrated manner.

The trail consisted of two not always parallel ruts of varying depth and gauge, caked hard, strewn with boulders, cut by holes and traversed by ditches. The cart had solid wooden wheels and no springs.

First we passed some stucco villas decaying behind tall enclosures. Sixty years ago, during the heydays of the dictatorship, Chapala had been a modish resort. The driver pointed, '*La casa de la hija de Don Porfirio Diaz.*'

'Look,' we said, 'that villa belongs to Diaz' daughter.'

'I am not going to be diverted by historical interest,' said E. The plank she was trying to remain on was narrow as well as wobbly.

'Doña Carmen comes here in the winter,' said the driver, 'but the *ferrocarril* her father built for her is broken.'

'A railway?' said E. 'A railway, where?'

'From Guadalajara.'

'Where is it now?'

'Broken. Now we have the road.'

'What road?'

'The road from Guadalajara.'

'But it doesn't go on.'

'Yes, to Guadalajara.'

'What *is* he talking about?'

'The Señora wants to know whether there was a road or railway from Chapala.'

'Yes, Don Porfirio's railway. Now the road.'

'We meant round the lake.'

'Round the lake one goes by boat.'

'The hell one does,' said Anthony.

'How did Don Porfirio and Doña Carmen go?' said I.

'Don Porfirio and Doña Carmen and the Excellencies did not go farther than Chapala.'

'Very sensible of them,' said E.

Soon we were in open country. On our left lay the lake, almost colourless under the still vertical sun; on our right, behind a fringe of fields, a row of humpy hills covered with lush green shrub. Nasty clusters of black carrion birds hung watchful in the sky. The trail, conservative in the rhythm of its vagaries, continued small hole, big hole, boulder, ditch; small hole, big hole, boulder, chasm. In turns we walked, we rode, we pushed, propped luggage, steadied shafts, picked up E.'s book and helped the mule. We sat by the chasms in discouragement. After some time, pigs appeared and baby donkeys, then a banana grove, and presently we reached a subtropical village. Women with children at their breasts peered at us from leaf huts.

'Anthony, is *this* your friend's place?' said E.

'What is this village called?' said I.

'The place of *el gringocito d'Inglaterra*,' said the old man.

'What's that?'

'A dear little dirty American from England,' said I.

'From the map it must be San Antonio Something,' said Anthony.

'Map!' said E. 'Don't tell me.'

'What about that American?' said Anthony. '*¿Dónde? ¿Dónde?*'

'Not American,' said I. 'Work him out in terms of *un cher petit boche d'Autriche*.'

'Oh,' said E., 'a nice young Englishman.'

'Let's call on him,' said Anthony.

'What a dreadful idea,' said I.

'My dear Anthony,' said E., 'you have much to learn. If this hypothetical personage chooses, for no doubt some very good reason of his own, to live in such a place as this, he does not do so in order to be called upon by the likes of us.'

'He may be lonesome,' said Anthony.

'Englishmen in subtropical villages never are.'

After another hour, we came to another much larger village with proper mud houses and a market place. For three hundred yards, potholes were agreeably replaced by cobblestones.

'Now what about this place?'

'Ajijíc,' said the driver.

'I dare say,' said E.

Then the trail resumed its character with a will. The countryside grew wilder, weltering rays struck the lake and the water glistened in milky rainbow colours. Birds appeared. On we dragged and shook and rumbled with no end in view. Then a train of mules came into sight, broke into a gallop, raced towards us in a cloud of dust, reined in and effected a trembling standstill. A man leapt from the saddle. He bowed to E. and handed her a large mauve envelope.

On crested paper, above a triple-barrelled signature, we read:

Villa El Dorado,
San Pedro Tlayacán

Your Madams,
Distinguished Esquire,
¡Your entire servant, being apprised to his profoundest confusion of Your unbecoming way to his undignified house, the disgraced rascals through obdurate tardiness having returned the insufficient boat without Your Unparalleled Favours to his eternal shame, is sending three unworthy mules, scant shelter and a humble sustenance for Your

137

Facile progress and implores You to dispense him for the abomination
of the travel!

Q. B. S. P.
Otavio de . . . y . . . y . . .

'Your friend seems very civil, Anthony,' said E.

The mules, fine well-groomed beasts, were hitched troika-
fashion on to our equipage; a third was to be Anthony's
mount. The shelter was two parasols, and the sustenance a
large Edwardian tea-basket in full polish. This was deposited
on the ground.

Our new attendants withdrew some distance where they
settled in expectancy. E. and Anthony were as unfamiliar
with the mechanism of this product of a pre-plastic age as
Don Otavio's retainers, so I sat on the roadside, lit the spirit
lamp and proceeded to make tea. The caddy had been freshly
filled; there was thin bread and butter, there were cucumber
sandwiches, ginger nuts, Huntley and Palmer biscuits. There
was a jar of Patum Peperium. Thus we proceeded much
refreshed on our travel. Thanks to the new turnout, the
progress of the last hours was a good deal faster and for E. and
myself more agonizing, the parasols adding greatly to our
insecurity and the indignity of walking having now become
unthinkable. So it was with relief that at sunset, without
warning and in a last excruciating spurt of gallop, we swung
into the drive of the Villa El Dorado.

A youngish man stood on the terrace of a very ugly house.
He ran out to meet us. He was wearing white flannels and a
charming shirt decorated with sea horses. A bunch of gold
holy medals tinkled in the open neck. His hands and
complexion were white as asses' milk; his face, a long oval
with slightly softened contours crested by a plume of silvery

138

hair, was a generic face: one of those inherited handsome faces of Goya's minor courtiers, where the acumen, pride and will of an earlier mould have run to fatuity and craft; a set face, narrow, stiff and sad. He turned out one of the kindest men I ever met.

'Hello,' he said, 'hello. I am Otavio XXX. I am so glad you got here at last. Nobody has come from Chapala by road for thirty years. You must be tired. That horrible cart, so like a tumbril.' Here he let off a burst of orders in Spanish. 'I *am* sorry about the boat being late.' He kissed E.'s hand and gave Anthony two sketchy taps on each shoulder, the formal simulacrum of a hug. 'Don Antonio! Joaquím and Orazio were down last Saturday to Monday, they speak of you as a brother.'

We thanked him for sending us tea and mules.

'You were able to use the basket? I am so happy. It belonged to my mother.' His manner was simple and so, after all, was his English. 'Now you must have some drinks. Or would you like to go up to your rooms first? No, not here. Over at the hacienda it is on the other side of these trees.' He let off more orders. 'Here is where I live now. The house is a replica of a villa at Monte Carlo my mother used to stay in when she was a girl. My father had it built for her as a wedding present. Now she has left it to me. The hacienda belongs mostly to my brothers. I look after it for them. They do not live here. No one has lived on the hacienda since the Revolutions, but my brother Enriquez and his wife come down for the weekends. Would you like to see it now before it is quite dark? I am afraid we have no electric light. We had our own plant when I was a boy, with an Italian who ran it. He was shot by mistake by Villa's band.

'Yes, these are lime trees. My great-grandfather planted

139

them. He had them brought from England. Now that our land is taken, my brothers and I are going to have an hotel at the hacienda. Do you not think that a good idea? We hope to have some sympathetic travellers from abroad. This is a *guanábano*. The fruit is good. You will be able to enjoy it at Christmas.

'Of course you must. You must stay a very long time. And this is the Hacienda San Pedro. I so hope you will like it.'

Thus, in the twilight, we saw the apricot façade, the open loggia, the garden and the lake, the fallen figure and the upright one.

'But it is lovely,' we said, 'lovely, lovely.'

'It is yours,' said Don Otavio.

Chapter Two
A WELL-RUN HOUSE

Par ici! vous qui voulez manger

Le Lotus perfumé! c'est ici qu'on vendange
Les fruits miraculeux dont votre cœur a faim;
Venez vous enivrer de la douceur étrange
De cette après-midi qui n'a jamais de fin.

OURS IS not an age of luxury, nor one of domestic comfort. Order and space, the sine qua nons of daily freedom, are rarities of great price, exorbitant in effort and in money. Without space, order is hard to maintain; and space is hard to keep warm and polished. Never before has housework been done by so many and so badly. Reluctant amateurs and semi-professionals scurry to and fro in a hum of Hoovers but fail to bring about the perpetual resurrrection of the inviolate bedroom, the well-set table and the somnolent kitchen from under the hourly detritus of existence. Men come home to no privacy, women to no leisure, and over the careless flow of hospitality falls the shadow of its aftermath.

Latins do not seem to share that sense of struggle. Their wives and mothers swing impeccable establishments, and put up the jam besides, without that air of participation in the rearguard's last and unsuccessful stand; but women of the Anglo-Saxon middle classes seldom have the Carthusian cast of mind and steadfastness of will conducive to a tidy house. Their drawers brim with single stockings and their sinks with tea leaves; they feel they waste their time, which indeed they do, and either settle in the mess like duck in duck soup, or grapple on, morning after morning, until the world becomes the size of their unmanageable home and their sole memento vivere the grease, the crumbs, the ashes where so short ago the pleasant company had sat, and their families are driven from house to flat and from flat to the confinement of the hotel bedroom.

Don Otavio de X y X y X has been ruined these thirty years. He has seventeen servants to look after him. Mexico is its own place and lives its own age, or composite of ages, and whatever that may be, it is not the age of post-war England; and in Mexico, San Pedro Tlayacán is a backwater. All the dirty work is done by many for a few. By so many, for so few, that the work must surely cease to be so dirty. Someone sits on a stool in the shade waving a painted fan before a charcoal fire; someone else is walking in the garden carrying Don Otavio's box of sweetmeats; in the back yard four people sit chattering with vegetables in their laps, a child has wandered off to prod the nests for an egg, another person is pushing a straw whisk about the patio tiles raising a few geranium petals: and thus here the enchanted ease, too, is spread over the many.

Don Otavio keeps house all day. He appears on the terrace of the villa and claps his hands. *Niños*, the papayas must be picked. *Niño*, there are roses again in the water tank. Has the boat gone for the butter? Has Jesús made it up with his wife? Has Carmelita been able to do something about the spell on the tomatoes? Would she like the priest? The white turkey is not well: *niña*, the brandy flask, and a teaspoon. Is the cook herself again today? *Niñas*, there is that ibis sitting on the washing. He wants to see the jam; he needs a bigger vase; the lamp in the hall was smoking; he would like his purse; and a little cinnamon, please, in his chocolate. What, out of beeswax? There's another hole in the billiard table; his brother is coming out tomorrow, they might have a suckling pig. He will have his dinner on the east terrace, in the moonlight. No, it is chilly; will they bring him a shawl? Dinner is to be laid in the back drawing room. For four. No, perhaps for nine.

Everybody hops and skips and pricks up their ears. There is endless talk, to and fro, about everything. And meanwhile, prodded and subsiding, spurred and delayed, through regular drinking bouts and exceptional drinking bouts, through fits and visitations and fiestas, the household jogs on its course like a donkey through his working day. Early fruit and coffee, the birds noisy in the trees, water pumped up from the lake, the servants' tortillas and the servants' *frijoles*, beefsteak and chocolate at the Villa, tea and eggs at the hacienda, the patios watered and the linen spread out on the lawn, the mule with provisions in from Jocotepec, the long midday meal and the longer afternoon lull, lemonade and iced tea, the nets cast on the lake before sunset, the wild fowl settling in the rushes, the lamps brought in and trays with Manzanilla and fried *charales*, Don Otavio's card table set up, the servants' tortillas, the servants' *frijoles* and somebody singing, dinner at ten and the shutters fastened down for the night.

Everything is done for us. *Aquí nada nos falta.* We are those sacred animals, guests at a Mexican gentleman's house, or rather at a Mexican gentleman's gates, for Don Otavio keeps to the El Dorado and we might be said to have the run of the hacienda if so hearty a term could be applied to that halcyon sweetness of existence. Don Otavio cannot know how happy he has made us, or he would not try so hard to improve on our happiness: messengers appear from the villa with offers of saddle-horses and canoes; with a camellia – it bloomed this morning; with pot-pourri – my aunt at Guanajuato makes it; with a bowl of pork-and-barley – it is the speciality of this saint's day, you may not find it entirely repulsive; with enquiries – have we slept at all, was there anything fit to eat for breakfast, are we tolerably in spirits? Then, after Mass and the toilet, Don Otavio himself strolls over for a talk. It is always the right moment. He glides into a chaise longue beside one.

'Yes, yes, the Empress Carlota, poor woman. My mother's favourite uncle was one of her ADCs. He died at Querétaro.'

'No, my father's people were Juaristas at that time. Poor Don Masimiliano.'

Then, again at the right moment, or rather a little before, Don Otavio rises, '*¿Con su permiso?*' and withdraws with smooth abruptness.

We lunch and dine together, and at nightfall Don Otavio and I play four hands of piquet in the El Dorado drawing room, a very large room, bare and stuffed at the same time, where every piece of furniture that is not a straight-backed chair or a footstool is a full-sized Victorian sideboard, and the crucifix alone is machine-made and modern. We play five centavos a point and chalk up the score. So far, thank God, I am a little to the good. Anthony has warned me to stay so.

'Don't you lose or there'll be this terrible rumpus,' he said. '*I* know. You haven't been through what I went through at Guadalajara. Punctilio, see?'

It appears that Don Otavio cannot take money from a lady under his roof, and nor may he pass over a card debt.

'Try and cheat a bit,' said Anthony.

'Well, you know, I think Don Otavio *does*. I daren't look.'

★

144

The seventeen servants sleep in a house of their own: that is, those who do not sleep at the villa and the two or three who, apparently by choice, sleep across thresholds with Marshal Bazaine's cumbersome 1860 rifles at their sides, so at night we are alone at the hacienda in our flight of rooms. Anthony has taken happily to the vast apartment that used to be the bedroom of Don Otavio's father, the Governor, a man we gather of ample and fulfilled ambitions who made himself one of the right hands of Porfirio Diaz, raked a huge fortune out of politics and acquired another by marriage to Don Otavio's mother, who brought him besides ten thousand acres in Jalisco and a string of titles, the major portion of the Province of Colima. He died in the nick of time, two months before the outbreak of the Revolutions. Don Otavio has given us to understand that he, himself, has taken more after his mother.

'My father had a difficult disposition.'

'Did you see much of him then? You must have been quite a small boy, Don Otavio?'

'We always went with him.' From the hacienda to the Gubernatorial Palace at Guadalajara, to the capital, to Chapultepec for an afternoon's cabinet meeting, down the Pacific slopes to the estates in Colima, on tours of inspection of the southern provinces, over the Sierra Madre to the mining towns of Durango, to Vera Cruz, to Paris in the wake of Diaz, to Seville for Holy Week, to Homburg, to Carlsbad and to Monte Carlo, by steamer, in private railway carriage, on horse and mule and Daimler, the family and household had followed. Don Otavio's mother, Don Otavio's maiden aunt, his three brothers, a cousin who acted as his father's private secretary, the bodyguard, his brothers' English tutor, his mother's confessor who to save the anti-clerical face of the regime would be passed off as the librarian by his father, Don Otavio's governess and a score of servants.

'Doña Maria Carmen, such a sweet woman, you would have adored her.'

'Now you can't remember Diaz' wife?'

'She was my mother's and my aunt's dearest friend and my second brother's godmother.'

'Diaz died in 1915? He must have been eighty.'

'He was eighty-four. Doña Maria Carmen came back from Paris twenty years later. She was much younger. They let her live in her house at Mexico. I always saw her and my aunt to Mass when I was there. She only died the winter before last. *Such* a sweet woman.'

'Don Otavio,' said E., 'you must have seen great changes. Like a man born in France in 1770.'

'We were ruined when I was a boy, and we had many troubles. When there was the rising at Guadalajara and my father just dead, we had to bar the shutters. My brothers' tutor put out the Union Jack and they passed our door. So many of our friends were murdered in their houses that day.'

'And how do you feel about it all now?'

'We may still get compensation for our land. Some people did. My brothers are working on it.'

'How do you feel about the present Government?'

'My brothers say the President is a very reasonable man.'

'Don Otavio, I have meant to ask you, where *did* you learn your English?'

'Well, I could not be sent to Downside like my brothers, and Mr Beasely left us soon after the beginning of the Revolutions, so there was only the Spanish governess. But my mother made me keep it up. She always spoke English to me for part of the day.'

'She means your written English, Otavio,' said Anthony.

'I do not write it. There was no one to teach me.'

'But you sent us a letter.'

'Oh that. That was a *lettre de politesse*.'

'So it was. But who wrote it?'

'Well, I did in a way. You see, my governess only spoke Castilian and French but she thought I ought to be able to write social notes in English. For deaths and invitations and occasions like that. She wrote out a dozen models for me in Spanish and made me put them into English, and use a dictionary for the spelling. I kept them.'

'Did your governess foresee our arrival by mule cart?'

'People who could read came by boat. I do not copy the models, I only look at them for the tone. It is not difficult. After all, formal letters are much the same in all languages.'

'I've never seen one,' said Anthony.

'When we are going to have the hotel, I shall have to write business letters.'

'Anthony shall help you. He will write you some models. They'll be quite a change from your governess'.'

'Thank you. That is very kind. Yes, I don't think hers would be really suitable. They are more supposed for equals.'

'Don Otavio, have you read many modern English novels?'

'My mother read *David Copperfield* to us.'

'And since?'

'I do not read often. My Guadalajara sister-in-law has *The Forsyte Saga*. I began that. *¿Con su permiso?*' Don Otavio rose and vanished.

'How would Otavio make out in the US?' said Anthony.

'Don Otavio has seen so many changes that he has failed to notice them,' said E., 'the difference between lived and recorded history.'

Chapter Three
TEA WITH MR MIDDLETON

Great, valiant, pious, good and clean,
Sublime, contemplative, serene,
Strong, constant, pleasant, wise!

LAKE CHAPALA has tides and is subject to sudden and alarming squalls, but in the late afternoon it is smooth like gelatine and shot through with unexpected reverberated colours, ruby and amethyst, cornelian and reseda. I rowed E. and myself into Jocotepec. We had not told Don Otavio for fear of escorts and assistance. Anthony had become as lazy as molasses and refused to budge from his chaise longue on the Governor's west loggia.

'What do you want to look at an Indian village for?' he said.

'I feel a great need to buy my own postage stamps and matches,' said E.

'When you can get them here with no trouble?'

'That may be the reason.'

'Well, have a good time. You might get me some cigars, if there are any. I can't go on smoking Otavio's.'

On the landing stage at Jocotepec stood an upright figure in a tweed suit and a planter's hat, holding a telescope. 'How do you do,' he said. 'Come and see my garden,' and marched on before.

On the lake shore was a bungalow with a veranda, and before the veranda was a garden, an English garden, fresh and restrained, a lawn and a lily pond, sweet peas and daffodils, lavender and primrose and lobelia all blooming demurely in and out of season at the same time.

'The worst of it out here are the bees,' said our host; 'hybridize everything. And of course the climate. If you don't look out you get delphiniums ten feet high.' He clapped his hands. An Indio appeared. '*Mozo, te.* And *llamar* missis.'

Presently a youngish woman came out. 'Richard. They seem to be having trouble with the kettle, Richard,' she said.

'What?' said our host. 'What? Again?' and ambled into the house.

'I can't speak the lingo,' said his wife. 'Richard does. Now you sit down; you've had enough of Richard's flowers. It's nice to hear a human voice in this dreadful savage country. Richard likes it, he's used to places like that. I like London but I'd like to live at Nice, wouldn't you? Nice and quiet. Cheap too. Richard has promised me to when one of us dies. I'm only his second wife, you know; we got married during the war . . .'

'Blanche,' said her husband's voice from the door. 'Give us some tea. So you are staying at the X.s' place?'

'We love it.'

'Shiftless fellow, Otavio. Lazy. The way they've let those grounds of theirs run down, shocking. And he won't take advice . . . You saw what his man did to those lime trees? Now if I told Otavio once to leave those limes alone, I told him a dozen times. No mind. They'll never make something out of that place.'

'Their land was confiscated, wasn't it?'

'And a good thing too, if you ask me. They don't know how to look after their land. Never did. Money, money, money, and sitting in a chair all day at their clubs waiting for it to roll in. Diaz did what he could, but he couldn't do much with these Creoles. Hand in glove with them too at the end through that priest-ridden wife of his.'

'They are all RCs here,' said our hostess.

Her husband gave her a look. 'Not that the present so-called owners are any better. The natives plant a few acres with what they think they'll need, and let the rest lie fallow. A new child weaned means planting another couple of acres of maize, that's their idea of food production. The Government's been importing grain for the towns.'

'What do you think of the present Mexican Government?' said E., looking up like Pavlov's dogs.

'A pack of thieves. No worse though than the last lot. All that can be said for them is that they stick to their own muttons. Don't poke their damn noses into everything; a man can still build himself a greenhouse without having to get a permit from some fool ministry.'

'At home, Richard votes Conservative,' said his wife.

'Mind your business, Blanche,' said her husband.

'But you do, Richard, don't you?'

'Not that you can call it government. Centralized administration in a country of this sort, I ask you. Universal representation. It doesn't work. Natives don't want it, don't understand it, and they haven't got it. Whatever those jabberers at Mexico may tell you. A pity this place was ever allowed to set up on its own – not that the Spanish knew how to look after their people – what they need here is local administration: civil servants who know their jobs, a medical staff, honest magistrates. But where'd you find them?'

'In a Crown Colony,' muttered E.

'Get on with your tea, Richard,' said his wife.

'There hasn't been anyone fit to run a village police station since they kicked out Diaz. I was out here in '09 and I can tell you that the country was a damned sight better off than it is now. Diaz was a good man. Pity he got unstuck. Trouble with him was that he was weak. These dictator fellows always are. Didn't stand up to the army lads, didn't really stand up to the radicals, didn't stand up to his wife and her grand wastrel connections. The old boy was a bit of a snob, never got over his getting married into that set, but he was sound enough for all that. Now take Otavio's papa, there was a tough old bird for you though you wouldn't think so looking at Otavio. I won't say he wasn't out for number one, or that he was exactly one's idea of a public servant, but he kept things going. Hanged half the bandits in the province and put the rest into the militia. Not new, but it served. He started a railway service between Guadalajara and Chapala that ran about as well as things ever do in this country.'

'What *did* they want a railway for out here?' said I.

'Well, quite a lot of people had places on the lake then. For one thing there was Diaz' girl with that villa at Chapala. Oh I wouldn't say it *paid*, but the old man knew what he was doing. More than those sons of his ever will, twiddling their thumbs and waiting for compensation; Enriquez and Jaime at Guadalajara dickering with the law, Luís at Mexico trying to sell building lots nobody's ever laid eyes on, all with large houses and expensive wives and huge families, and Otavio running around San Pedro like a chicken without a head chattering to a pack of servants. *He'll* never see a penny of that compensation – if it ever comes – his brothers'll see to that. As it is they've pretty damn near done him out of everything. His mother meant him to have the place as he seems the only one who cares for it and the others have all got professions, for what they are worth. Well, they palmed him off with that joke of a villa and kept the hacienda, and left him to look after it for them while they made off with the cash. Enriquez, that's the eldest – you'll find him quite an impressive chap – even took the motor boat. Oh, Otavio is the best of the lot when all's said and done, even if he doesn't know how to stand up for himself. And now they're going to turn that place into an hotel. A bear-garden full of trippers on the lake. That was Enriquez' idea. Typical. I dare say it'll all come to nothing. Unless they can wangle the road from Chapala.'

'Oh yes,' I said, 'that road.'

'It was voted seventy years ago. The money was raised twenty-three times.'

'Richard!'

'It always vanished in some way or other. Even Otavio's papa couldn't do anything about it.'

'Richard!'

'What is it?'

'Someone at the gate.'

'Yes, yes.' Our host raised his voice, '*Adelante, adelante, vengo.*'

A boy advanced.

'*Vengo. Vengo. ¿Qué quiero?*'

'*Telegrama, Señor,*' said the boy.

'Oh yes, yes.' Our host stretched out his hand. 'Blanche: my spectacles.' He looked at her over their rims. 'Mrs Jackson's mother missed her boat at San Francisco.'

'Poor Mrs Jackson will be ever so upset.'

'I told the old girl not to go by South-Pacific. If I told them once . . . Oh. *Tengo.*' He fished in his waistcoat, produced a copper and handed it with the telegram. '*Tengo, tengo, esto por Señor Jackson, traer esto pronto casa Jackson.*'

'*Si, si Señor,*' said the boy, '*regulár,*' and went off.

'Shiftless fellow, Jackson,' said our host.

'Now, Richard, it wasn't his fault the roof wasn't finished when Mrs Jackson's mother came out. You took the mason for your hole in the lily pool.'

'Do you have many people living round here?' I said.

'Eleven,' said our host. 'Seven of them Americans. And there are some Germans and a Frog. He died. Didn't know how to look after himself.'

'Richard sees all their telegrams. They come to him first; he told the post-mistress. There are not very many . . .'

'We are a small colony out here,' said her husband, 'and must do all we can for each other.'

'He reads the postcards, too. Every morning, at the post office. But we never see anyone. Everybody lives miles away.'

'My wife doesn't like to go out; she's afraid of the natives. Very foolish of her.'

'I should like to sit on the beach, if I had someone to sit with me. The natives stare so.'

'Now, I'll tell you what you want to do,' said our host, 'you don't want to stay on at Otavio's. For one thing the place isn't an hotel yet and well, I mean to say, well, you don't want to be the fellow's guests for ever, and if I know those Creoles that's what you are. Typical of them, poor as church mice, not that the X.s haven't got something salted away somewhere.'

'Don Otavio has been extremely kind to us,' said E. on a rising note. 'Anthony, my young cousin, second cousin I should say,' something seemed to compel her to shed full light, 'made great friends with two of Don Otavio's nephews, and their uncle was good enough to ask us all to stay with him. The boys are going to visit Anthony in his home at Baltimore next summer.'

'Quite. Yes, yes, quite. Now there's a furnished cottage here at Jocotepec, just the thing. There are three of you, you said? Just the thing. You won't find it large; it's got a little patio though, not a view exactly but it's only the other side of the road from the lake. Furniture isn't much, but you wouldn't expect that out here; sooner or later you'll have to build anyway. The X.s always did themselves well, the old man had a Liverpool firm to do the plumbing. In '95 it must have been. I suppose those great big bathrooms still work?'

'They do. Perfectly.'

'Thought so. Well, at Jocotepec you'll have to have a boy to fetch your water. And mind he doesn't charge you for the donkey. Your landlady lives across the patio, nice woman, Elvira, if you can shut her up. I'll talk to her tomorrow morning.'

'Richard!' Our host's wife showed again the signs of disturbance caused in her by a native at the gate.

'What is it? What's he want?'

'Oh, it's Andreas,' we said, '*adiós, Andreas.*'

'*Con permiso de Ustedes,*' said Andreas and came forward.

'*Adiós Señora. Adiós Señora. Adiós Señor. Adiós Señora,*' for it is considered extremely rude not to greet every person present individually. 'Don Otavio salutes the Señoras and told me to row them home. The waters are a little agitated. I have brought the Señoras' blankets.' He held out our coats.

'Now isn't that like the fellow,' said our present host. 'Nannying you, interfering ass. And that reminds me, you want to get one good servant for your house and keep an eye on him. One. Whatever they may tell you. If you have more they'll start waiting on each other. Now what about having a look at the house tomorrow? You'd better come to luncheon. Bring your cousin. We lunch at 1.15.'

154

Chapter Four
LE DINER EN MUSIQUE

Au pays parfumé que le soleil caresse,
J'ai connu, sous un dais d'arbres tout empourprés
Et de palmiers d'où pleut sur les yeux la paresse,
Une dame créole aux charmes ignorés.

A T SAN PEDRO, we found a band in the garden playing good and loud.

'It is Doña Anna's band,' said Andreas. 'Doña Anna is calling on the master.'

'Is the lady a bandleader?'

'No, Señora. Doña Anna is a lady who lives on the other side of the water. A rich rich lady, she has music all day. It is the band from Ajijíc, the best band in Jalisco. It is Doña Anna's band now. The *mariachis* go to her house every morning. On feast-days too.'

'And do they also follow her about?'

'Yes, yes. Where Doña Anna goes go the *mariachis*.'

'Did you get me any cigars?' said Anthony.

'No.'

'Did you see your Indian village?'

'No.'

'We may be seeing a great deal of it if we don't look out,' said I.

'*You* didn't show much character,' said E.

'No,' said I.

'Otavio's been clucking like an old hen,' said Anthony. 'Why you didn't tell him you were going into Jocotepec. It seems there is a character, Mr Middleton or Middleman or something, you are supposed to call on and look at the garden.'

'We did see the garden.'

'Oh you did? Good. Poor Otavio was so upset, he said Mr Middleman's or Middleton's feelings were going to be hurt.'

'And you're going to see it too, dear. We are all to lunch there tomorrow.'

'Rush around in the middle of the day? Not me.'

'Spineless fellow, Anthony,' said E.

'And what's more you're going to live in a cottage at Jocotepec with a back-patio and a landlady and one servant you have to keep an eye on, and your bath water will come by donkey. No, not by donkey, by boy. At least that's what you are paying for.'

'You're kidding,' said Anthony.

'It is not an empty threat,' said I.

'A cloud as large as Mr Middleton's hand,' said E.

'It isn't *his* business,' said Anthony.

'I am an American,' said E. in an uncertain tone, as though she were practising for her level; 'I am an American. I will not be pushed around.'

Below, the band was still blaring away at the *Mañanitas*. 'Anthony, what *is* this din?'

'Oh, I don't know. They came in a lot of boats with this widow an hour or so ago. She's a knockout. And wait till you see her pearls. They're grey. I've never seen grey pearls. Dinner's an hour late and we're going to have suckling pig.'

Presently Don Otavio came over to say his word.

'I hope you will like Doña Anna. She is a great friend. She has had a sad life, poor woman. One must be kind to her.

She was married *à l'espagnole*, always shut up. Her husband did not let her go anywhere. It is unusual. He died two years ago and now that she is out of mourning she can do as she likes. She is trying to divert herself a little, it is natural. That is why she is keeping the *mariachis* with her all day. She needs gaiety after all these sad years and she is very musical. People at Guadalajara don't like it. It is true that Doña Anna is an original woman. She was a very great beauty. Now of course she is old.'

'And now tell us all about the autocrat in the garden. Has he always lived at Jocotepec?'

'Mr Middleton came here to retire. He was an engineer. I think he spent most of his life in Africa. He made the garden all himself. It is a very wonderful garden, is it not?'

'A very wonderful garden.'

'He plants everything in the spring. It is the hot dry season when everything dies. Mr Middleton says it is laziness. He very kindly lets me have some of his cuttings, but Jesús says they are things that cannot grow here. Mr Middleton does not like that. He says Jesús' flowers are too large.'

'Do you like Mr Middleton, Don Otavio? '

'Mr Middleton is a very distinguished English gentleman. And very clever.'

'He asked us to lunch with him tomorrow.'

'I shall see that the boat is ready. Mr Middleton does not like to be kept waiting.'

'He said something about a quarter past one, but he can't mean that. What time do they have luncheon?'

'At a quarter past one. And dinner at a quarter to eight. Mr Middleton keeps his own hours.'

'That cannot be so easy here.'

'It is inconvenient. The butcher does not kill before noon,

and the fish only comes in at three. The servants are unhappy about it.'

'What if they are asked out?'

'Mr Middleton does not like to eat in other people's houses and Mrs Middleton does not go out. She is afraid of the Indios, poor woman. It is a sad life for her. If only the road were mended, she could go for a drive. Now, I must not leave Doña Anna, *con su permiso*?'

When we came down, we found dinner laid on the terrace outside the main drawing room with the *mariachis*, all brasses ablow, sitting on the balustrade. Mexican establishments, like those of Tsarist Russia, do not have an apartment especially assigned to the purpose of eating. Table and appurtenances are moved about and meals laid *où le cœur vous en dise* according to the season, the menu, the company and the mood: luncheon in the east room today, Buttermere, the honeysuckle is blooming by the window. It is a genial arrangement and, provided one is neither short of space nor service, one that gives much scope to food and wine – omelette, ham and melon in the shade out-of-doors at noon; strawberries on the lawn; beef stew in the kitchen; madrilene and salmon on a nocturnal terrace; saddle of lamb and walnuts in the dining room; hock under the stars, port in the northroom, claret in the library, the iced magnum by the fire . . .

We found Doña Anna a woman, in her late forties perhaps, in full beauty and a cream of pearls. She wore crêpe de Chine pyjamas of the cut of those worn some decades ago in the South of France by the first women who wore trousers. By her side sat a sulky youth; handsome too, but brutish and as little civil as the customs of his class and country permitted. Doña Anna met us with the kind of zest that produces the same instant animation as the first tumbler of neat vodka, and that later, if kept up, palls, flattens and oppresses. Her voice was lovely, her Spanish rapid like a conjuring trick. Anecdote and comment flowed, as did alas the sweet Sauterne, ever a weakness of Don Otavio's table. The lake, people on the lake. The chief witch of Sahuayo and her gradual domination of Doña Anna's household. Doña Anna's unmasking of the witch. The Sunday murders at San Juan Cosala, the new funds for the road, last winter's bullfighting season – none of the new lot can hold a candle to the great *matadores*, do you remember Lallanda, do you remember Carnicerito? The Old Times. Doña Anna's wedding trip to Granada – never saw a thing. The Court at Madrid – very dull. The Queen, poor woman ... Otavio's Mama – how she spoilt you, *¡niño!* Dances at Mexico – *seguro, before* I was married ... Doña Anna did not mince her words. She was witty in a robust way that was both good-natured and contained a touch of worldly brutality. She ate with a good appetite.

Domingo and Andreas and Don Otavio's own Juan trotted round the table hissing with excitement and stress. The sequence of a length of courses always baffled them. When the suckling pig had been cleared, they came running with the fish. '*¡Niños!*' said Don Otavio, ringing his hands, '*Por caridad.*' Doña Anna gave them a smile and helped herself to a small piece. Her manners were very polished and without Don Otavio's tinge of Latin Cranford. The tale of her haremed life seemed hardly credible, of the two she appeared the woman of the world and Don Otavio the provincial recluse. The youth sat by her side like a lump, yawning and scowling into his plate.

'He's had a tiring day, poor boy,' said Doña Anna, 'out with the motor boat since breakfast.'

The band had been playing into our ears from the soup. Mexican folk music has to be endured to be believed. It strives to be at once virile and melancholy, and succeeds in sounding military and yearning. Tambourines throb, brasses blare, strings quiver; the rhythm is mechanical and obtrusive, and it is always played very loud.

'Doña Anna, do you have the *mariachis* all day?' said E.

'They usually come to my house at nine. Of course they don't begin till I am awake.'

At the seventh rendering of a piece called, I believe, *Siempre Jalisco*, the musicians, to more sensitive ears than ours, appeared to be running down.

'Play up, *niños*,' said Doña Anna.

They seemed to do so. After a while there was another just perceptible decrease in volume. Doña Anna leapt from her chair, wrenched a trumpet from an Indio's hand, and slapped his face.

'If you cannot make music, go home and plough,' she said and returned to her seat. Music and conversation were resumed.

Presently the servants were called in and performed some dances. The most appreciated one consisted in throwing a hat on the floor and delicately stepping round it. The men looked very graceful and serious doing this; the women stood and watched. Later the band played items vaguely partaking of the nature of the tango and the waltz, and we danced. Anthony with Doña Anna. The youth sat and looked daggers.

'Anthony had better look out for a knife in his back,' I said to Don Otavio.

'Oh no, no. There is no harm in Don Fernando, poor

boy. Naturally he does not like to see her dance. Young people are so strict. He does not approve of her going out so much now. Of course Doña Anna insists on his going with her.'

'She might have chosen a more amiable escort.'

'Her brothers are dead. Doña Anna *is* an unconventional woman, her wearing trousers upsets Fernando.'

'It seems hardly for him to mind.'

'One can understand it. Don Fernando has been a good son.'

'Doña Anna is his mother,' I said smoothly.

'Of course. Well, yes, Don Fernando might have been a nephew.'

Next waltz I said to Anthony, 'I've been on thin ice.'

'I thought you were. E., too.'

'We have such conventional minds. Evil springs to them.'

'I learnt better.'

'I'm beginning to appreciate your Guadalajara training.'

At midnight Doña Anna made her farewells. Then she set off, *en cortège*, to the waterfront. First went two Indios with lanterns, then came six men carrying the oars, then Doña Anna on the arm of her son with Don Otavio by her side, then more boys with lanterns; behind them a straggle of retainers with cloaks and cushions, and at last the band playing full blast. They went down the alley of limes, into the garden, into the night. Slowly they vanished: lights and music and the white of Doña Anna's crepe de chine. All evening we had laughed, with them and apart, and now it was sad.

'There,' said E., 'goes the last relic of Mexican feudalism.'

Chapter Five
MRS RAWLSTON'S
FIRST APPEARANCE

J'ai quelque jours dans l'océan,
Mais je ne sais plus sous quels cieux,
Jeté comme offrande au néant
Tout un peu de vin précieux.

OUTSIDE THE HACIENDA gates, a field beyond the road, rises a fat, round, dark green hill covered with mossy shrub that shields us from the wind, traps the sun and blocks the view of anything beyond. The hill is one of a chain flanking the north shore of the lake, and the level land between the waterfront and this low range is only the breadth of a few acres, widening at certain points to accommodate a village or an estate, at others tapering to a strip of beach beside the road. Halfway up our hill is a votive chapel reached by a path constructed for horses and ladies; beyond, it would be an easy scramble to the top. To get there, walk along the ridge and see what lay below, and see it at break of day, had been for some time a project of Anthony's and mine, one of the things one always talks about and never does. That night I was woken by the rain. It was still the season, and on Lake Chapala the rain comes in the hour before dawn and ceases with the sun. Perfection could go no further. I got up and roused Anthony. We stepped over Jesús and his rifle in the hall, into a frail, glistening morning. Beads of water more than dew lay on everything like the larger jewels of this hemisphere. We walked up to the chapel much too fast and by the time we got there the day was already warm. Inside the sanctuary a pair of goats were resting by the altar. The climb began – there seemed to be springs in the air, water became translated into bubbles of light; the sun only five-and-twenty minutes old gave us no quarter.

'If Otavio knew, he'd send us hats,' muttered Anthony.

We reached the top. I straightened myself with caution, having a fear of heights, looked up, and there was a sparkling world – to one side hills glowing with fruit, and beyond, gold, fresh, rich, the plains of Guadalajara; to the other the lake with its nine islands and curving shores, still and opaque.

'What a place. What a country. If only one could stay. If only one could live here.'

'Yeah,' said Anthony.

'You are going back in three weeks,' said I. 'How can you bear it? Cellophane, television, the deep-freeze unit, getting and spending. The whole old bag of nothing.'

'I see what you mean,' said Anthony.

'And it's going to be grey. Five, six, seven months of the year. And cold. And then very hot. Never this. Never this perennial June, the light clear brightness. How we shall miss it.'

'You talk as if you had to leave when I do.'

'No. But in less than a year I shall be gone. And that will be the end of Mexico for me. We don't fly across oceans the way you do. I shall live in Italy, if the gods permit; and I hope to be very happy there; and I shall always regret this.'

'You wouldn't want to live here?'

'I didn't tell you about the man we saw thrown off a moving bus. I shall not forget that either. Some of the stories last night were like that. Not that the West isn't terrifying enough, as we know. Only here, we are not engaged.'

'I should like to live here,' said Anthony. 'Very much. If you could, but you can't. It's your friends, they think too much of you and, if you know what I mean, not enough. I mean they respect you a hell of a lot and they don't respect you at all. I don't want to be always looked at as this oddity. It wouldn't matter to them if you did wrong. They wouldn't know. Nor if you did right either. You might get to feel kind of lost about things.'

'Don Otavio's and Doña Anna's, and Andreas' and Domingo's, impact on our consciences is slight, and so is ours on theirs. That is what is called living without the pressure of an accepted social pattern. I suppose everybody needs their equals and betters. But, my dear, isn't that chopping the world into very small pieces? There are other standards, values we share. See how nicely we all speak to each other, that is a shared value. And what about the essential brotherhood of men? We're all Christians here. No of course we are not. There is nothing to share and you are right and it is true that we can only take in this country. We've nothing they want, unless we give what Mr Middleton gives – he told us he doctored the natives. That would be called service, but it is also self-service. So you are right again. And now you must help me to get off this mountain.'

'Do I hear the authentic voices of Old Virginia?' said E. 'I have not heard it since Nancy Astor and I never hoped to hear it again.'

Below in the garden a very old woman wearing the rags that only a few dare wear was talking to Don Otavio. 'Now don't you give me any of that, Tavio. You tell your *mozos* to leave my goats alone. If they want to lie in your chapel to get out of the sun, poor beasts, it's only human and none of your business. They won't do that chapel any harm. Better they than those dirty children slithering on their knees.

'Don't you talk to me about desecration. Those goats were feeding on that hill when you were in your smocks, Tavio, and your mother had your hair in curl papers. Yes, she had, and you remember it. And nobody was having any chapels in the middle of the countryside. Never understood what your aunt put up that chapel for. Thought you Catholics had to have a miracle before they let you do that. Haven't you got yer own chapel on the hacienda? It's not as if I ever see *you* climbing up that hill. You just tell those *mozos* now to leave me goats alone. Oh, there they are. Come along, dears. We go home now.' Absently, but firmly, she took hold of a rope at whose ends two long-haired goats were straining. Both the brutes and the old lady seemed impervious to the pulling. 'And that reminds me, any of your new friends play bridge? Don't you know? Well, find out. Send one of them over to me this afternoon. The Saunders are coming; we need a fourth.'

'Well,' I said, 'that lets me out of Mr Middleton.'

'Why you?' said Anthony.

'Because E. doesn't play and will have to protect us at Jocotepec, and Don Otavio thinks she needs an escort. And because it is not true that we rather bear the ills we know than fly to others that we know not of. I shall enjoy myself this afternoon.'

'Are we to be at the beck and call of every eccentric on this Mexican lake?' said E.

'It is a very fine lake; it is larger than Lake Geneva. And

this is the tone you must take at Jocotepec. Don Otavio – we
heard everything. And now you must tell your new friends
about your old friend.'

'Mrs Rawlston is a very wonderful old lady.'

'We do not doubt it. Has she also got a wonderful garden?'

'She has a most *beautiful* garden. It is famous in the
Republic. Mrs Rawlston came when she was a girl. She came
to be a governess. Her family were ruined in a war. I think it
was the war about the Negroes. She married one of her
countrymen here. He had mines, but she and the children
always lived on the lake. They built a house halfway between
Tlayacán and San Juan Cosalá. It must be sixty-five years ago.
Mrs Rawlston's husband was shot during the Zapata rising.
The servants left to join bands, the children were at school
abroad, Mrs Rawlston stayed through the whole Revolutions
all alone in that big house. She slept in the garden with a gun,
she said she did not want to be murdered in her bed. Of
course they were quite ruined. Now the children are both
married, one at Mexico and one at Monterrey. Mrs Rawlston
does not like her son- and daughter-in-law. It is a lonely life
for her, poor woman, but she is a very important person on
the lake.'

'As important as Mr Middleton?'

Don Otavio realized that he was confronted with that
unfamiliar thing, a joke. He took it with a smile. 'More
important. But Mr Middleton does not know.'

'Do they get on?'

'Their houses are not in the same place. They have esteem
for each other. Perhaps we need not tell Mr Middleton that
you are going to Mrs Rawlston's today.'

'We will tell him that I caught a touch of the sun on that
hill.'

'No, not sun. It would not be wise. It is one of the three things Mr Middleton cures. Sunstroke, dysentry and malaria.'

'Does Mrs Rawlston cure also?'

'No. Mrs Rawlston goes to law. She makes the Indios sue the Government when she thinks they ought to. She goes to court herself, and pleads and does everything. She does not like lawyers.'

'Her Spanish must be very good?'

'One understands everything she says, and she says much.'

Chapter Six
BRIDGE WITH
MRS RAWLSTON

. . . in nice balance, truth she weighs,
And solid pudding against empty praise.

M RS RAWLSTON lived in a large, dark, ugly, dishevelled
house, full of raffia and pots of jam in the hall,
desolate and at the same time cozy.

'Come on in, Mrs B.,' she said, 'we're all waiting for our
bridge game on the porch.'

I had been rushed through luncheon by Don Otavio and
packed off on mule back, forty-five minutes of it through the
subtropical afternoon.

I found two English people on the veranda, necessarily
sprung from somewhere.

'How do you do,' they said.

'How do you do,' said I.

We settled round a wobbly card table. Mrs Rawlston
waved me to the seat opposite her own. 'You a good player,
Mrs B.?'

'A very bad one, I'm afraid.'

'Better cut for partners,' said Mrs Rawlston. We did, and
she drew me.

'Blackwood, Peter?' said the Englishwoman.

'Blackwood,' said the Englishman.

Mrs Rawlston picked up her pack and dealt.

'I believe it is my deal, Mrs Rawlston,' said the
Englishwoman.

'What's that?'

'I believe it is *my* deal,' said the Englishwoman in a clear voice.

'Never mind, let's get on with it,' said Mrs Rawlston. 'It all comes to the same in the end.'

'By,' said Mrs Rawlston.

'Pass,' said the Englishwoman.

'Pass.'

'Pass.'

'Two no trumps,' said Mrs Rawlston.

'Pass,' said the Englishwoman.

I hesitated.

'I said two no trumps,' said Mrs Rawlston. 'Two, mind you.'

'Now, now, Mrs Rawlston,' said the Englishman, 'we can't have that.'

'You must forget you heard,' said the Englishwoman.

'I'm not sure what I'm supposed to do, anyway,' said I.

'Remember I passed first round,' said Mrs Rawlston.

'Now really, Mrs Rawlston . . .'

'Three spades,' said I.

'Spades?' said Mrs Rawlston. 'Got any?'

We made the first rubber in two hands. There seemed to be a feeling that it was not deserved. I moved to the seat opposite the Englishwoman.

'Blackwood, partner?'

'I don't know,' I said, 'it seems to get one up so awfully high. I never dare bid fives and sixes. I suppose if one wants to go for slam . . . What *do* you think?'

There was silence.

'Mrs Rawlston can see your cards,' said the Englishman.

'I'm so sorry,' said I.

'Shove a bit of paper under that leg, Peter,' said Mrs Rawlston; 'floor's uneven. That's better.'

'No clubs, partner?' said the Englishwoman.

'No. Oh I'm so sorry, yes,' said I.

'Revoke,' said Mrs Rawlston. 'Three tricks for us. Put 'em down, Peter; my piece of paper's blown off. That wind from Vera Cruz is up again.'

'Surely, two, Mrs Rawlston.'

'Three tricks for a revoke. Don't get one often these days, people reading Culbertson and counting up their hands the way they do.'

'I am most frightfully sorry,' I said; 'it is too bad of me.'

'A diamond,' said Mrs Rawlston. 'No, let's make it a heart. Two hearts; did ye hear me, Peter? Where did you leave that mule, Mrs B.?'

'The San Pedro *mozo* took him home. They are going to send the boat for me.'

'Well, I am going up to four hearts,' said Mrs Rawlston; 'I don't see why not. Those friends you got with you at San Pedro are Yankees, ain't they?'

'Only Mrs A. Her cousin is from the South. Maryland.'

'I call it a Border State,' said Mrs Rawlston.

'Mrs Rawlston, I just bid five clubs.'

'You did, did you. Now what shall we do, Peter, risk it?'

'Your *cards*!'

'I'm so sorry,' said I.

'Six hearts,' said Mrs Rawlston.

'Double,' said the Englishwoman.

'That always sounds so brave,' said I.

'*Your* lead, partner,' said the Englishwoman.

Wildly unnerved, I led a high heart.

'Our opponent's suit.'

'I am sorry! What have I done? And you *doubled*. How can you forgive me. I'm really quite impossible.'

'It does not matter at all.'

'Game and rubber,' said Mrs Rawlston. 'Let's have some tea. Peter, how much would it cost us if Mrs B. had led a club?'

'She would have cashed her ace and king; made the impasse in spades, got rid of her singleton, drawn a trump and established her queen, led another round of spades and made her partner trump your diamond.'

'No, no, no, I couldn't possibly have done all that.'

'Five down, doubled *and* vulnerable.'

'Tea,' said Mrs Rawlston, 'I made you all some beaten biscuit.'

'Not beaten biscuits! Mrs Rawlston,' said the English-woman.

Tea was delicious. Georgian silver, lovely china, covered dishes full of baked creations with homely exotic names, spoon bread and batter bread, soda biscuits and popovers, as light as down, with the warmth of the oven upon them, melting in the mouth, before the fresh, cold sweet butter.

'Mrs Rawlston makes her own butter, too. Don't you, Mrs Rawlston?' said the Englishwoman.

'Always beat me own butter,' said Mrs Rawlston. 'Milk's the trouble in this country. No one knows the first thing about cows. When those San Pedro boys were kids, their father raised a Black Angus for them. A Black Angus for milking! Silly old man he was. Always rushing round after one thing or another, and all he ever got was money. Boys were scared to death of him, all but Enriquez. Couldn't even keep his wife from her popish tricks. Drawing room always full of cringing tutors; Jesuits more like. Mrs B. is staying at San Pedro.'

'Oh, yes,' said the Englishwoman.

'Clever boy, Tavio. Always got his own way. Big brothers were sent off to school, little Tavio stayed home with mamma. When she died, Enriquez and Jaime and Luís and their families had to leave their home and earn their living, who stayed home again? Tavio. Then this aunt, the nun, said she'd leave him all she had to leave as long as he entered the Church. She's still got plenty, if she can make those priests keep their paws off it. Tavio didn't say yes and he didn't say no. He just didn't get married, in case. "Well, Tavio," I tell him, "where's your black coat? Ain't you ordained yet, or whatever you Catholics do when you turn parson? Been a long time making up your mind, haven't you? Twenty years, is it? And in no great hurry to support a wife either. Well, you got yourself fixed up real nice, Tavio – the run of the place, everything done for you, snug as a bug and not a thing on your mind. With your fine bachelor's quarters at Mexico, too. Well, I'll say this for you, you were a good son and you've got nice manners." And I might add, he sets a good table and he gives to the poor.'

'Thank you, I *will* have another of these delicious scones, Mrs Rawlston.'

'What you do for your milk and butter, Peter?'

'We send Josefina into Chapala twice a week.'

'City stuff. Now, my son-in-law eats lard. Just what you'd expect, as I tell him.' Mrs Rawlston turned to me, 'My son-in-law is a German. Can't stand 'em.'

'The prejudice is not unique.'

'"Lard," I said to him, "that's all you used to have in your own country, ain't it? Then why don't you eat honest Christian butter on your bread when you have it? Ain't that what you came here for? Don't you know good stuff from bad? Ain't that why you Germans always come running into other countries, because you don't like it at home? And then you get so fat you have trouble getting yourselves out again. Don't you know when you're not wanted, you Germans?"'

'Arc you going to have your daughter and grandchildren this summer, Mrs Rawlston?' said the Englishwoman.

'They're all at Cordoba for *his* holiday. I don't see why I should have my house full of Germans because my daughter was fool enough to marry one. I told them so. Now why did Diana have to marry that German for? Losing all their wars, too.'

'Oh come on, Mrs Rawlston, you know that Diana is very happy with him.'

'Maybe. I wasn't when they all came and lived with me after Pearl Harbor because he was kicked out of his job. He had nowhere else to go, Diana said. "Why don't you go and fight for your country, Karl?" I told him. Not he. Mope in my house, read my paper, month in month out – though I didn't mind his reading it half so much the day after Stalingrad – until he got himself that big job at Mexico he's got now. I said to him, "Job, Karl? Why don't they lock you up? Don't they know any better?"'

'Oh now, Mrs Rawlston, Karl Waldheim was no Nazi, poor chap.'

'He's a German, ain't he? Good enough for me. Now have you all quite finished? Drink up your tea, Peter. Come along, let's get on with our bridge game.'

'Mrs Rawlston, may we have another look round your lovely garden?'

'Nothing new in it since lunchtime, dear; and Mrs B. can come over in the morning and look at it if she wants to.

Come along, it'll be getting dark soon. I don't get a bridge game every day these days.'

It was getting dark. An oil lamp was brought and fluttered fitfully in the wind from Vera Cruz that had sprung up good and proper, and so did the cards. Every so often a whole deal would be lifted off the table by a gust.

'Pick 'em up, pick 'em up. All comes to the same in the end,' said Mrs Rawlston.

Birds shrieked in the rushes; settled for the night. Stars rose. The boat came from San Pedro. Frogs croaked. Mrs Rawlston had revoked three times.

'Never mind, doesn't count, lamp's too low to tell spades from hearts.'

Our score sheets had long been blown away.

'Wind bother you?' said Mrs Rawlston. 'Any of you want to go in? Light's no better and for meself I see no sense in stuffing indoors on a fine summer night. Always sleep out of doors. Got kind of used to it in the Revolutions. Had to then. Or those Indio soldiers would have gone and stolen my fruit. When there was a moon they'd come, or in the small hours – they're scared to death of the dark – and I'd pop out on them. "Now what d'you think you are doing," I'd say to them, "going about the countryside robbing people's gardens and murdering them in their sleep? Haven't you got no homes of your own? That's no way of making a revolution, that's petty larceny. Ain't you ashamed of yourselves, you great hulking men, how many are there of you: thirty – can't ye count: with your silly knives and your great clumsy guns, what you think you look like? And me an old woman all alone. What you want to go and kill me for, you louts? Don't

you have enough killing on your fiesta days?" That'd fix
them. Never touched my fruit, poor devils. They're not bad,
those Indios. Revolutions went a bit to their heads, murder
every day and no one to tell them their places. Early years
weren't much; some of Villa's bands were tough. Later we
got the *El Cristo Rey* gangs. They were much the worst. Kind
of revivalists. Did everybody in who wasn't for the Church.
Out for blood *they* were and no nonsense. Thousands and
thousands of them all over the country. They'd come
streaking into the villages on horseback with those great big
banners and that cry they had, CHRIST IS KING. My, people
were scared. Came after me, too. "What you think I am," I
told them, "a heathen? I believe in Our Lord same as you do,
and better, without your papist fripperies." I had my own
gun then, no use talking sense to the *Cristeros*. Had to use it
too, and, *what's more*, take cover. They fired a round into the
garden and left me for dead. Always in such a hurry they
were. Well, so now I sleep out of doors, rain or shine. Kept
my gun too. I guess it would be the death of me if I slept
inside a house now. You don't change your habits at eighty-
nine. Yes, eighty-nine come November; and seventy-two of
them in Mexico. Born in the year before the War between
the States.

'Dummy? I? Again? Want some of my prunella any of
you? Made it last fall. Diana says it ain't half bad, never touch
it myself. I like my drink from abroad.'

'No thank you, Mrs Rawlston,' said Peter.

'No thank you,' said I.

After the seventh rubber, the Englishwoman rose. 'Mrs
Rawlston, it has been a lovely evening. Thank you so much.'

'Not going, are you? Won't you stay to supper so we can
have another hand or two afterwards?'

'I'm afraid we have to go,' said the Englishwoman, 'the dogs are waiting for us.'

'That's too bad. Mrs B., you'll stay another minute, I have something to give you for Tavio.'

Scores were reconstructed by memory. I had played four rubbers with Mrs Rawlston and it was found that I was seven pesos to the good. If ever money was supposed to burn in a pocket, this did.

'Well, goodbye, dear Mrs Rawlston, and thank you again so much.'

'Come again soon, Peter.'

'*You* must come to San Antonio, Mrs Rawlston.'

'Goodbye,' said I.

'Goodbye,' said the Englishwoman.

'Goodbye,' said the Englishman.

'Mr Middleton's bite was worse than his bark,' said E.

'It was all laid on,' said Anthony, 'landlady on the doorstep, lease made up.'

'Mr Middleton met us at his gate watch in hand,' said E.

'I had my share of barks, too,' said I. 'Muffled barks.'

'Did you not enjoy the Saunders'?' said Don Otavio.

'They did not enjoy me.'

'Oh you,' said E. 'Stuffing beaten biscuit. I'd give anything for real beaten biscuit.'

'I gave too much. Now tell me what happened. Are we safe?'

'Don't worry. No cottage for us. I settled it.'

'My dear. And how did you put it?'

'By evasion.'

'E. said we couldn't decide anything without you,' said Anthony.

'So it is *not* all settled?'

'And you would let him know tomorrow.'

'Oh, E. You didn't?'

'Well, you see, Mr Middleton's bark was *not* muffled.'

'Aw,' said Anthony, 'let's write him a note and forget about it.'

Chapter Seven
DON ENRIQUEZ UNFOLDS
A PLAN

But fruits of pomegranate and peach,
Refresh the Church from over sea.

D ON OTAVIO is going into Guadalajara for the day. Don
Otavio's departures are worthy to be seen. The engine
of his brother's motor launch, brought in the night before
from Chapala, has been revved thunderously since dawn.
Early Mass is an hour earlier, and the Padre is rowed over
from San Juan Cosalá. For his efforts the Padre is given
breakfast at the hacienda. While the Padre eats, the parrot is
locked in the linen room as his language cannot be trusted
and Don José is an old man. The barber also appears an hour
earlier. Soledad and Carmelita are summoned to the El
Dorado to assist at the toilet. People cross and recross the
lawn with various items: the bulky entrails of the water filter
to be repaired at Guadalajara, tins of petrol for Don Otavio's
car waiting at Chapala, crates of fruit and sheaves of flowers
for Don Otavio's relatives; provisions, cushions. These are
stowed in the launch, taken out again, looked at, rearranged.
At nine the garden fills with spectators, servants and petitioners. At ten, Don Otavio's chauffeur appears on the lawn
dressed in white ducks and a beach shirt, bearing a rug; at a
quarter past, Don Otavio's valet bearing in his arms Don
Otavio's female Maltese terrier, curled and decked out with a
large satin bow. She is to spend the day with Don Otavio's
favourite sister-in-law. At half-past ten, Don Otavio issues

from the house, splendid like the moon, all in white silk, his silvery hair brushed upwards, a Charvet tie over his holy medals, bearing nothing. A volley of advice springs from his mouth. His progress to the waterfront is punctuated by miscellaneous requests: the cook would like a funnel, Carmelita a length of ribbon, Juan some scented oil. Don Otavio grants them all. He steps into the launch. Two live chickens with bound legs are deposited at his feet. The engine gives a terrific roar, dies down, throbs again. Pietra, the chauffeur's wife, who at this instant decided to accompany her husband, is handed into the boat. Domingo comes running with a little girl in a revolting bandage that is to be changed by the nuns. Don Otavio draws her onto his lap. A *mozo* from Jocotepec who wants a lift leaps onto the prow. Thirty people break into *que Dios les proteja*, Don Otavio raises a hand in gracious salute, and the boat glides out.

The name of the girl who looks after us, who brings in the morning tea and closes the shutters, who whisks away the barely worn shirt and linen suit and lays them out again in the evening smelling of sun and meadows, is Soledad. She is the most exquisite of creatures. The texture of her skin – rosy *café au lait*, matt and aglow, the almond oval of her face, the mouth that looks as though it had opened only with this day, the delicate hands and wrists, the perfectly shaped feet, the grace and balance of her movements: everything about her is of finer clay. It is that flowerlike exquisiteness compounded of fineness, innocence and youth, that is found in the more elusive animals, a hind, a fawn, more rarely in a human being and hardly ever in a member of the white race. Soledad's expression is open, serene, inherently detached. She has a sweet smile, neither remote nor here; warmth not dependent for its kindling on surroundings; and uses a light singing voice all day. We look at her with awe. Such creatures seem hardly human; that they are, must be their tragedy. What can become of her among us? Mind does not touch her, nor vulgarity, but men will, and age. Twice mortal, her destiny should be the milk-white steed, translation in a cloud. She will be married to a village lout or by a rich man.

My own great-grandmother was Spanish, and though her beauty could hardly have been of the quality of Soledad's, she was supposed to have been a very lovely girl indeed when she was married, taken to a northern country and received into an alien creed. I remember a very small, very wrinkled, old woman, indeed a little like Soledad's own mother, who never left the house in which the authority was her children's, and whose sweetness of nature was judged to be harmless. She hobbled about passages tatting lace, carrying a plate of pudding to her upstairs drawing room. In spite of my shrinking from age – I was five – she and I drank our chocolate and ate sweets together entirely in the manner of equals.

This morning Soledad has a message for me from Guadalupe. Guadalupe is the X. y X. brothers' old wet-nurse who now looks after the fowls. It has transpired, Domingo and Andreas have overheard at table, that I have been to Rome, and Guadalupe requests the favour of my company to converse upon the subject. Guadalupe, with whom so far relations have been of the most tenuous, regrets having been unaware of the presence under their roof of a person who has been to Rome. At the moment she is engaged with a lapful of goslings, but if I would accommodate myself to the fowl-patio?

I love Rome perhaps more than any other place in the

world. The very name at this immense distance, falling so lightly, so unknowingly from Soledad's unconscious lips, stirs memory and longing.

'*Buenos dias, Señora.*'

'*Buenos dias, Guadalupe.*'

'You have been to Rome, Señora?'

'Many times.'

'Many times! It is very pious.'

My answer to this is suitable. I was aware that the Eternal City has always been all things to all men. Goethe lived within its walls for eighteen months and successfully avoided seeing a single monument of Christian art. A reverse course is taken by the pilgrims of today who, the dust of the Seventh Basilica hardly off their knees, crowd into the Forum. The Colosseum is claimed both by the followers of the Apostles and the followers of Gibbon; others regard a visit to the Cradle of Christianity and the Fount of Law as a baroque treasure hunt and will look at nothing before Bernini. I thought I guessed Guadalupe's need.

'And did you see the Virgin every time?'

I had not guessed it. 'I saw the Pope,' I said guardedly.

'Yes, yes, the Pope. A very good man no doubt. He looks after the Virgin. Did you see Her?'

One spring and summer I had a flat there, facing and level with the ninety-foot cipolin column of the Immaculate Conception. From sunrise to starry midnight, the statue of Maria Imaculata and the huge winged bronze Bull of St Luke almost at arm's reach had looked into my windows and my terrace. 'There is much of the Virgin in Rome,' I said.

'Of course. There would be. Was She well? Has She all She wants? What did She wear?'

'Rome is a large place,' said I.

'Very large and very splendid. For the Virgin. You *did* see the Virgin, *niña*?'

'I don't think the Virgin is really visible in Rome. You are not thinking of Lourdes, Guadalupe, where people have seen her?'

'Yes, the Virgin is seen at Lourdes also. But the Virgin lives in Rome, everybody knows that. In a *palaçio* called El Vatican. She has Her own railway now. It is very magnificent. You will tell me everything about it.'

'Now Guadalupe,' I said, feeling that prevarication would serve no further, 'you know that the Virgin is in Paradise, not in Rome. Even Rome is not that. And the railway was built for the Pope. Don't you know about the Assumption? You *know* the Virgin went to heaven.'

'The Virgin left Rome? Just when She had the new railway? It was made all for Her. I gave two pesos to the Padre for the Virgin's Railway. You are very confused, *niña*, with your talk of Lourdes and Paradise and the Pope taking the Virgin's Railway for himself. As soon as these goslings are asleep, I shall say three rosaries for you. To clear your mind.'

All three of Don Otavio's brothers and their wives are expected tomorrow and Don Otavio is all aflutter with housekeeping. The cook has been drinking again and not yet herself. Jesús' wife causes anxiety too, as she is said to have an eye on Don Otavio's Juan. Juan is terrified as Jesús has already knifed three youths from Ajijíc. The others show a tendency to lay down work and give themselves to watching the outcome of these events.

'Do not let us have troubles, *niños*,' Don Otavio implored them, 'while my sisters-in-law are here.'

'I'm surprised Jesús hasn't had a go at Mr Middleton,' said I, 'the way Mr Middleton goes on about Jesús' garden.'

'It is not conceivable,' said Don Otavio.

'Troubles come when they wish to,' said Domingo.

'The horses have stolen the vegetables,' said Andreas.

'*¡Niños!*' said Don Otavio. '*¿Con su permiso?*'

'I've been over to the villa,' said Anthony, 'you should see the liquor Otavio's bringing out. Scotch; French brandy; cases of it. It's all Don Enriquez' really, he keeps it here. And a whole side of beef's come from Chapala. I saw it.'

'What a one you are for snooping.'

'I gave the cook your Alka-Seltzer, E. They're making ice cream in the damnedest gadget you ever saw. Kind of bucket with a crank. But I do wish that Joaquím and Orazio were coming.'

'Aren't they?'

'Hell, no. No one young at all. This is serious. Didn't you know? Don Enriquez is bringing out the agreement about this hotel proposition and they are going to pore over it. That's why Luís is coming all the way out from Mex City.'

'Anthony, you know too much.'

'*We* ought to be at Jocotepec,' said E.

'*Con permiso de Ustedes*,' said Juan. 'Don Otavio wishes to know whether the Señores would be good enough to keep the parrot with them for a little while? Don Otavio is doing the flowers.'

'We have our uses here,' said I.

★

Don Otavio, followed by Soledad bearing linen and Jesús' children bearing vases, crossed the loggia.

'Always with a book,' he said to E. 'You must have so many.'

I looked up from mine and listened.

'This one is always enjoyable,' said E.

'I am so glad,' said Don Otavio.

'You ought to have met Mr Collins, Don Otavio. He set such a standard of polite letter-writing.'

'Who was the gentleman?'

'A clergyman of the Church of England.'

Don Otavio covered a slight stiffening with a courteous smile.

'And a personage of Jane Austen's.'

'Oh; he lived on the lady's estates,' said Don Otavio with the relief of full comprehension. '¿Con su permiso?'

They arrived in Don Enriquez' motor launch an hour before luncheon. An awning had been put up and a table spread with refreshments. Don Otavio, freshly powdered, in a Charvet shirt and a plum-coloured sash with a tassel wound around his waist, E., Anthony and I were waiting on the lawn.

Don Enriquez, in a white silk suit and utterly in his prime, was a fine, massive, worldly figure – masculine, at ease, intimating power and craft. Don Jaime looked like an ecclesiastical shadow of his elder brother: tapering, emaciated, with an austere face and a haunted expression that might have been ascetic but was above all hungry. Don Luís looked quite louche, with more than a touch of the motor salesman about him. Don Jaime wore a dark lounge suit, and Don Luís a brighter one. All three brothers were heavily powdered.

Their wives were slight, elegant, and beauties. Doña Victoria had fine hard features, and Doña Concepción a ravishing face. They wore plain white piqué dresses, almost tennis dresses, in what used to be called simple good taste, but Doña Concepción wore ruby earrings and Doña Victoria wore diamonds. They wore no make-up, except on their eyes and mouths.

Don Luís' wife had stayed at Mexico having another baby.

They brought a number of servants. Don Enriquez brought a string of snipe for Don Otavio, and Doña Concepción the last number of *Vogue*.

We stood about the lawn with drinks, chattering and making a good meal of tacos until it was time to go in to luncheon. Don Otavio looked after everybody, but Doña Victoria appeared to be acting as hostess. Don Enriquez seemed too much at home to care.

Don Enriquez treats Don Otavio with affectionate condescension. Don Jaime treats him with almost concealed contempt, and Don Luís with open emulation. Doña Victoria is rather waspish to her brother-in-law, and Doña Concepción is charming.

Seeing Don Otavio among his family, we were suddenly struck by the utter anomaly of his position as an unmarried man.

He moved about his brothers with affection and respect. With perhaps most respect for Don Jaime and most affection and no less respect for Don Luís, and seemed to regard Doña Concepción as an equal companion and Doña Victoria with awe.

For some reason, both Don Enriquez and Doña Victoria are all over Anthony.

'Tavio has not taken you to the Island yet? *Qué tal, chiquito,* what have you been thinking of?'

'*Querido*, no one has been to the Island since Papa died.'

'Yes, and that is why Don Antonio would enjoy it. It is quite savage. We all used to love it when we were boys. The inhabitants never go to the mainland. They cannot have seen a white face since we're grown up.'

'Enriquez, Don Antonio *is* grown up,' said Doña Victoria.

'He has Joaquím's age.'

'At which you were married and had a son.'

'And they have not,' said Don Enriquez comfortably.

'I wish Joaquím's tastes lay still outside the *Circle des Jeux*,' said Doña Victoria, 'we ought to make *him* take Don Antonio to the Island.'

'How are Joaquím and Orazio, sir?' said Anthony.

'Very well and expensive,' said their father.

'Don Enriquez, as a lawyer,' said E., 'what do you think of the present form of government in Mexico?'

'No worse than most forms.'

'If it has one,' said Don Jaime.

'Oh, the *politicos* have their line. Their purpose, I should say.'

'*Their* purposes,' said Don Luís.

'You will find the country still a land of opportunity,' said Don Enriquez.

E. returned to her plate.

'Otavio, must we have the beef covered in tomato sauce, too,' said Doña Victoria, 'when the fish was already done *a la veracruzana*? Was it not fresh?'

'Angelita is not herself. Jesús' wife is cooking. This is the only way she knows.'

'She felt fine after the Alka-Seltzer,' said Anthony. 'She said it was the quickest thing ever.'

'Yes, she had quite recovered, poor woman. So she went and had some more *tequilita*.'

'Oh dear,' said Doña Victoria.

'They all need a little change, poor things, they are waiting for the *Diez y Seis de Setembre*,' said Don Otavio. 'The fireworks already started this week. I heard them this morning.'

'What kind of fiesta is that?' said Anthony.

'Independence Day,' said E.

'Theirs?'

'Ours,' said Don Jaime.

'Doña E. has a very great knowledge of our history,' said Don Otavio.

'We are getting quite insular these days,' said Don Enriquez, 'with nobody able to afford to travel.'

'My sons have not even been to Paris,' said Don Jaime.

'Well, you forget, *querido*, there was also the war in Europe.'

'I know,' said Don Jaime. 'We had to send our girls to the Sacred Heart in Canada.'

E. laid down her fork. 'What would you say was the effect of the war on Mexico?' she said.

'We got a few scraps of business thrown our way,' said Don Enriquez.

'Quite a few,' said Don Luís.

'A lot of shopkeepers who had never eaten bread before made a lot of money,' said Don Jaime. 'And now you see them all over the place wearing shoes.'

'The bars are full of them,' said Don Luís. 'One really can't go out any more.'

'You cannot imagine what it was like for clothes,' said Doña Victoria.

'*What* we all looked like,' said Doña Concepción.

'Buenos Aires and Rio were in the same boat of course. Some of us tried New York one season.'

'Well, the colours were more gay,' said Don Otavio.

'Yes, there was that.'

'France cannot be a country in decline with Paris still able to force the women of the Latin and Oriental races into black,' said E.

'*¿Por favor?*' said Doña Concepción.

'I admire *your* country,' said Don Luís to E., 'so many nice things to import from. Only not enough people to buy them here. There's Coca-Cola of course, a very wonderful business, but the concessions are all for the Presidential Family.'

'The Swans are reserved for the Dons,' said I.

'Our presidents have too many brothers,' said Don Enriquez.

'Don Jaime, what do you really feel about the present Mexican government?' said E.

'*De quel point de vue, Madame?*'

'I don't expect you approve their methods and ideals?'

'Their methods render their ideals quite immaterial.'

'I have a new bracelet, Tavio,' said Doña Concepción.

'Will you show it to me after siesta? I have something pretty for you to see too, *chiquita*.'

'Would you say it was a *stable* government?' said E.

'Our *politicos* hang on,' said Don Luís. 'The new kind would rather share than quit.'

'More stable than anything poor old Don Porfirio ever

dreamt of,' said Don Enriquez, 'with us supposed to be out and the Indios taking no part.'

'I take it there is no body of informed middle-class opinion or pressure?' said E.

'Pressure for office,' said Don Luís.

'This country was founded by Spanish gentlemen and their servants,' said Don Jaime.

'*And* galley slaves,' said Don Enriquez.

'The Indios used to take part,' said I, 'think of all those risings.'

'They'd always follow a general with a band,' said Don Enriquez. 'But those days are over. Our politicians have tasted comfort. Nobody's going to ride over the mountains any more. Besides, the US wouldn't let us. The Revolutions are done with.'

'The causes for them, too?' said E.

'Don't those politicians like shooting any more?' said Anthony.

'A man can shoot private as well as public, boy,' said Don Enriquez.

'How could the United States stop anything?' said E. 'Economic sanctions? They would hardly affect the lives of the people such as they are.'

'But frustrate the efforts of the *politicos* – nothing to spend their money on,' said Don Enriquez.

'Certainly no one would want to invade Mexico now-adays,' said E.

'The Germans planned a parachute landing on this lake,' said Don Jaime.

'Oh, the Germans,' said Don Enriquez.

'And has your father got a Cadillac too, Don Antonio?' said Don Luís.

'Nobody could really take Mexico,' said E., 'whatever the weapons.'

'You took half our country,' said Don Jaime with a sudden burst of complete seriousness.

'A very deplorable business,' said E. 'Lincoln to his eternal honour voted against it in Congress. But the Peace of Guadalupe Hidalgo was made a hundred years ago. It was a very bad peace, but it *was* peace. And that is a long time for it.'

'It is a long time to have kept half our country,' said Don Jaime.

'You can hardly expect us to return Texas and Arizona and California now.'

'It would not be reasonable,' said Don Enriquez.

'Because they have become so rich?'

'Because one cannot put the clock back,' said E.

'Why should it only move in one way?'

'If it could move in the other, Texas and California, as well as the rest of Mexico, might find themselves once more under a Spanish Crown.'

'We all came from Spain,' said Don Jaime.

'Not *all* your grandmothers, Jaime,' said Don Enriquez roughly, 'not by a long chalk.'

'*¡Chicos!*' said Don Otavio.

'Doña Sibilla, what is your real opinion of M Christian Dior?' said Doña Concepción.

'I suppose he *is* very great?' said Doña Victoria.

'Perhaps a little avant-garde?' said Doña Concepción.

'Not entirely a classic?' said Doña Victoria.

'Mama always went to Worth,' said Don Otavio.

'*Con su permiso*,' said Doña Victoria, and we all rose.

★

Everybody went at once to their rooms. The two couples had been put up at the hacienda and Don Luís at the villa. Don Otavio came running back. 'Would you like to look at my new *Vogue*?' he said to E. 'I know you don't take the siesta.'

'Thank you. Very kind. Thank you.'

'I am afraid Concepción says it is not a very exciting number.'

'Anthony, do see she doesn't lose it,' said I.

Doña Victoria and Don Jaime stayed awake too. They settled in the shade of a papaya and began a game of bezique.

Two hours later Doña Concepción and Don Luís reappeared, joined the others, and the four swiftly settled round a bridge table. Presently Anthony came out, chose himself a chair, and sat with them.

E. crossed the lawn, bearing in one hand Professor Brogan's work on the French Republic, in the other a volume of *Phineas Finn*.

'What did you do with that *Vogue*?' I called down.

'Oh my God!' said E. 'Where is it?'

After another while, Don Enriquez strolled out, freshly valeted, and boarded his launch. He was off to pay his respects to Mrs Rawlston.

I went to find Don Otavio.

'Angelita is worse,' he said.

'I was afraid so. Don Otavio, I wish you would let me do the cooking tonight.'

'It cannot be thought of.'

'I have had to cook before, you know.'

'I believe it is taught in some of the modern convents. At least in Canada. The Sacred Heart at Montreal has cooking classes. Of course my nieces did not take them.'

'Think what Jesús' wife will do to the snipe.'

'Jesús' wife will not cook tonight. Jesús beat her. They have had a *disgusto*.'

'Who *will* cook? *Is* there anyone not prostrate with alcohol and domestic strife?'

'Guadalupe, poor woman.'

'Will Doña Victoria like Guadalupe's food?'

'Nobody will.'

'Well, then?'

'It would not be suitable.'

'Oh, nonsense, Don Otavio. I shall have everything ready for Guadalupe to keep hot and you needn't tell anyone.'

'We could tell Concepción.'

'Of course we could. And Anthony. So it is settled. Domingo and Andreas shall help me and Soledad's mother can keep the fires going. You see I am already familiar with the workings of your kitchen.'

'No, no, I cannot let you. What would Doña E. say?'

'That she was proud to be a citizen, native-born, of a democratic country. If she noticed the difference, but she won't. I hope you will. Because I cook very well.'

'It is a very great kindness, Doña Sibilla. Now I must go to the cellar. *¿Con su permiso?*'

'What are you going to give us to drink tonight?' I said, keeping my tone light.

'I thought of bringing up half a dozen of that nice Sauterne. It is not at all bad. And some sparkling burgundy with the birds. Luís likes it. And a little champagne with our pudding. It is only Argentinian, alas, but very sweet.'

'Don Otavio,' I said, 'Anthony tells me that you still have some very wonderful claret. Some of the 1900 Margaux and Lafites, *if* I can trust my ears. Well you know, they won't keep much longer.'

'Yes, yes, those old red wines. They are very bitter. The French Ambassador, M. de Clerveaux, gave them to my father. Nobody liked them very much.'

Here courage failed, and the cry from my heart remained unuttered.

'Guadalupe, this is no time for prayers,' said I. 'Stop those Aves and chop me some onions.'

'. . . *Santa María Madre de Dios . . . llena eres de gracia . . .*' Guadalupe made frantic signs for me to keep quiet.

'All right, all right. But must you hold your beads too?' I thought of a *curé* we knew in Tourraine who used to tell his pious housekeeper who, as he put it, *courrait à la messe à toutes les heures, "Si vous voulez servir le Seigneur, allez vous faire Bonne Soeur; mais si vous voulez me servir, moi, faites votre cuisine,"* and I longed to tell Guadalupe.

'. . . *y en la hora de nuestra muerte Amen.* Ready, *niña*, here are your eggs, boiled half soft as you said. Twelve Aves. I was not praying.'

'And do you all time your cooking by saying Hail Marys?'

'The Ave for eggs. The Pater for cutlets, the Creed for frying. It is longer.'

'Such a practical religion ours. Little the Protestants know.'

Anthony popped in, keeping me informed of what went on.

Don Enriquez has returned at nightfall and taken Doña Concepción's seat. Doña Concepción has gone upstairs with Don Otavio. The rest are still at bridge. Doña Victoria, Don Jaime and Doña Concepción are players of international tournament level. Don Luís and Don Enriquez, in that order, are first rate but not in the others' class. Don Otavio is not bad and he, Anthony, just good enough to be able to tell.

'And my, they are fast,' he said, 'a hand a minute. And they only go for the fat hands. A peso a point. It isn't bridge, it's big-time gambling. And they say they won't play poker when they're just the family.

'You don't have to worry. They won't play with us. You and I and Otavio are supposed to have a nice game of rummy after dinner.'

'It doesn't look much like a business visit,' said I.

'They're taking it easy. You wait – they'll be in a fine tizzy in a day or two. Everybody is already pow-wowing with somebody on the sly. Don Enriquez went to see Mrs Rawlston to find out what the chances are for the road this year. She's supposed to know everything that goes on down here. And Otavio has a hunch he'll be told he must marry, so Luís has been offering him his wife for hostess, but Otavio isn't so keen on that either. He's sent a messenger to this aunt at Guadalajara, he's supposed to be a great favourite. Don Jaime has sent a message too, only Otavio isn't supposed to know about that, but he does.'

'And how do *you* know, Anthony?'

'From Juan. Juan is friends with Don Enriquez' valet, and Otavio says everything in front of Juan.'

'And are you in turn a witness to Juan's soliloquies?'

'Hell, no. I ask.'

High fast bridge went on, with the interruption of dinner, until half-past one. But this morning there is a conclave. It is held in the drawing room of the El Dorado, and the women are present.

'They're only going to settle preliminaries,' said Anthony. 'Money isn't coming up today.'

We bathed. Refreshments had again been spread on the lawn, but it was long past two and nobody to partake. Mr Middleton had called while we were in the water and left a message that he wished to talk to us about arrangements for our coffins and would we come to tea tomorrow. At last Doña Concepción emerged from the villa. She asked Domingo for a vermouth and flung herself into a chair.

'I am so glad for Tavio about this hotel,' she said to me. 'I hope it will come off. He will enjoy it so. He likes looking after people. We used to tease him that he ought to enter a nursing order. He has had such a lonely life, poor boy. Did you know he had a vocation? His mother was so pleased. Then there were the Revolutions. My husband said it was difficult enough for people like us without having a priest in the family. My father-in-law was not popular. So it was all put off. Tavio was heartbroken. He went to Mexico for a time. I am afraid he made some very bad friends there. When he came back everything had calmed down, and he could have entered the Church then. My husband says it may be quite useful to us now. But Tavio was no longer sure. Perhaps it was not a true vocation, and all worked out for the best. Who knows?

'Yes, I should love another vermouth. Tavio has never been happy in the world,' Doña Concepción went on with the garrulity of weariness, 'and if it *was* a true vocation, and he missed it, that would be a very terrible thing, would it not? Our aunt, Isabella-María – she is really Sister Madalena in Christ, but she is only a lay-nun; the Holy Father made her a countess when we all lost our titles, my husband says we haven't really lost them at all, but as we cannot use them any more it comes to the same, does it not? Men are so peculiar about those things, don't you find? It was very kind of the Holy Father and he only did it because Aunt Isabella-María is so very important to the Church, but of course papal titles are papal titles, one couldn't possibly use them, only South Americans do – well, Aunt Isabella-María says we must have patience and that we do not know the ways of God. I pray a great deal for Tavio. You see, he has no mother to pray for him, that makes always such a difference, doesn't it? Not that she isn't interceding from where she is. Now it looks as though Tavio might enter the Church after all. But it would have to be Orders. You see, he never studied. My husband and brothers-in-law say they would much rather have him an *abbé*. Aunt Isabella-María has been very good to Tavio. She likes him to live at San Pedro. He loves it. My husband does not. Luís would like to live here, but he and Doña Asunción are very poor. They have nine children. Nine alive, I mean. Enriquez and Victoria of course stay here whenever they want to. This is what the trouble is about this morning. Oh, I wish they'd come out; it must be past lunch time. Doña Sibilla, do you have to have many rooms to make an hotel?'

'Rooms are rather essential.'

'How many?'

'It depends. If you are thinking of San Pedro, I should say there were just the right number for its size. About twenty bedrooms, are there?'

'Eight would *not* do?'

'It seems hardly worth starting an hotel on eight.'

'That is what Tavio and Luís keep saying. My husband got very angry with Luís. He says it has nothing to do with him as he lives at Mexico, it is we and the Enriquez' who come out here from Saturday to Monday. Enriquez says he must have nine rooms reserved for himself and his family. My husband thinks we ought to make sacrifices, after all we need not take the governess each time, but even so five rooms are hardly enough for us. Victoria says Tavio ought to let them have the first floor of the villa to themselves, and put us up on the second. Tavio did not like that. He said an hotel was one thing but it was not suitable to give up his home too. Victoria said it was ridiculous for a bachelor to live in a house that size and she had much better manage the servants. Enriquez said the hacienda was *his* home and it was natural to want to keep a few bedrooms. Luís said it was absurd to want to make money and at the same time live like cardinals and Enriquez said he never grudged a man his comforts and told Luís to mind his business. It was all very dreadful and difficult. What will they all do? I left. I do not think they noticed.'

At luncheon everybody was a shade more polite to us than yesterday. Don Enriquez was himself, Don Otavio was quiet and Don Luís thinking. Only Don Jaime showed strain and Doña Victoria annoyance. It was during this luncheon that Jesús stabbed Juan.

There was a wild shriek from the kitchen quarters, and had we not heard Jesús utter another one and seen him rush past the loggia with out-flung arms, we should never have known what had happened. None of the people present ever told.

When we reached the kitchen Juan lay on the floor, his eyes closed, in quite a deal of blood. Angelita, Guadalupe, Soledad, Soledad's mother, Pedro and Domingo stood about with averted eyes and sullen blank faces. Carmelita, Jesús' wife and Andreas had slipped out as we came in.

We bent over Juan.

'Is he badly hurt?' said Don Otavio. He was dead white and shaking from head to foot.

'What's going on here?' said Don Enriquez.

There was silence.

Fortunately Juan moaned, and moaned dramatically.

Don Enriquez shrugged, and he and Don Jaime walked out.

'Give me some water, quick, *niños,*' said Don Otavio.

'And some scissors,' said Doña Concepción.

'Run and get the box with the medicines from my bathroom,' said Don Otavio.

No one stirred.

Anthony ran. Don Otavio, Doña Concepción and I did what was necessary. It became obvious at once that it was a deep flesh wound and nothing at all. The knife had gone in at the back, and come out again at the side without entering the ribcage. We spoke reassuring words to Juan. He kept his eyes shut and lay quite still.

'No, no,' I said to Anthony who had produced a rather surprising store of his own, 'we're not going to monkey with streptomycin. This is clearly a case for iodine, clean gauze and a couple of days in bed.'

'You're *not* going to have a doctor?' said Anthony.

'You can see it is nothing,' said I.

'The doctor lives twelve miles from here,' said Don Otavio.

'And drinks this time of the month,' said Don Luís.

'Juanito, would you like the kind witch from Ajijíc?' said Don Otavio.

Juan gave a faint nod.

'We will send for her at once. Which one do you want? Consuela or the lady from Germany?'

'The lady from overseas,' said Juan and, struck by his powers of speech, opened his eyes.

'You see, *niños*, Juan is not dead. He will get well. All like before. Pedro, Juan is your friend, is he not? Come and help us now.'

There was no response.

'Pick up that knife and put it out of the way,' said Don Luís.

The knife was lying on the floor. A long knife with a wooden handle, more like a good butcher's knife than a weapon.

'Pick up that knife, I tell you,' said Don Luís. 'Can't you hear me?'

They made no sign.

'Aw, what's the odds,' said Anthony, and picked up the knife.

'They are afraid,' said Don Otavio.

'They are all like that,' said Don Luís. 'Our law arrests the witnesses of an accident, or anyone who has anything to do with it afterwards. And as these kind of things are never brought to trial, they usually stay in jail for years. It's an old, old law. Of course it only goes for public incidents, there's no need for them to behave like that here. But it's no use, I don't suppose they've even heard of the law, they're just terrified. It's become an Indio habit. Unreasonable as cattle.'

As Juan was still convinced that he could not move, and the others refused to take the slightest notice of him, Don Luís, Anthony and Don Otavio had to carry him to bed.

'Where does he sleep?' said Anthony.

'Across my door,' said Don Otavio.

'Hardly the place to receive the lady witch from Germany,' said I.

'We can put his blanket in the room where Domingo and Andreas sleep.'

'Well, Anthony,' I said later in the afternoon, 'this puts the lid on *your* source of information.' The conclave was sitting again after the siesta. 'Fortunately I have my own. I know now what these preliminaries were; and they're not settled. Doña Concepción was tired and talked. I don't think she will again.'

'That's OK. Juan's a lot better. That Fräulein Sauer has been to see him. The poor bastard is sitting up eating *frijoles* and jabbering about escape from death. But say, that Kraut is no witch. I asked her, and she gave me this lecture on like curing like, and diseases making their own remedies like something out of the *Reader's Digest*. Otavio wanted to send her home in the boat, but she said what did he think her two good German feets were for. German boots, more like.'

That night, I cooked again. The atmosphere in the kitchen was one of great reserve. Guadalupe and Soledad's mother exchanged polite conversation for my ear. Jesús' wife sat on a stool shedding tears. No one addressed her. The drawing room, on the contrary, was animated. The conclave had risen early. Don Otavio came out of it looking impenetrable and sleek. There was bridge and rummy, and later on sweet champagne.

'What will happen to Jesús?' said I.

'He will hide in the hills for a little while,' said Don Otavio. 'He must be so ashamed. Then he will drink for a bit, and when he has recovered from that he will come home.

Then he and his wife will have to make it up. That will take a few more days.'

'And meanwhile we are without a gardener,' said Doña Victoria.

'It will not be so long this time. They will want to it be all *regulár* before the Sixteenth. They want to enjoy that.'

'Is that a comfort?' said I. 'What will they all be doing *on* the Sixteenth?'

'Yes, it is a trying holiday,' said Don Otavio.

'Before the Revolutions we used to go abroad to avoid it,' said Doña Victoria.

'Holy Week is worse,' said her husband.

'And the Fifth of May,' said Don Jaime.

'Holy Week lasts longer,' said Doña Victoria.

'We have Fifty-two Sundays and Seventy-nine Holidays,' said Don Jaime.

'All observed?' said I.

'All observed. Of course some of them only for one day.'

'Which are the most important?'

'*La Purisima*,' said Doña Victoria.

'*Nuestra Señora de Guadalupe*,' said Don Otavio.

'*Viernes Santo*,' said Doña Concepción.

'*Corpus Domini*,' said Don Luís.

'The Government insists more on the Military Holidays,' said Don Enriquez; 'the Battle of Puebla, the Taking of Mexico from the French, the Investiture of Querétaro.'

'The Indios like the Days of National Mourning,' said Don Jaime.

'What are those?' said I.

'The Anniversaries of the Murder of Francisco Madero in February, the Execution of Hidalgo in July, the Execution of Morelos in December, the Death of Juarez in July . . .'

'Is the Execution of the Emperor Maximilian a holiday?' said E.

'He is not *persona grata* at present,' said Don Enriquez.

'Was he ever that?' said I.

'He *was* a disappointment,' said Don Enriquez.

'The *greatest* holiday is the Day of the Dead,' said Don Luís.

'*El Día de los Muertes*, of course,' said Doña Victoria.

'Of course,' said Don Enriquez.

'What would have happened if Jesús had killed Juan?' said I.

'The same. He would have to stay away a little longer.'

'There would not be the usual formalities attending murder?' said E.

'A knifing,' said Don Enriquez. 'Our police isn't very interested in that kind of thing.'

'We should have half the population sitting in jail twiddling their thumbs,' said Don Jaime.

'Servants are hard enough to get as it is,' said Doña Victoria.

Later that night, Anthony came to my room and reported. 'It's all been fixed,' he said. It appears that Don Enriquez and his wife are going to have three rooms set aside for them at the hacienda, and floor space for their boatmen, the valet and the maid, which still leaves a possible number of bedrooms to the hotel. Their sons and daughter, and the Jaimes and their children will be put up by Don Otavio at the villa whenever they choose to come. They will be his guests, and he'll have the running of his house. Don Jaime will receive the profit from the rooms he forgoes to occupy at the hacienda. They all seem pleased by the arrangement: everybody thinks he has got what he wanted. Don Otavio loves to have Doña Concepción and his house full of nieces and nephews, and Don Jaime docs not come very often.

'It's really quite brilliant,' said I. 'I wonder who thought of it.'

'I did,' said Anthony.

'You?'

'Yes. So much nicer for Joaquím and Orazio, too. Doña Victoria keeps such an eye on them when she gets the chance. I doped it all out and told Juan, and Juan told Otavio, and Otavio made Luís propose it as a disinterested party.'

'A rare role. What about Don Jaime's extras?'

'Me again.'

'Anthony, you *should* live in Mexico.'

'Oh, S.,' said E., 'I've been talking to such an interesting German woman this afternoon. A bit of a rough diamond, but most instructive about Dr Adenauer. Who is she? The doctor?'

'The witch. Anthony thinks she's a fake.'

'S., we have been much mistaken about the aims of Western Germany,' said E.

Chapter Eight

DOUBLECROSSINGS

Nous avons au grenier un nombre suffisant,
Ce me semble, de vieilles planches?

M R MIDDLETON stood on his veranda, watch drawn. 'Three and twenty minutes to five,' he said. 'Hear you had quite a rumpus yesterday. Gardener killed his wife and two of the *mozos*, and wounded some of the housemaids. If I were Otavio, I'd make it an excuse to sack the man. Shocking gardener. Fellow hadn't even heard of a mulch.'

'Hello,' said Blanche Middleton, 'hello. I didn't sleep a wink last night thinking of you.'

'Only one *mozo* was wounded – the merest gash; and no one, I am grateful to say, was killed,' said E.

'Natives exaggerate so,' said Mr Middleton. 'No way of getting accurate information about anything. Great nuisance. Usually make a point of finding out myself. They didn't have the sense at San Pedro to send for me.'

'They sent for a German from Ajijíc,' said Anthony.

'Oh, the homoeopathic quack. The woman's a fool, but the natives are impressed. My crocuses are out. Come and look at them.'

'Richard, tea's ready. You said it was seven minutes past your tea time.'

'Twelve now. Well pour it out, Blanche, pour it out. So you're having all the X.s down at the hacienda? What do you make of them? Enriquez, I dare say, is behaving like God Almighty. Fellow can't even keep his wife in order. Be quiet,

Blanche, it's been all over the clubs for years about Doña Victoria and Doña Concepción's brother. Nobody seems to mind. They're a rotten lot, the bunch of them. Doña Concepción has had her romances too, but she's more discreet. Felipe, the other chap, is always hanging round. I wonder he hasn't come down with them this time. Oh of course, they're thrashing out that hotel deal.'

'E. calls it the Conclave,' said Anthony.

'How is it going?'

'We wouldn't know,' said Anthony, with his sweet smile.

'Well, I've been to Guadalajara and *I* can tell you a thing or two. Enriquez was going to put up the capital and *he* was going to pocket the profits. If there are any. I'm going to give them a piece or two of advice, hope they have sense enough to take it. The others were supposed to get just something in proportion with their share in the place. Nobody seems to know what Otavio's is. Some say it's less because he's got the villa, some believe it's more because he was supposed to have had it all. Any rate, he was to get something extra as he's supposed to run the hotel. Not really run it; he'll have a manager and a fellow to cook the books and whatnot, these people never think of raising a finger themselves if they can help it. But he'll keep an eye on things and play host. Otavio'll be worth his keep with the trippers, I dare say. Now it seems that Enriquez hasn't produced the capital he said he would – you wouldn't know how hard it is to lay hands on a bit of cash in this country – and there is this RC aunt of theirs suddenly chipping in with a good round sum, in Otavio's name if you please. Otavio is to go full shares with Enriquez, and get a director's salary as well. That makes Otavio top dog of the show. It was sprung on them all last week. Enriquez doesn't really care two pins – after the first shock – the more capital the better and he can always get his way with Otavio. A fly could walk over that fellow. But the other two must be feeling rather in the cold now. Enriquez alone was one thing. They've smelt money and they'll have to be squared. After all, they must own about half the place between them. It's more tricky than that because there are all sorts of mortgages and family loans, and they say Luís sold his share sub rosa to Enriquez years ago. I dare say it isn't true or Enriquez hasn't paid. Fact is, nobody quite knows where he stands. Jaime may. He's supposed to have it all at his fingertips. He's got the brains, Enriquez's got the guts in that family. Slippery customer, Jaime. You can't tell what he's after. Sometimes it's money, and then again it's not. His eldest girl could have married the government wallah who cornered all the oil. Jaime wouldn't hear of it. I wonder what he'll do now. So far he's always stood in with Enriquez in a family bust-up. Luís doesn't count. He's been thinking crooked for so long, he wouldn't know a straight deal if he saw one. So now you know what it's all about.'

'Thank you,' said Anthony, his face grave.

'Mr Middleton,' said E., 'you left us such a peculiar message yesterday. At least in the unreliable native version.'

'Quite,' said Mr Middleton. 'I was going to ask you whether you had ordered your coffins? I dare say you haven't. Well, I advise you to do so at once. There's quite a handy little man just out of Jocotepec, cheap too, who doesn't take all week either, with a bit of prodding.'

'May I ask you,' said E., 'what causes you to take so gloomy a view of our life expectancies? Poor Anthony here is barely twenty, you know.'

'I always make a point of telling newcomers to have their coffins made. The other day we had two men from the

Botanical Institute at Bombay to tea. Interesting chaps. One of them wrote a book on mimosa, all theory I dare say. I had to tell *them* too. Nobody seems to take in that by Mexican law they have to be buried within twenty-four hours, coffin or no coffin. Well, you'd be hard put to get one made in that time, native workmen being what they are. This is one of the few laws out here you can't get round. I have mine, of course, and one for my wife; and I insisted on having a suitable coffin made for our servant. Naturally the coffin remains my property if he leaves.'

'All those great big coffins Richard keeps in the cellar,' said Blanche; 'they give me the creeps.'

'You have to air them now and again,' said her husband; 'the wood warps so. People never think of anything. When that American chap died of flu last spring – DTs if you ask me – his wife came running round asking for mine. As if I hadn't told them. Blanche bamboozled me into letting them have it – for the last time, Blanche – and would you believe it, it took me five weeks to get that woman to replace my coffin. Of course she drinks too. So don't say you haven't been warned, and don't come asking for mine.'

'Then has everybody out here got their coffin, sir?' said Anthony.

'Well, Waldheim has two. One here, and one at Mexico. I told him. Sensible chap, Waldheim. One can always count on the Germans. Reliable people. Pity the old girl is so down on him. Won't let his boys go to the German school at Guadalajara. Took them out at the beginning of the war, and stuck them into the American school instead. Sloppy kind of place. After the Fall of France, Waldheim, who is a bit of a wet rag, pulled himself together and put the boys back into the German school. After the Battle of Britain, Mrs Rawlston took them out again; after Tobruk, Waldheim put them back; Mrs Rawlston pulled them out for Lend-Lease and Waldheim put them back for Singapore. Boys changed schools twelve times before D-Day. After that Mrs Rawlston just kept them at the American school. Now she doesn't like their manners. Well, she can't expect to have it all her way, as I keep telling her.'

'I never heard you say *that* to Mrs Rawlston, Richard,' said Blanche Middleton.

'The cottage was to have been the thin wedge for the coffin,' said Anthony in the boat.

'Mr Middleton is what my mother called an impertinent man,' said E.

'I am grateful,' said Anthony. 'Think how bad Juan is at figures. What a hash he would have made of those mortgages.'

It was obvious at once that something had gone wrong. Don Enriquez was pacing the lawn by himself, and the brow of Jupiter was clouded.

We sought Don Otavio, and learned that he had left for Guadalajara half an hour ago in his brother's motor boat. And for the present we learnt nothing else. Doña Victoria was closeted with Don Jaime. Doña Concepción had gone to lie down. Don Luís was walking alone with a light tread.

Presently a message came for him to see Doña Victoria, and he started like a guilty schoolboy.

'Money *has* come up,' said Anthony.

We were told that Don Otavio was spending the night at

his aunt's house and would not be back until some time next afternoon.

Later Doña Victoria came out onto the terrace, looking like Phèdre. Dinner was strained, and the house not the same without Don Otavio. The courses were shuffled the wrong order; afterwards Doña Victoria and Don Jaime played bezique.

Don Enriquez sat alone over his cigar. 'Where *did* he get it from?' he said once in a loud voice, addressing no one in particular.

'No soap,' said Anthony later on that night. 'Juan says Otavio left in such a hurry, he didn't say goodbye to him. He says Pedro heard his master say that Don Luís had put a bombshell on the table. Juan is very puzzled.'

Next morning there was no conclave. People stayed apart, drifted into groups and came apart again, and nothing seemed to happen. As the day wore on, it became clear that everyone was waiting, more or less openly, for Don Otavio's return.

'I told the little one to take my car to Chapala,' said Don Enriquez; 'that should make him faster.'

After breakfast Doña Victoria spoke to me. She was extremely nervous, one might almost have said frightened, but her words were her own. 'I am afraid we must have seemed most inhospitable last night,' she said. 'My husband has made such efforts to keep up San Pedro, and now we found out that his plans have been crossed in the most unscrupulous manner. My husband has worked so hard and he is the head of the family. It is most incorrect and treacherous.'

Doña Concepción sought Anthony on the lawn. 'Don Antonio, will you do me a very great favour? Will you take this letter in for me and post it? I know it is unusual, but it is quite all right. See it is addressed to my brother. Will you take

it yourself? The servants are so unreliable. Will you see that
the postmistress puts on the mark before your eyes? You must
always do that or they will steal the stamps and throw away the
letters. This is an express letter and has expensive stamps. Even
so it will take days, Santísima María. But I don't think we
should telegraph. And Don Antonio, will you not tell anyone?'

Doña Concepción went at once to where Doña Victoria
was sitting; she looked up and followed Anthony with her
eyes.

'Do you think they know about Mr Middleton and the
Jocotepec telegrams?' said Anthony to E. 'Oughtn't I take
this letter to him first? We Anglo-Saxons are a small colony
out here and must do all we can for each other.'

At noon, Don Luís brought a gin fizz to E. 'Rum lot, my
family,' he said, 'you'd think you'd be doing them a favour
by helping them out a bit and they treat you like a criminal.
No real sense of business in our country.'

Dressing for luncheon, Don Enriquez exploded in front of
his valet, and consequently Juan was found to be more
enlightened, though still puzzled, as to the nature of Don
Luís' bombshell. What Don Luís had put on the table were
centavos, Juan told Anthony.

'Shouldn't have called it *centavos*, either,' said Anthony.
'*Twenty-five thousand pesos* the bastard produced in hard cash.
I should have liked to see their faces. Now what's eating
them? There isn't that much reason to be put out? Of course
it was cheek of Luís.'

'One begins to see the point of primogeniture,' said E.

'This lets Don Luís in on the profits,' said I. 'The place
couldn't carry so many shareholders, and they particularly did
not want Luís. I suppose if they refused his money, he could
refuse permission to have the hotel.'

'Yeah,' said Anthony. 'But twenty-five thousand pesos ain't hay.'

'Where did he get them from?' said E.

At teatime Don Jaime unburdened himself, obliquely, to E. 'If you were about to launch an enterprise,' he said, 'and someone you *knew* had nothing insisted on investing a substantial sum, what would be your conclusion?'

'That there was someone else behind your man,' said E.

'Yes. I am afraid so. And what would be the motive?'

'To get in on your venture, of course.'

'That, or revenge,' said Don Jaime. 'Where did he get it from?'

It was nearly dusk and there was still no sign of Don Otavio. Doña Victoria was standing on the waterfront, now almost haggard with anxiety. Then there was the sound of a motor. The boat came in sight, landed; Don Otavio stepped out with Doña Victoria clutching at him. The two came up the garden, Don Otavio grave, Doña Victoria a woman changed by relief. Don Enriquez walked rapidly down to meet them. The rest of us stood on the terrace, watching. Doña Concepción crossed herself. She turned to me. 'You know we are in trouble,' she said. 'Luís has a large sum of money and it is a great worry. Tavio is bringing Aunt Isabella-María's advice. Oh, *where* did he get it from?'

Down in the garden, Don Enriquez suddenly rocked with laughter: he slapped his thighs and thumped at Don Otavio. He looked up to us. 'From our pious aunt!' he shouted.

Chapter Nine
A FAMILY AND A FORTUNE

How pleasant it is to have money, heigh ho!
How pleasant it is to have money.

THE REST of the family had been more slow to see the joke, and dinner that night was still glum.

'Am I to understand,' said E. when we were alone, 'that this eminent lay-nun is a doublecrosser?'

'No, no, no,' said Anthony; 'it's all out now. Luís got the dough out of the pious aunt two months ago for some crackpot scheme of his. It went bust even before Luís had time to get in.'

'I dare say an experience unique in his career,' said E.

'So Luís hung on to the money. The old girl is furious. She made a screaming row with her confessor. You see the dope had told her to put Luís on his feet for the sake of his nine children.'

'What are they going to do about it now?'

'The pious aunt wants her money back. Otavio brought a letter telling Luís. Some letter. The others are pretending they know nothing about it. They're going to offer Luís a thousand pesos to stay out. They're that relieved it wasn't some tycoon who wanted to do them out of the whole place, they're going to play it soft. What beats me is what Doña Victoria was so scared about. Luís is asking five thousand. *He* hasn't seen the letter yet. They think they can settle for two. Otavio has got them on him. From the pious aunt.'

'Ready money cannot be as tight in Mexico as Mr Middleton would have us believe,' said E.

It was settled, thanks to Don Otavio's firmness, for fifteen hundred.

'Who is going to get the extra five?' said E. and I at once.

'Otavio is returning them to the pious aunt. She always tips him.'

Everybody appeared in high spirits and agreements were signed that morning with a flourish. Don Jaime brought off a small coup of his own. He had meant to ask for a modest share in the profits in return for an investment of five thousand pesos, but in view of the reception given to Don Luís's offer had decided to desist. He now took advantage of the reversal of mood to ask for this profit *without* an offer of capital and so impressed Don Enriquez and Otavio by his loyalty in not springing cash on them that they consented at once.

Mrs Rawlston came to lunch. She seemed upset about something. 'You all set now to rook each other and the public?' she addressed the company.

'Mrs Rawlston is always herself,' said Doña Victoria.

'Is this not a pretty dress?' said Don Otavio.

'That's right, Victoria,' said Mrs Rawlston; 'put every cent you've got on your back.'

'Mrs A., you a Democrat?' she asked E. over the rice.

'We are all *so* fond of Doña E.,' said Don Otavio.

'I am,' said E. 'My father voted for Woodrow Wilson twice; I cast my first vote for James Cox against the unfortunate Herding; I voted for John W. Davis against Coolidge . . .'

'*Against* an incoming president?' said Don Luís.

'That's kind of a Republican family you married into,' said Mrs Rawlston.

'Personally, Mrs Rawlston, I am a strong Roosevelt woman.'

'We have had better, and we have had worse. I haven't been home since the Arthur Administration. 1884. Well, have you heard the news? Mr Middleton's had a pair of blacks to his house. Should have thought Mr Middleton knew better. Richard Middleton a nigger-lover! Wouldn't have believed it. I sat down straight away and wrote to tell him what I think of him. Blacks in his house! Sitting down to tea with them, and poor Blanche pouring it out.'

'You cannot mean the two gentlemen from Bombay, Mrs Rawlston? They are distinguished plant psychologists, and I believe high-caste Hindus.'

'They're black for all that, ain't they? I saw them. Thought I heard you say you were a Democrat, Mrs A.?'

'Now what are you all celebrating about?' She turned to Don Enriquez. 'How soon are you going to open this hotel?'

'Very soon. Everything has been arranged.'

'Have you got the road? Have you got a manager? Got a cook that can stay sober for two Sundays on end? Got any customers?'

'There are still a few details. We only settled the most important.'

'Got any linen? What about knives and forks? And china? Any of you thought of that? Thought of anything beside yourselves? Luís gave you all a fine scare, didn't you, Luís? Who did you think the money came from?'

'Some combine from the north,' said Don Jaime.

'Bet you all thought it was Felipe. I can see you did.

Didn't *you*, Concepción? Your brother never knew what to do with his money, and they say he's got a grudge against you, Enriquez.'

There was no silence: speech flowed promptly from all sides almost before Mrs Rawlston had finished and I did not allow Anthony to catch my eye.

Some of Mrs Rawlston's details came up that evening, and came up in front of us.

'We shan't have the road this year,' said Don Enriquez. 'It doesn't matter: you can have the run of my boat. I shall put it in the company's name.'

'We shall have to buy new things,' said Don Otavio. 'Juan and I will make a list.'

'It will be expensive,' said Don Enriquez.

'Victoria, what about Mama's silver? And the big Sèvres?' said Don Otavio.

'What silver?' said Don Enriquez.

'The silver and china that were taken into Guadalajara when the *Carrancistas* were all over the lake,' said Don Otavio.

'*Madre de Dios*, do we still have all that stuff in our house, Victoria?'

'You must have seen us use it, *querido*.'

'You would not think of putting the family plate in an hotel?' said Don Jaime.

'I entirely agree with Jaime,' said Doña Victoria.

'So do I,' said Don Luís. 'I know a Northern American firm that sells hotel equipment. Nice, cheap things. They are going to make me very special prices. I brought their catalogue.'

'We will use Mama's,' said Don Enriquez at once. 'Don't

look at me, Victoria; it is *my* mother's silver. Worse things can happen. The Saints know who is eating off yours now as it was stolen in the Revolutions. By your own servants, too; or so your father told me.'

'Very well, Enriquez. You never think of your daughter, do you?'

'Oh, my daughter, my daughter. She is a handsome girl. Who knows? Perhaps I shall marry her to some foreign fellow who doesn't expect twelve of this and a dozen of the other. Why should I throw good silver after my daughter?'

'Now really, Enriquez,' said Doña Victoria.

'These days all foreigners who aren't heretics are either poor or South Americans,' said Don Jaime.

'There were such nice Irish girls at school,' said Doña Concepción.

'The Irish never had anything worth having,' said Don Enriquez.

'A bigoted lot,' said Don Jaime.

'Of course, there are always the French,' said Doña Victoria.

'All the really good fortunes are still intact,' said Don Jaime.

'All Frenchmen are atheists,' said Doña Concepción.

'Atheism is no heresy,' said Don Jaime.

'It doesn't show,' said Don Luís.

'Atheists are nothing but relapsed Catholics,' said Doña Victoria.

'Reconversion is a very wonderful opportunity, a very great grace for a wife,' said Doña Concepción.

'That is true,' said Don Luís.

'We have looked to Europe for too long,' said Don Enriquez; 'there are many rich Catholic families in the United States of Northern North America, are there not, Doña E.?'

Chapter Ten
A PARTY

Nous avons joué de la flûte, et personne a voulu danser.
Et quand nous avons voulu danser plus personne ne jouait de la flûte . . .

T HE SANDS were running out.

On Sunday there was a party. Joaquím and Orazio and their sister arrived the night before; also four of the Jaimes' almost grown-up children and Doña Concepción's brother, Don Felipe, a lean, overbred, dissolute-looking man in his forties. On the day, boatload upon boatload of men looking like Goyas and women looking like Doña Concepción disembarked at noon. Comparatively modest refreshment had been set out in the garden; more elaborate preparations were going on behind the scenes, and the band from Ajijíc, lent by Doña Anna, was hiding, silent, in the bushes. We had understood it to be an evening party. Don Otavio and Doña Concepción explained that Mexican parties always begin in the morning and in an apparently offhand manner. You are not expected to expect your guests to like it well enough to stay. If they do, meals will appear at the proper times with apparent spontaneity. There must be a supply of drink against any length and number, but only a fraction of it suitable for a brief call visible at first. In due course, dinner for forty will be served and the guests contrive to adjust their clothes with the same air of improvisation.

'What if the party doesn't go?' said Anthony.

'That is very sad,' said Don Otavio. 'Then there is no music. They are told not to play.'

'Does it happen often?'

'It happens.'

'Then does everybody go home?'

'Oh, no. That would not be polite.'

'So they stay for lunch and tea and dinner all the same?'

'They stay. But it is not the same.'

'It is not the same at all,' said Doña Concepción.

The men sat in the shade and smoked; the women chattered all over the house and lawn. They talked to E. and me about their schools; Roehampton and the various branches of the Sacred Heart. E. had been to one of them, greatly embarrassing the history class, and I had been to the Ursulines, so we were able to hold our own.

'Doña E., how is it possible that poor Antonio is heretical when you are not?' said Doña Concepción.

'Well, his grandfather came from the South, and mine from Ireland,' said E.

'Yes, yes. But it must be so dreadful for you to have a Protestant in the family. Do you try to convert him?'

'No,' said E.

'*Such* a pity,' said Doña Victoria.

Huge amounts of food and case upon case of spirits were consumed, but no one was in the least the worse for liquor. At four, the band began to play and kept it up till midnight. After dinner there was dancing. The married women danced, the young girls did not. Anthony was gently refused by Don Enriquez' daughter, 'You must wait until I am *casada*, Don Antonio – housed.'

The guests went after their full span but at what was still a decorous hour, and the next morning the three brothers left San Pedro. The women stayed on and entered a five days' Retreat for a Special Intention, the success of the hotel. The

Sixteenth of September was celebrated along the lake with much alcohol, bloodshed and fireworks in full sunlight. Waves of newly white-collared Indios arrived at Chapala by motor bus. Nationalism and rowdy xenophobia were rampant. The lanes echoed with drunken groans and screams of *Viva Mexico*. For a week, children danced nightly around Mr Middleton's bungalow shouting *GRINGO*, the opprobrious term for Americans. At Jocotepec, at the culminating point of the festival, several local mules joined loudly in the *Grita de Dolores*, the ritual cry burst into by the crowds at the stroke of midnight amidst a bedlam of bell-ringing and firing off of firearms; the unfortunate animals were arrested for patriotic blasphemy and taken off to jail where they languished for days before their drunken owners noticed their absence and set to bail them out. Jesús had not returned.

'He sold his mother's cow,' said Don Otavio, 'so he will go to the North of North America, to Texas, to make his fortune. He has had a general disgust.'

'What about his wife?'

'She can marry Juan.'

'Divorce?'

'No, no. She and Jesús were not married enough. The Church does not like the Indios to get really married. There would be so much adultery. It would be a very great sin.'

At the end of the week Anthony left, borne off by water and motor car to Guadalajara and thence by air to the USA, and a few days later our time had come. Don Otavio embraced E.; I was embraced by Guadalupe and Soledad, and we both gave a solemn promise to return at Christmas.

'Why must you go on travels, *niña*?' said Guadalupe. 'It is expensive and not wise. Is it for a vow?'

'No one goes anywhere except to Guadalajara and

Mexico,' said Don Otavio, 'and to San José Purúa for the gout. Foreigners go to Acapulco to bathe, but it is very hot and nasty. If the hotel does well, Luís and I shall go to Juan-les-Pins. We hear it is very nice now. Oh, why must you leave San Pedro?

'No. You are very much mistaken. There is nothing to see in the Republic. Nothing. You will be very uncomfortable and not at all happy.'

Chapter Eleven
MAZATLÁN: AN ORDEAL

Non, je ne suis pas heureuse ici.
PELLEAS ET MÉLISANDE

O UR FIRST destination was Mazatlán, a tropical port on
the Pacific in the state of Sinaloa, a clearing house for
sugar, gold and fruit, forgotten now, lagoon enclosed, idyllic.
We had been charmed by a description in an old travel book,
and although the place lay some six hundred kilometres off
our intended route – slow progress through the Central
Provinces to the Ruins in the South – we decided to go, and
to spend a month at Mazatlán.

There is no road into Sinaloa from anywhere. Aeroplanes
are small and few, but there is a railway. The Southern-
Pacific Railway, in fact, which twice a week starts from
Guadalajara, climbs down the Sierra to the West Coast and
runs along the Pacific all the way to California. This is what
we took.

We very nearly missed it. I was standing in a queue waiting
to register a trunk. All auguries were fair. There were only
half a dozen people in front of me with few encumbrances
each, and there were four registration clerks scurrying about
in a flurry of helpfulness. There was a full hour before even
the official time of departure. Taking a train is a nervous
ordeal to me: I sat on one side of the trunk trying to read a
newspaper; the porter, a young man half my size, sat on
the other. E. had gone to the platform to find our seats. The
station was squalid. Hundreds of people were sitting on

the ground, wrapped in blankets or straw mats, asleep, cooking food, nursing babies.

'*Viajeros*,' said the porter.

'Then why don't they travel?' said I. 'It must be unusual to make camp before you have started; in peace time at least.'

'The travellers are waiting for the trains,' said the porter.

'Are the trains as late as that?'

'Not the trains. The travellers.'

'Late? They look as though they'd come very early.'

'Yes, early. Late and early. The travellers come at all times.'

'Don't they ever come in time for the trains?'

'Who would know that?' said the porter.

'Don't they find out?'

'Why take so great a trouble? This is a nice station. All in the shade.'

Forty minutes passed and the four clerks were still attending to the first person in the queue. I got off the trunk, edged forward and peeked. The clerks were trying to put steel bands around a somewhat dishevelled bundle. The contrivance for clamping the steel bands did not seem to work. One clerk hugged the bundle in his arms, two held it laced in steel, the fourth advanced with the apparatus in the manner of a monkey imitating a dentist approaching the chair. He pounced: something snapped, steel bands writhed in the air, the bundle burst agape; then everything was dropped on the floor, comments were exchanged, the clerks rested from their labours. Then one approached the bundle and the identical process was repeated all over again. I edged back, unable to bear more.

Another twenty minutes and perseverance must have borne its fruit for the owner of the bundle strode away empty-handed, frowning at a slip of paper. The next man in line had not filled in his forms. Had no forms. He was told where to get them. He went. The clerks lolled back.

'Why don't they go on with the next person?' said I, looking at my watch.

'It is not his turn. It is the turn of the man who has no forms,' said the porter. 'It would not be polite. This is a very regular, modern railway.'

The man who had no forms returned. 'You must fill them in,' said the clerks.

'I cannot write in forms,' said the man.

'You must go to a scribe,' said the clerks.

There was a pause.

'It is Sunday,' said the man.

'You should go yesterday,' said the clerks.

'Yesterday I had no forms,' said the man.

'That is true,' said the clerks.

There was another pause.

'The ticket clerk writes in forms,' said the clerks. 'We will ask him to do it.'

'I can take the train another day,' said the man.

'We will ask the ticket clerk. He is very obliging.'

'No, no. I shall take the train some other day; it is no matter.' The man asked for his crate, it was lifted on to his head and he walked away.

The next man had forms and a straw trunk, neatly strapped and padlocked. The clerks produced the coil of steel band.

'*Not* more steel bands?' said I.

'Steel bands for everything,' said the porter.

'That trunk is locked.'

'Steel bands for every piece of baggage. It is the regulation.'

'One does see why the thieves prefer to walk off with the

whole piece. Now what about that train? It *is* an hour past its hour.'

'Do not preoccupy yourself with the train, Señora. The train will not go for a long little while. It never leaves without everybody. It is a very regular train.'

The clerks had lit a spirit lamp and were dropping melted lead on the recalcitrant steel bands. The lead burnt a small hole into the straw trunk. The clerks poured some water from a carafe into the hole. The owner of the trunk giggled excitedly.

I will say *Lycidas* to myself; from beginning to end, very slowly this time, before looking up, I resolved. The porter seized my hand. 'Come,' he cried. He wrenched at the trunk. 'Come! The train!' We ran through the gate. The train was pulling out. I was pushed on. Two carriages further up, E. was being assisted down. Our hand luggage lay piled at various points of the platform. I tried to get off. The porter howled, E. saw me and was pushed on again. Two strangers grasped the trunk about its middle and, running, shoved it into an open door. Bystanders picked up bags and typewriters and flung them into passing windows. Peso notes fluttered in the wind of increasing speed.

E. and I met and sat down.

'You had the passports.'

'*You* had the tickets.'

'*You* had the money.'

'I should have got out at the first stop,' said E., 'and telegraphed the American Consulate and Don Otavio.'

'Our *first stop*, my dear, is nine hours from here, at Tepic, in the *Terra Caliente*. Tepic, I have just learned, is a Nahoa word meaning hard stone.'

'Don Otavio wasn't at all enthusiastic about Mazatlán,' said

E.; 'frankly, S., I don't think any forgotten tropical port is worth this.'

'Let's have lunch,' said I.

The Pullman was full of people we had not seen in markets and buses, or met at San Pedro Tlayacán. The kind of people Don Jaime described as not having worn shoes long: petit bourgeois Mexicans, mestizos all, the fairly recent products of the towns. The men were broad-hipped, soft and sweaty; the girls pretty; the women running to fat after seventeen. Every family had brought fruit, a provision of sweets and a bottle of *tequila*. The atmosphere was polite, complacent, reserved. No passenger passed another in the corridor without exchanging the compliments of the hour. Whenever someone stumbled against our trunk (now inevitably obstructing an aisle), he would apologize for touching our property. The whole train rang with *dispénseme, con permiso, si Vd. lo permite, a sus órdenes, servidor di Ustéd.* In the section opposite to ours, sat an enormous mestiza lady with folds and folds of purple chins and skin, and her two daughters who had very bad complexions and spent their time putting powder on their faces. E., an addict of the *Bibliothèque Rose*, called them *Mme Crapaude et ses deux filles laides.* Outside, valley after valley slid by in the September sunshine: tobacco, tequila plantations, maize, mangoes, more maize. The afternoon wore on. E. read *Persuasion*; Madame Crapaude engaged me in snatches of dull conversation; the daughters prinked. We were running through a volcanic region, unplanted, uninhabited, cleft by mounds and crevasses the colour and texture of pumice stone. Then the scenery widened, became wholly panoramic with no foreground at all: clouds and clouds of mountain peaks and, beside the rails, a sheer drop of some thousand feet. The train slowed, dipped, and with all brakes drawn began descending at an exceedingly steep angle. We were creeping down the side of the Western Sierra Madre.

Mme Crapaude's *deux filles laides* squealed.

'I believe this is a very great engineering feat,' said E. 'We had the same problem in the Rocky Mountains. No rail-bed can take that kind of stress long. You remember the Colorado Pass Rail Wreck in '39?'

On the map, Mexico looks like the headless part of a large fish, hacked across the middle. Its shape and situation are roughly that of Italy only that Mexico is about seven times as large. Like the Italian peninsula, it is attached in the north to the mass of a continent, and stretches southwards into the sea. Like Italy, it is wide across the top, then tapers down; like Italy it is flanked by two long, opposing coast-lines. Unlike the boot, it is not straight but curves around the gulf like a dolphin's back. And the peninsula is not a peninsula: the fish's tail is not washed by the sea but joined to Central America by a short, forked land border with Guatamala and British Honduras.

Not a peninsula in fact, but in shape and feeling. It is often thought of as the bridge between the North American Continent and Central America; this, apart from the inhabitant's conviction of being part of North America, is misleading, as the concept of a bridge implies a smoothness and regularity which the land mass of Mexico lacks to a fantastic degree. Two-thirds of its length are filled by the plateau (another misleading term), and from the north this is accessible enough. It used to be said that one could drive from Texas on to Mexico in a coach-and-four: the drive-in is hundreds of miles wide, the rise from sea level gradual. The southern exit is a different matter. It is narrower, very steep and furrowed by canyons. It has one – recent – road. And of course the plateau itself is not level, but a rugged base for other mountains. The surface of this singular tableland is slit by gorges, gashed by ravines, rent by chasms, blocked by volcanoes and crossed by expanse beyond expanse of lateral ranges. If progress north to south is thus impeded, access from west or east is hardly possible at all as the long sides of the plateau are the two stupendous sierras dropping perpendicularly into the sea and, across these, the coasts can only be reached at a few hair-raising points.

Soon darkness mercifully veiled the secrets of that descent. Nothing similar occurred to dim the sharpness of the recollections of a century of rail wrecks that issued from E.'s memory.

That night I lay in my bunk across from where Mme Crapaude's daughters had squeezed themselves into one upper, dozing wakefully, lucid and lonely. The train jerked, pitched, halted, in our slow advance over one of the world's most uninhabited mountain passes. *Que diable allais-je chercher dans cette galère?*

We were due at Mazatlán at 5 a.m.; in itself a prospect not conducive to a quiet night's rest. The stops became longer. At last I decided we were going to be late, and fell asleep. I was woken by voices. Cannot get through, I heard. Line's washed away; we'll have to go back. And indeed after another wait the train began to reverse. It had become impossibly stuffy inside the bunks, so by six o'clock everybody was up and dressed, sticky and dirty with only a tepid trickle to wash under in the stinking lavatory, and ready to face the situation. No one knew what that was. Engine trouble, said some. A bridge was down. There had been floods though the rains *ought* to be over, and the line was under water. A local tribe, inimical to railways, had tampered with the ties. Meanwhile we had gone back a stretch and come to a halt in what the breaking light of day revealed to be a swamp; and further light, a supposed station.

The name RUIZ was peeling off a board nailed to a degraded hut, housing no doubt some signals and the station-master's family. This hut was the extent of the station buildings. There were no further huts, no platform, no facilities; no village in sight. There was no shelter of any kind. We were now across the Sierra Madre, and Ruiz would be in Nayarít, the territory of the Nayarítos, the only aborigines who managed to dawdle over their conversion to the Catholic faith from the Conquest well into the eighteenth century, and Nayarít lay in the coastal plains and therefore in the hot zone. Even at that early hour there was no need of such geography to make it clear that this was going to be as hot a day as any of us had ever feared to live through. Mosquitoes, too, were already up and about. A number of pigs now assembled round the train, and presently boarded it, looking and begging for food. They were dripping with liquid yellow mud. Information as to the length of our sojourn at Ruiz was not unanimous. Some said six hours, some ten; some said we would leave at midday, some at nightfall. Some said next morning, others in three days. The last train from the north had been four days late. There was also the hypothesis that we would be returned to Guadalajara. None of this was improbable.

The morning got under way. We all sat. E. and I consciously. It is hard on a Westerner to sit in a train that does not move. He may have a book, he may have something to talk about, he may be comfortable – we were not – and all the time he will be aware that something is missing, that something is wrong. It will jab and nibble at his nerves, scatter his concentration, tumble his equilibrium. If only the damn thing would move: the heat, the dirt, the boredom, all would be tolerable. *Oh, if only it would move!*

'Is *nothing* being done about this?' said E., standing up.

The Mexicans munched and sipped and chattered – *seguro*, it was hot. Mme Crapaude wielded a desperate fan. They were discussing developments with detached interest. We were in touch with Guymas – by the telegraph – with Tepíc, with Guadalajara. Someone was on his way to repair what had to be repaired. Repairs were going on almost now.

'Cannot anyone go and *see*?' said E.

But the rains had churned the earth and, getting off the train, one sank at once ankle-deep into tough, sucking clay.

At ten, everyone had resorted to wet handkerchiefs against their foreheads; relief was still hoped for in shifted positions and adjusted windows, and E. still eloquent on the various phenomena of heat prostration.

By eleven, nobody spoke. The mud on the pig's backs had caked bone-dry. Had I still been capable of fellow-feeling, that spark would have gone to Mme Crapaude's heaving form. Stupor did not lull, it made one with the heat and the duration and the box one sat wrapped in, the thick, grey, steaming bale of cotton wool: every heartbeat was the same, and every heartbeat was worse; there was no end in view and no end could now be envisaged.

After an existence of this the train moved smoothly out. There had been no warning. One conductor had to run for it, another got left behind. After a short pull, we stopped again, and at a station of similar aspect. Blocks of ice were piled on the roofs of the carriages, and once more we were off, headed towards the coast. It was 3 p.m. We had spent nine hours at Ruiz.

Mme Crapaude's daughters shook out their powder puffs.

E. and I misused our freshened faculties in figuring out how much of the delay we were likely to make up.

'We were already a few hours late when we turned back this morning,' said I.

'*And* late starting.'

'Well, it's all straight and flat now. We ought to make Mazatlán in two or three hours. Four at the outside.'

The rains must have been heavy. Stretches of track were still under water. Cautiously we crept through steam and heat, green flat swamp and an amorphous vegetation. Impossible to tell tree from shrub and shrub from creeper. They were all creepers: spineless, rank rather than luxuriant. I had never seen tropical flora before, and was disappointed by the lack of colour. Mile upon mile upon mile: no people, no houses, though now and again a clump of cattle standing patiently, belly-deep, in water. One could see their faces and count their horns. We were not making up time.

'We shall never know where that ice came from,' said E.

Night fell abruptly at seven. The carriage lights were opaque blue, we sat on in weary gloom among the made-up bunks: other wretches were staying on that train. At last the lights of Mazatlán gleamed in the thick night. Quite a number of lights for a forgotten port. A halt, a reverse, shunting, and at ten o'clock, seventeen hours late, we were in.

Mme Crapaude clasped E. and me to her moist bosom, her daughters extended flabby hands, men clapped our shoulders: *que Dios las proteja, que les vaya bien.*

A station lit by flares. Greedy hands and impassive faces. A driver who had been to Texas and would not move off before having collected a commission on us from mysterious agents. A long drive in the dark, first on open road, then through lengths of straight, built-up streets. The emergence of the waterfront: a huge, iron-grey, concrete esplanade, a physical blow in its stark ugliness; beyond it the Pacific making its great noise. The hotel. A Victorian Moorish structure, vast, balconied. In the hall, a row of hatted gentlemen reclining in rocking-chairs by spittoons. A thick smell of dead-town, faded splendours and present bankruptcy. An indifferent clerk shoving a key, opening a register.

'If you wanna eat, better eat quick.'

The desolate dining room, pilastered, gilt. A dais for a band, empty. A wooden fan like a windmill whirring over our heads from the stuccoed ceiling.

'What does it mean? Who was it built for?' said E. 'Forgotten? I should say it was. Wiped off every civilized person's memory. But it must have been on someone's mind at some time: these chandeliers and this mahogany and that pier didn't get here by accident.'

The fish is off. The meat looks purple and is off too. The ice is also purple, but scented. It tastes of plaster stirred with hair oil.

'At San Pedro—' said I.

'Do not mention San Pedro,' said E. 'It would make me cry.'

A turn on the treeless front, so like an English seaside pier, shorn of its amusements, its animation, transposed into a tropical environment.

Tomorrow we shall see the lagoons. Tomorrow we shall find somewhere to live. I did not look at E. when I said it. Now sleep. It was then that we came to face the incredible room.

Double-doors led into a large, finely proportioned apartment. Two immense, naked, fly-blown windows fronted the Pacific without shutters or curtains but for one tattered velvet rag torn off halfway. Plaster and paint were flaking off the walls and ceiling. Three huge fourposters were standing haphazardly about the room, their oak thick with beetles. Roaches in the springs and spiders on the floor. A mahogany dressing-table, a kitchen-chair with a broken seat. No drinking water. The bathroom, a dank cavern. One tap was missing, the other yielded a murky trickle. The lavatory was half-dismantled for some no doubt essential repair. Nothing appeared to have been dusted for a very long period, and everything was on a really grand scale of dilapidation.

'Do you see what I see? Or is it because I am so tired?'

'At the best inn's best room,' said E. 'This must have been the most splendid hotel of the Diaz era.'

'S.,' E. said at dawn, 'what is this ruthless roar? Is there a subway?'

'It is the Pacific. It looks grey. And quite flat, except for those breakers. Exactly the way it looks at Santa Monica, California.'

'The reward of travel,' said E.

The glare became unbearable. I went to procure relief. 'Just anything,' I asked, 'any odd piece of stuff to put over those great windows.'

'Curtains?' said the manager. 'Should I worry about curtains? Our ceilings are coming down.'

We saw a more modest and more liveable hotel in the centre. We saw some clean, comfortless rooms at three and sixpence a week on the waterfront. We found some quite edible eggs, beans and coffee for a very low price at a luncheon counter. We found that it was hot, but not intolerably so. We saw the unprepossessing town, boom-built during one bad period, run to seed in another. What stood up was a blaring art nouveau cathedral and some municipal excrescences. Life seemed subdued, and there were no signs of port activities. We never saw the lagoons.

They could only be reached by taxi. Last night's driver was lying in wait, naming an impossible fare, ready for a good haggle. We lost heart.

So I bathed in the churning, tepid brine from a machine in a cement breakwater in front of the hotel.

We were very, very depressed.

'Where are we?' said E. 'You have been so competent with the map. Where are we in relation to *other* places? Do we have to take a journey to get out of here?'

I went to find the aeroplane agency. The next plane out of Mazatlán was in three days. It was full up. There was another one next week. It was full up too. I joined E. in the bar, the only part of the hotel whose decay reflected an Edwardian afterglow. The mahogany, though worm-eaten, still shone in patches; the brasses were polished. The barman was neither Mexican nor American; he was a barman. He made us some absinthe cocktails.

'You wouldn't want an Armagnac,' he said, 'or a Benedictine? No, I suppose not at this hour. It's ten years since anyone has asked me for an Armagnac. It's all rum these days, and gin. One has to be thankful when it isn't tequila.'

'There wouldn't be a boat out of Mazatlán to somewhere today?' said E.

'A boat? Out of Mazatlán? There are no boats at Mazatlán. The port is silted. Didn't you know?'

'Nobody told us.'

'They don't talk much of Mazatlán nowadays. Silted these twenty years.'

E. looked at me. 'The train?'

'The train.'

'Today?'

'Today.'

But the Southern-Pacific was not due again until Saturday. It was Wednesday.

'We may as well have two more of these excellent drinks barman,' said E., 'if you will be so kind as to make them for us.'

'Why don't you take the train of the day before yesterday?' said the barman.

'Can one?' said E.

'The train of the day before yesterday is late. It did not come through on Monday. It will probably come through tonight. If you go to the station this evening, you cannot miss it.'

'Now we can send a wire to Don Otavio,' said E.

The train of the day before yesterday was full of wilted Americans. They had been frantic; now they were dead-beat with their three days' confinement.

'The line was under water, and we crawled, just crawled all the way from Nogales. Have you ever heard of such a thing? No, ma'am! You wouldn't want to make that trip twice.'

'Not in ordinary circumstances,' said E.

We got into Guadalajara the next evening, only five hours late.

Don Otavio, and Andreas and Juan, and Don Enriquez' Pedro were on the platform.

'I am so happy. Your rooms are ready for you. You must be so tired. You shall go straight to bed. Soledad will take you a tray.'

We drove into Guadalajara, which seemed like Paris, for a drink. Then we drove out to Chapala in Don Otavio's car. The air was fresh and smelt of hay. We went gently because cows were sleeping on the road with their calves. They had left the fields seeking the warmth of the still sun-drenched stones. They opened their eyes at us but did not get up. At Chapala we changed into Don Enriquez' motor boat. On the lake, the night was very clear, and filled with shooting stars. The mild water sparkled, phosphorescent, around our prow. Fish leaped, shone, and fell again. The shore lay softly, peaceful, half-divined. I was in that as it were tertiary state of fatigue where the nerves and senses lie bared to direct contact with the world and there is no longer distance or matter between the vision and the absorption, where the mind races, recording, lucid but empty, and beauty can become ours through osmosis. We landed and saw the façade of San Pedro standing in the moonlight.

Part Three

TRAVELS

Dites, qu'avez-vous vu?

Chapter One
GUANAJUATO OR
SIC TRANSIT

*Ah Madame, soyez tranquille. Vous voilà dans la Bonne
Province Française.*

HERE THERE is always cause to sit up and rub one's eyes. One had come to expect different things in different places, Aztec temples in a hybrid Metropolis, echoes of Medieval Spain among swamp and hut, derelict spas in South Sea squalor, Byzantine Idylls twelve air hours from the USA, Don Quixote in a bank and the Marx Brothers in the Post Office. One expected to be cherished like a mascot, cradled in luxury, or crawl like vermin, unregarded, over immense distances exposed to every inclemency. One did not, could not, expect to find oneself in a quiet little town, *une brave petite ville, bien calme bien propre*, eating one's table d'hôte, *en pension*, napkin in ring, at the *Posada del Progreso* with the notary and the mayor's clerk.

Mexico is still a country without a middle class. There are revolutionaries, but no lay mediators. There is public feeling, hideous waves of nationalism, on occasions. There is no public opinion.

There are of course a certain number of people who though literate and shod are neither Creoles nor *Anciens Riches*, but they do not make up a class; individually they either have few civic cares, or try to make a beeline for office. There is no trace of that *fundamental* power of a mediator class: the exercise of pressure through disinterested moral

239

criticism distinct from any direct prerogative; that restraining mystique which has been a practical political reality from the Roman Republic through the modifications of the English monarchy to the Dreyfus case. And where this class and influence are missing, change, good or bad, usually comes – as it so largely did in the Latin Americas – through violence, through mob risings, schism among the military, palace revolution.

Revolutionary movements in those parts have always been curiously fickle. An interested individual would make use of a grievance to collect followers. The leader kept his end in view, the followers indulged themselves with a martial outing and forgot theirs. Thus, Mexican Indians had plenty of grievances – though of course few weapons – against Spain, yet secession from that country was only instigated and achieved when the conquerors had become too numerous for the spoils, and the Creole section of the ruling class set out against the Spanish-born and more privileged members.

A mediator class would have been hard put to emerge in Mexico. Where was it to come from? Who were to be its members? Occupied Indians, or the gentlemen from Spain? The men who sought their fortunes and served their Faith and King in a faraway country, or the aborigines whose cultures were levelled and whose existence moulded into peonage? The Conquistadores and their descendants had their hands full. The Inquisition hovered over their consciences as the home government watched over their pockets – at any moment they might be accused of harbouring heresies or of salting away gold. They never sent enough gold as it was. Even land grants were full of strings; the audience might allot vast acres to a faithful servant, and then direct the proceeds towards the upkeep of some church. So the years passed: fighting, ruling, pleading. They were very much alone; severed from the established world, cut off from their place in the order of their time, every step was a new step, and yet they were hamstrung, pinned to Spain, by a hundred bureaucratic ties. They were no intellectuals, but they were men of intellectual appetites. And they lived them. The distinction between the spirit of adventure and the spirit of enquiry had not yet been drawn. There was the first Bishop of Michoacán who admired Sir Thomas More and thus wrote to the Council of the Indies for leave to set up a model of More's Utopia amongst the Tarrascans. They were versatile men. They were scholars and poets, that is, they had plenty of Latin and read their Plato and composed Italian verse, but for all that they were neither artists nor philosophers. Their accomplishments were part of their renaissance make-up like a nineteenth-century young woman's watercolours, and they did not dream of imparting them to the conquered country.

The respective descendants of Toltecs, Aztecs and Tarrascans, whose ancestors bore probably as little resemblance to each other as British shepherds did to contemporary Athenians, lived in common tutelage. They worked where they were told to, razing temples, building cathedrals, mining; laws were made for them; a style was imported for their place of worship; they were received into their new religion – in violation of its basic tenets – as second-rank Christians, spiritual minors, held incapable of distinction between heresy and dogma, and thus neither subject to the Inquisition nor responsible for the purity of their faith.

Accepting the proposition that salvation is attainable within the Faith alone, that measure was an inevitable expedient, as it would have been beyond the scope and time of any tribunal to deal with the Indians' many heresies, and as impossible to prevent them. The Indians were delighted to accept a new god, but reluctant to relinquish many of the old ones. Being allowed to muddle on with their mixed pantheon, they stayed contentedly enough in the new faith; and, as it turned out, became in time extremely fervent Catholics. In the course of a few centuries, the old gods faded into insignificant and occasional relics before the lustre of the Trinity, the Virgin and the Saints.

Huitzluiputzli is still about, got up sometimes in wing and crown, tucked away under the altar against a rainy day; yet if the Mexican Indians are still somewhat polytheistically inclined, most of their deities can now at least be found in the *Book of Martyrs* and the Christian calendar.

So the Indians became devout Catholics, and learnt to speak Spanish. The Spaniards remained devout Catholics, and went on speaking Spanish. The first generation brought no wives so there was, if not much intermarriage, a great deal of interbreeding. The Indians ceased to be pure Indians, and the Spaniards became Creoles. The country also did its part, and in due course the Creoles, through various stages of Mexification, became Mexican Creoles. After some hundred years of living together, neither Indians nor Spaniards were quite what they had originally been. In some ways they have become like each other; in others, they share nothing at all. The gulf between conqueror and conquered has settled into the gulf between class and class. Each still draws from a different tradition; neither has tried to learn consciously from the other's. When they are on good terms, they call each other *niños*, children. There they live side by side, in domestic proximity, familiar and remote, trusting and aloof, like so many *frères de lait*, boys, one from the village, one from the manor, who shared the same wet-nurse.

Of course Guanajuato cannot be what it seems. We know what is supposed to go on under these surfaces of probity and provincial calm, the wickedness (Who has not read their Balzac?), the repressions (Their Mauriac? Their Julien Green?), the crimes. Every assizes reveals these respectable backwaters as the scene of yet another trial of the Ogre of Didier-le-Marché or Argemont-sous-Congre. Yet there *is* the surface. In France it is a natural cover, in Mexico it is not natural in the least. The elements are lacking. How this town has managed even to seem what it may not be is a mystery. Perhaps it is a conjuring trick: the eye follows and the mind boggles.

Guanajuato is in central Mexico. Guanajuato in Tarrascan means Frog's Hill. The town is entered through a canyon. The altitude is seven thousand feet, the climate fair. Architecturally, it is very pretty: steep streets of white houses of a simple seventeenth-century Moorish cast, winding up and down a hillside. Its history was exceptionally savage, and its past prosperity fabulous.

It has one endearing absurdity, a neo-classical theatre with a great portico and nine muses standing waving on the cornice, the earnest product of somebody's recollections of the Madeleine, the Parthenon and the present Comédie Française, and his more solid study of what may have been the Municipal Theatre at Toulouse built under the presidency of Jules Grévy. It is quite small and executed all over in bright green stone. This hallucinatory touch gives it – against every intention of the architect – a cosy and exotic charm. The town's advertised chief sight is the Ossuary, a vault in which the bones of the very poor repose in a promiscuous heap, and the roughly embalmed bodies of the dead of intermediate means are stood upright against the walls. This place is open to visitors at regular hours. (Gratuity.)

Much of the worst fighting of the Revolutionary Wars was done in central Mexico. In 1810 Guanajuato, which has a tremendous fortress, was held by the Spanish and besieged by an army of Independents headed by Hidalgo himself. Don Miguel Hidalgo y Costilla, the present national hero, was, one might remember, a Creole parish priest. After a hard siege, the assault – an appalling struggle as both sides fought with utter courage and ferocity. It ended with fire set to wooden doors, hand-to-hand fighting in the patio and a kill on the roof. Then the victorious Independents sacked the town. Three days later the Guanajuatans reacted by breaking into the fortress and murdering the only people they could, the Royalist prisoners, some two hundred disarmed Spanish soldiers. Thereupon other Spaniards marched upon the town, set siege to it in their turn and in due course captured it from the Independents. *They* ordered the execution of every person captured, man, woman or child. And when a few months later Hidalgo, Ignacio Allende and some other Independence leaders were taken at Chihuahua and executed, their heads were sent to Guanajuato, put in iron cages and hung up outside the fortress. There they stayed exposed for ten years. Then the Independence Movement won, New Spain became the Republic of Mexico; the heads were taken to Mexico City in a crystal urn and given a state burial. Then ex-Lieutenant Augustín Iturbide, a very young mestizo and another of the revolutionary leaders, made himself Emperor of Mexico. Young as he was, Augustín I was married, and had his wife and himself solemnly crowned and anointed at Mexico Cathedral. The First Empire lasted three hundred and seven days. Augustín abdicated; was exiled; went to England; returned, and landed again in Mexico and, in the more summary fashion of that country, was shot. One wonders whether Stendhal ever heard of Augustín Iturbide.

Then the country became a constitutional republic. The first President changed his name from Fernandez to Guadalupe-Victoria, in honour both of his victory and the national patron saint, the Holy Virgin of Guadalupe. Then he abolished other people's titles. Soon, two Franciscan Friars rose against the obtaining form of government; General Santa Anna, a Creole jack-in-the-box, rose to defend it; and there began the War between the Centralists and the Federalists. Provinces revolted, bands gathered, armies were on the march, sieges laid. And so it went on.

Tobacco, maize and wheat now grow on the hollowed hills of Guanajuato, and canary seed is the district's chief export staple. La Valenciana, El Melado, Las Reyas – once those hills held the richest deposits of gold and silver known to mankind. It was in the days of the immense prestige of gold when no question yet had arisen as to the intrinsic value of precious metals, and these mines changed the history of Europe and had their part in shaping the world we have today. For a century after the Conquest, the gold from Guanajuato was shipped to the Spanish Crown. The Iberian peninsula did not become more fertile; if anything, rather less food was grown; but as the inhabitants of more fruitful regions were delighted to exchange consumers' goods for handsome metals, Spain could command every commodity. A fraction of the silver extracted from La Valenciana paid for the men and timber that built the Armada. Spain became a power and of course a menace. Generations of Englishmen looked at it with the apprehension later felt by generations of Frenchmen looking at Germany. The scales of the Reformation were weighted. The very focus of Christendom was shifted from Rome to the Escorial, and thus from a mellow Latin worldliness to the barbarism and ascetic discipline of a risen Moorish Prussia.

A little gold is still extracted at Guanajuato. It is bought by the USA, who to prevent depreciation has guaranteed to take the output. It is shipped to Kentucky and buried again under Fort Knox.

La Valenciana is now empty of silver. On top of the hill commanding the town, the canyon and a spacious valley, sun-drenched in the sparkling air, stands San Caetano, the church built as a thanks-offering in the heydays of the mine, Churrigueresque, domed, honey coloured, extravagant and melted, every stone glowing with the stored warmth of two hundred sunny years. We had come with a bottle of wine and a loaf, and sat below the shading walls, listening into the intense stillness of a crystalline early noon, eating and drinking, blinking into the valley, E. talking of the Decline of the West: Spengler having, it appears, dedicated a long chapter to La Valenciana; the mine, not the church.

Chapter Two
QUERÉTARO: A MODEST INN

Où l'on pourra manger, et dormir, et s'asseoir

THE JOURNEY — by first-class bus — from Guadalajara to Guanajuato, broken by a day and night at Leon, an industrial centre remarkable mostly for its rural aspect, had been so pleasant that we were rash enough to try to get from Guanajuato to San Miguel de Allende despite the fact, somewhat contradicted by the existence of a bus service, that there appeared to be no road.

We were on our way to Querétaro. Guanajuato, San Miguel and Querétaro form a triangle. There is a good road between Guanajuato and Querétaro, and a road of sorts between Querétaro and San Miguel. None is shown on maps, local or general, between San Miguel and Guanajuato. As the distance between these two is by far the shortest, it seemed silly to go first to Querétaro, then all the way back to San Miguel, and then all the way back to Querétaro again. This I explained at length to the ticket-man at the bus station, who showed no signs of confusion but agreed with sympathy.

'How far is it?' said E.

'*This* way, only about a hundred miles.'

'How long can a hundred miles be?'

It was a second-class service. Arrangements on second-class buses are above-board enough: the insides are roped off into two parts — the front has seats and is reserved for passengers and their smaller animals, the back is for bullocks, crates, and such goats, pigs and sheep as have out-grown lap size. Seats are not reserved. But they are scrupulously left to those who have boarded the bus the night before and there is moreover plenty of standing space. The vehicles themselves are older first-class buses, repainted and looking practically the same with the engines overhauled and capable of good speed; such deficiencies as there may be are only in the springs and brakes. Stops are by request.

There *was* a road-bed, in a fairly advanced stage of construction, much of it really passable. There was nothing that could be called a surface, and there was no grading, so the changes of level were at a degree unusual in public motor transport. At the worst stretches one got off, the beasts grazed and the male passengers gave a hand in steadying the bus on its descent over a flight of boulders.

'You suppose it does it *every* day?' said E.

All in all, it was a long hundred miles.

San Miguel de Allende proved unrewarding. The town seemed both uncouth and arty; full of great clumsy monuments in home-made peasant gothic, and coy little bead shops. There were signs (quite absent elsewhere in the central provinces) of a half-fulfilled bid for tourists; the plaza was up, and gusts of dust blowing over everything. Perhaps it was a bad week; nearly everyone I have talked to since about San Miguel said they loved the place and that it had much charm. We, after a few days' rest, went on to Querétaro.

Arrival at these provincial towns follows a certain pattern. Whatever the size of the place, the bus stops, for good, a mile or two from the centre. A carrier will rise from the kerb, pile your luggage on his back (always one carrier to however many trunks) and set off at a brisk running pace in a direction known to him. Naturally, you follow. At first there is a good long straight and you can see your bags bobbing three hundred yards ahead.

Then, in a breathless trot, trying to catch glimpses of your new surroundings, you enter the town. Now the *cargador* begins to whizz round sharp corners at which you pause in agonized indecision and after half an hour reach the plaza where you will find him in shady repose outside the entrance of the main hotel.

A word on these provincial inns, the *posadas*. They are run by honest, mildly prosperous, commercial Mexicans for other mildly prosperous, commercial Mexicans. Travellers not fitting this description can go to one or two more modest establishments of essentially the same character, or they can go to the German *pension*. Pilgrims sleep in the street; English and American tourists usually love *Haus Heimat*. The *posadas* are most jolly. The ground floor is always a large, unkempt parlour opening into the patio without much transition, full of overgrown plants, wicker chairs, objects without visible use, birds free and caged, and a number of sleeping dogs. Here the innkeepers jot their accounts, sort the linen, drive bargains with the poultry woman and the egg child, arraign the servants, play the gramophone, drink chocolate, chat and doze; and here the guests sit, smoke cigars, have their hair cut, shout for servants, play the gramophone, drink rum and chocolate, chat and doze. Everybody has their own bottle, sent out for by the *mozo*. The innkeeper would think you mad to pay him bar prices; every time you draw cork he will supply you – compliments of the house – with glasses, limes, salt (without which spirits are considered to be unswallow-able), pistachio nuts, fried anchovies, toasted tortillas strewn with crumbs of cheese and lettuce, stuffed cold maize dumplings and pickled chilli peppers.

The three more substantial meals are taken in the COMIDOR, an uncompromising rectangle marked thus and partitioned off the parlour by a glass door. The bedrooms are very clean, quite bleak and full of beds. There is always plumbing, recent and proudly displayed. The rule is a basin, shower-bath and a WC right inside the room. There are no screens, and not always a window. In that case one leaves the door open and soon gets used to it, nobody inside or out ever paying the slightest attention. The service at some hours is zealous and alarmingly imaginative (in one place they unpacked for us and we found every article regardless of use arranged in a symmetrical pattern on the floor); at other hours, early morning, siesta, after dinner, there is no service at all. The terms are something between eight and ten shillings a day for accommodation (the room to yourself if you are alone and the room for seven if you are seven) and all the food you can eat. There are no taxes, no service charges, no extras; that is there *are* extras: errands run, coffee, chocolate, drinking water, sweet bread, fruit all day long, but you do not pay for them. Washing is one and sixpence a dozen, whether the dozen be shirts, dresses, flannels, socks or handkerchiefs, and is returned in immaculate condition the same day.

Breakfast, round ten o'clock, is ham-and-eggs or eggs-and-chilli, followed by beef steak with sliced tomatoes, followed by black beans; tortillas, rolls, buns, sweet bread and cake; jam, honey and stewed fruit: papayas, muskmelon, bananas and prickly pears; coffee or chocolate. The coffee nowadays is often imported from Guatamala, and very good; the chocolate can be ordered in three different styles, French,

Mexican and Spanish. French chocolate is beaten frothy with cream, Mexican is plain thick black, and Spanish is black whipped with cinnamon. Some guests have four eggs, two beef steaks, three cups of chocolate and an extra basket of sweet bread. Their smaller children sit hoisted on the laps of girl servants – a servant per baby – who hold their mouths open and stuff them with slow conscientiousness course for course like so many little geese. For luncheon there will be a tureen of soup; then a dish of dry soup; then fish; a baked vegetable; a made *plat de résistance*, sweet peppers stuffed with bean-paste-and-beef, or choyotes with pork-mince-and-curds, or turkey curry; then a vegetable salad; some scraps of fowl; a green salad; fried mashed beans; a very sweet sweet; stewed fruit; mangoes, papayas, guavas, persimmons, muskmelon, prickly pears and bananas; and of course tortillas, bread, sweet bread, cake, coffee and chocolate. Before lunch the men drink rum and Coca-Cola, just before lunch they drink tequila, with lunch they drink beer and after lunch coffee and chocolate. The women and children drink Coca-Cola, bottled orange fizz, more bottled orange fizz, and chocolate. Supper in the provinces is at nine, and a shorter meal – chicken broth, omelette, a hot vegetable course, beef steak or cutlets, a salad, beans, fruit, breads and chocolate, perhaps an extra piece of cake for the children, but you may ask for many things that aren't on the table.

The cooking is good; the *matière première* excellent. The beef is tough, but not beyond the exercise of teeth. There are few sauces and little fat and flour, and very little *cooked* fat is used – instead, the piece of fresh butter on the vegetable, the drop of oil on the grilled chop as it goes to the table – and so the food, if abundant, is neither rich nor greasy. If one keeps off the sweets and the sweet breads (a pleasure to any person over ten), one will find that the meals are light, and a spoonful of fried black beans after several green salads not unwelcome. And although Indio babies munch red pepper, and chilli on maize cake is eaten by the poor like so much bread and cheese, Mexican cooking is not hot: there are a number of hot dishes, and these are very hot indeed and a bowl of *salsa ranchera* – raw chilli chopped with tomato and a little onion – is part of the condiment tray on every breakfast table; the run of the food, however, is bland and to suppose it overspiced and highly seasoned would be as erroneous as deducing this character of English cooking from the indices of curried mutton, Lea and Perrin's sauce and Mr Coleman's mustard.

Simple food then, robust, orderly, pleasant. Not the greatest simple food: the grilled sole, the spring vegetable so subtle that it may escape attention, the perfectly roast bird; but the older cycle of rice, beans and eggs, of garlic and tomato, gourds and squashes, poor meat, figs, roast fish, green herbs and lamb seethed in oil and lime. Cooking is at once the most and the least localized of the arts: it owes its development to commerce and to travel, and its preservation to stout regionalism; it must find its character in the resources at hand, yet may enrich these by some of the good things from outside. Every enlarging contribution was made by clever, articulate and travelled men, yet the burden is carried and handed on by obscure local women. The history of cooking, with its interchanges and migrations, is indeed hard to pin down. Certain styles of cooking run like a thread across the globe and certain folk themes appear over and over again at places unrelated to each other. The cooking of Mexico belongs loosely to the European Mediterranean. The link was obviously made by the Navigators and Spain; perhaps it was strengthened by some shared oriental affinities. The new food was a graft that took well. It suited the climate and the land, and joined quite naturally with the indigenous roots, just as that Mediterranean tradition itself was a happy hybrid of Greece and Carthage, Gaul and Moor, native corn and Persian fruit.

Querétaro is a country town, and the repository of some of the most splendidly modish examples of ecclesiastical late Churrigueresque. The streets are full of ex-convents, rope and harness shops; straw is everywhere and a cattle-show might be held at any minute. The town is one of the few surviving places built before the Conquest; architecturally this does not make the slightest difference as the Spaniards never left a native stone unturned but it adds extra length to the always lurid past. Querétaro, by another name, was founded by the Otomics, a relatively unaggressive people who refused to fight Cortés' troops with anything but bare fists, lost of course, and gave a dance for their new rulers. The town was taken from them by Montezuma, turned into a garrison and held through decade after decade against the Danubian hordes of the Aztec Empire, the Chimimecs. In due course and another name it was captured by the Spanish, and after some centuries of vice-regal rule became the official cradle of Mexican Independence and one of the major battle-grounds of that cause: *La Corregidora*, Doña Josefa Ortiz de Dominguez, the Joan of Arc and Pasionaria of the War of Independence, who housed, hid and abetted the conspirators against the crown, being the wife of the Mayor of Querétaro.

Chapter Three
THE EMPEROR MAXIMILIAN
AT QUERÉTARO

Presque toute l'histoire n'est qu'une suite d'horreurs

CHAMFORT

MAXIMILIAN OF HABSBURG was sentenced to death by court martial at Querétaro on 15 June 1867, and shot four days later on a hill outside that town. He was not the first man to die through violence in that vicinity, though during those four days many people tried to save his life. Juarez' headquarters at San Luís Potosí were connected by telegraph. The representatives of the civilized world interceded: Queen Victoria, the Queen of Spain, the Kings of Italy, Sweden, Belgium and Prussia pleaded for a commutation of the death sentence; President Johnson of the United States sent an envoy; Victor Hugo and Garibaldi each wrote an appeal; the French Consul and the Austrian Minister acted on their urgent instructions; the Princess Salm-Salm rode alone from Querétaro to San Luís to fling herself at Juarez' knees. He was not impressed. After three years in the field, fighting, retreating, fighting, pushed north by French artillery and Austrian dragoons in sky-blue tunics and white patent-leather cartridge belts, shifting the less and less impressive seat of a temporary government from market town to mountain village, pressed against the border, skipping into Texas, edging forward again: an outlaw, a guerrilla, a gathering power, President Juarez by military victory and capture of the Emperor was once more the de facto head of the Mexican

Government. He had been in the wilderness a very long time. There had been death and death and death again. And now he was asked to spare the life of one man. The moral pressure put on Juarez was great; perhaps it was too much, perhaps it came from the wrong quarters. He did not like Europe, and he was most self-consciously not a respecter of persons. He sent a telegram to Querétaro confirming the death sentence the day after it had been pronounced.

Now it seems so easy. One generous gesture – a pardon, relief all round, a phantom consigned to exile and the new regime opening with an act of clemency. Why did Juarez not commute the sentence? Why, as we are led to believe, did he not even consider it? It was not his moment of perspective. Even so, something must have come through these anguished messages arriving at San Luís. Did he, a professed defender of human values, not grasp that here was a great moral, or at least a great rhetorical opportunity? If he could not respond to the instances of the diplomatic corps, he might have responded to President Johnson for, although he looked upon Europe with the suspicions of a surly New World peasant, Juarez admired the United States and above all he had admired Lincoln in whose struggle he saw a parallel to his own, without probably ever guessing at the intellectual self-doubt, the humanity, subtlety and range of that very great man with whom Juarez shared an initial hardship of getting themselves taught to read. He might have been moved by Victor Hugo, a brother radical and enemy of Napoleon III's, and his so stirring appeal to their common ideals of liberty and justice. Perhaps they did not mean the same. Juarez was not brought up on the Voltairian principle of taking pains to make it possible for an adversary to express his noxious opinions, nor was he nurtured in the tradition of classical literature that condemns the tyrant and extols the moderation of the victor and at once discerns in him a new potential tyrant. He cannot have been much concerned with the victory of man over himself: freedom was the freedom to earn and eat one's bread, and all of human bondage was caused by forces from without. These forces Juarez had set himself to destroy. He had his first chance when he was given the Ministry of Justice and Ecclesiastical Relations in the Juan Alvarez government of 1855.

Juarez was an Indian, a patriot, a lawyer and a practising reformer, and as such held the inevitable convictions as to the ultimate good of his reforms and his own indispensability in establishing them. Indeed, at the beginning of Juarez' political life, in the Mexico of the 1850s, the prospect of any and every reform must have seemed both an improvement and a possibility beyond wildest dreams, and as Benito Juarez was not only tough, single-minded and obstinate like seven donkeys but also quite impermeable to material corruption, it was natural that he should have been considered the right man for this task by others and himself.

The antecedents of the Juan Alvarez presidency were the habitual ones, except for one of Alvarez' predecessors, Mariano Arista, who was not only constitutionally elected but furthermore the first Mexican president thus chosen who lived to take office. When revolts broke out against him, that unusual man, rather than involve the country in another civil war, resigned, actually left Mexico, stayed abroad, and died in poverty. After Arista's departure, General Santa Anna took over once more. It was his fourth or fifth term as dictator and generalissimo, and as he was by then considered an almost disreputable character, his claims to office are not clear. He had lost a leg in some battle, and used to thump the wooden one during his public speeches in appeal to national gratitude. He had also at one time surrendered the entire Mexican army after a twenty-minute skirmish to General Houston. For this, Santa Anna's countrymen had wished to shoot him, but he put himself under American military protection, signed away Texas to the United States, and escaped. Later he repudiated the Texan deal. Santa Anna spent much of his life sulking at his hacienda or wandering about abroad, but he always popped up at some moment or other and was welcomed with open political arms. At one time, Mme Calderon de la Barca's husband, the Spanish Ambassador, 'gave him [Santa Anna] a letter from the Queen, written under the supposition of his being still President, with which he seemed much pleased'. Madame de la Barca goes on to say, 'he has a sallow complexion, fine dark eyes, soft and penetrating, and an interesting expression of face . . . It is strange how frequently this expression of philosophic resignation, of placid sadness, is to be remarked on the countenance of the deepest, most ambitious, and most designing men'. During the present term, this fabulous mountebank did himself well. He began by selling a piece of land – some forty thousand square miles at the border – to the American government, and thus in funds, revived the Order of Guadalupe, one of young Iturbide's ephemeral imperial fantasies abolished these thirty years, and created himself Grand Master; then he recalled the Jesuits, recently expelled. Six months after his accession, with a kind of Punch-and-Judy effrontery, he proclaimed himself Perpetual Dictator by Decree. Revolutions broke loose and

Santa Anna's opponents marched upon the capital. Santa Anna sneaked away and two new liberal presidents, General Alvarez and Ignacio Comonfort, arrived at Mexico City at the head of their respective armies. They made it up. Alvarez stayed President, Comonfort took the Secretaryship for War, and it was in this government that Juarez held his first office.

The atmosphere of nineteenth-century Mexico was at once medieval and anarchical. No breath of Protestantism or Evolution had yet touched the spiritual authority of the Church; members of it were taking different sides in secular conflicts, the institution remained one-pointed, unique, its prestige intact. The Church in Mexico was very well off. It enjoyed many of the temporal prerogatives and exemptions abrogated then elsewhere; it held a quarter of the country's landed property; its members were privileged and its hangers-on numerous; what with the people pawns and the government's self-seeking farce, the Church alone was untouchable and its abuses no doubt as open, customary and extreme as they have so often been described.

Into this set-up Juarez inserted a long and lawyer-like bill, the Lex Juarez, purporting to deal with general administration. This bill contained some clauses curtailing the powers of the military and ecclesiastical courts which so far had had exclusive jurisdiction in all cases, civil or criminal, involving soldiers or the clergy. Since the bulk of the male population had at one time or another been pressed into the soldiery, and benefice of clergy was sometimes pleaded down to members of the families of housekeepers of incumbents, and since the ecclesiastical courts were liable to bias on points concerning property, and the military completely casual in their handling of non-military crimes, Juarez' thin end of the wedge was well chosen. *Ils avaient compris tout de suite.* There was an uproar. The Bishop of Michoacán cried heresy, half the army rebelled; the government kept them down with the other half; Juarez continued. His next law quite bluntly ordered the compulsory sale of all Church land. These holdings were to be sold publicly at an assessed value to private persons; the Church was to get the money. The Bishop of Puebla cried sedition; the clerical party raised a levy of fifteen hundred men. The Archbishop of Mexico tried to mediate by suggesting submission of the problem to the Pope. This so infuriated the nationalistic susceptibilities of the government that President Comonfort (Alvarez had meanwhile been pushed out) began to confiscate Church lands at once. The clericals, thereupon, joined forces with the military; the Church threatened with anathema persons buying ecclesiastical property at government sales; the government promulgated a new and very truculent constitution; and the War of the Reform, one of the most savage of Mexican civil wars, was on.

In 1857, Pius IX declared the government of Mexico apocryphal, and put its members under excommunication. Comonfort began to get frightened. He annulled the new constitution, arrested Juarez, and tried to form a compromise government. Then he took fright again, strengthened the National Guard, released Juarez, and re-established the constitution. Then he fled. The capital was in full revolt; other progressive leaders rallied at Querétaro and declared Juarez President of Mexico according to the provisions of the new constitution then again in force. The clericals elected an anti-president by pronouncement a few days after Juarez had sworn his oath of office. The point of time is important because Juarez, whose adherence to the letter of the law was the faith of an atheist lawyer in an age of anarchy, always stressed the legality of his government. Clericals and Juaristas fought each other at Querétaro, at San Luís; there was engagement upon engagement further north. Juarez had to withdraw to Guadalajara, and so began the first stretch of his two three-year terms of fighting his way across the country, years that, apart from their hardships and their cruelty, their monotony and their dangers, must have seemed to him an intolerable waste of time and gifts and opportunity, a bitter delay of all he wished to give his country. At Guadalajara he was captured and on the point of being shot. He escaped and fought his way up the Pacific Coast, entered the United States and returned to Mexico by boat. He landed at Vera Cruz and held that port for two years against siege from land and sea by the forces of a succession of counter-presidents ensconced at Mexico City. From this position, with really reckless obstinacy, Juarez issued the famous Reform Laws. They went very far. Disestablishment, of course, and religious toleration; abolition of any of the special privileges of the clergy. The laws also declared marriage a civil contract only; decreed the dissolution of all religious orders and communities; forbade the Church to own any landed property at all, forbade its members to receive any pay whatsoever and directed them to subsist on the voluntary contributions of parishioners. By that time, several hundred thousand people were under arms, campaigning as Juaristas, clericals or bandits. Bans of excommunication issued from every bishopric, priests were murdered in their presbyteries and secret nunneries established in the cellars of the faithful; all sides shot prisoners and the clerical General Marquez (the Tiger of Tacubaya) had doctors executed for treating wounded Juaristas.

Throughout 1860 Juarez' forces were gaining. People like Don Otavio's father began to join what they recognized as the right bandwagon. And early in 1861, the Juaristas managed to enter Mexico City. Of course Juarez at once implemented the Reform Laws. He had all remaining Church property confiscated, exiled the bishops, and expelled the Papal Nuncio and the Spanish Envoy. The bishops, the anti-president, some ex-anti-presidents with a number of Mexican émigrés fled to Paris and began the intrigues which made an invasion of Mexico seem so attractive to the romantic ambitions of the Empress Eugénie, so meritorious to the Vatican and so profitable to banking interests. Another of the Juarez government's troubles was money. Not unnaturally, there was none in the treasury, and there was also a relatively large foreign debt: ten thousand pounds – borrowed by Santa Anna – owed to Britain; inflated bonds held by France and Spain. Juarez suspended payment of interest. Hence the punitive expedition by these creditor countries, the French landing at Vera Cruz and the French campaign on Puebla. The war was on again. After a year and a half of it, the French entered Mexico City. President Juarez withdrew north with some troops and two faithful generals (one of them, Juarez' most ironic legacy, General Diaz). The French spread into the Central Provinces, Mexico became an occupied country and to the Chancelleries of Europe that problem and opportunity, a vacant throne. Hence the arrival of the Emperor Maximilian; hence three years later, Querétaro.

This in 1867 was Benito Juarez' past. (His future was five years of relatively undisturbed rule along his own lines, then sudden, natural death at the age of sixty-six. He was succeeded by a friend, Tejada, another lawyer, who carried the Reform Laws to an unpopular extreme and was kicked out in a civil war by another friend, Porfirio Diaz.) Could Juarez have made a different decision at San Luís Potosí? His lines then were dug deep; arrived at a given point, a man can only act as he must. The answers were all stacked for Juarez. Maximilian had conspired against the legitimate government of Mexico; Maximilian had himself issued a decree putting under sentence of death any Mexican bearing arms against the monarchy; Maximilian was backed by powers contrary to the public welfare of the country. His execution was legal; just; a warning. It was not very important. Regicide recoils? Juarez did not think of Maximilian of Habsburg as a prince but as a kind of exotic, fulldress counter-president. The two men never met. It was not in Juarez' grasp to realize that Maximilian was essentially an innocent man, another like himself tied to a conception of duty, and now a man without reality or following, a man alone. It would have made small difference. The principles involved remained the same: Maximilian had broken the rules. To Juarez who had seen too many die, the rules were more lasting than life, and more important, and in such a case one can never ask, which rules? That brave and tenacious man, who had not spared himself, who had fretted with such patience through the misspent years, who had been able to bring about so much against such odds, could not reverse *le juste retour des choses d'ici-bas*, could not stop the cycle of retaliatory deeds.

After a given point a man can only act as he must. Why did Maximilian go to Querétaro? Why did he not abdicate? Why did he not leave Mexico when he could? And why, if he did decide to fight it out, did he leave an open city and deliberately enter a town under siege?

Querétaro, when Maximilian decided to go there in February '67, was already invested by two competent Juarista generals. Within a few days of the Emperor's arrival the town became surrounded; and during the three months that followed between then and surrender the Imperial forces never managed to break through this cordon. Querétaro is not a particularly easy place to hold; it lies on a slight slope in the middle of a valley and has few fortifications; nor does the town seem to have been provisioned against an increase in garrison. Food and ammunition were short at once; later soldiers and townspeople came near starvation. The drinking water supply was cut off from outside and the river deliberately polluted with corpses. No reinforcements ever arrived, and the people could no longer wash their linen and clothes. Into this town, Maximilian withdrew from Mexico City, the pivot of the country's communications, cutting himself off from movement, manoeuvre and choice. He took with him some two thousand men; three generals, two died, the third led a sortie and never returned; a number of ADCs, one of them a Colonel Lopez who entered into some very suspicious negotiations with the enemy but was never paid; his doctor, good Basch, who was given a tiepin and kept a touching diary to the end; his secretary; and his confessor, Father Fisher, SJ, a great hefty violent man who had been a Lutheran pastor in Germany and a cowboy in Wyoming, and whom the Emperor had picked up in Mexico and sent the year before with a mission to the Vatican, where he had been made extremely short shrift of. The Hungarian palace cook and a friend, Prince Felix Salm-Salm, a German soldier of fortune who had just come from fighting the American Civil War under the Union Army, managed to follow through the lines of their own accord. Querétaro was Maximilian's decision.

Some accounts imply that the Emperor did not know that the town was under siege, that he was not told by his generals, who either did not know themselves or only half knew; others say that he was treasonably misled. These suppositions are equally fantastic. Incompetence, lassitude, muddled half-hearted treason, all of these; but to this extent? Querétaro is only a hundred and sixty miles north of Mexico City; communications were then still open, Maximilian had had a military education, geography was one of his hobbies, and who would have been served by so circuitous a piece of treachery? Nor could the withdrawal to Querétaro have been popular with Maximilian's followers. The pattern for a losing general's conduct was pretty well established. Depending on one's future intentions, one either slipped away, or fought one's way to the north or the coast where one kept a foot in Vera Cruz and bode one's time. One avoided going south as the journey was hellish and one never could tell what third force one might find risen in Oaxaca or Tabasco. At a pinch and with the road to the coast open at one's back, one could always try to hold Puebla.

For some time, Maximilian must have been aware of the overwhelming unreality in which he was still afloat. Nothing he did had impact. It was all over and he was still there. And he was thirty-five years old. His upbringing might have provided one strand: one did not desert one's post. *But what had become of the post?* Whom was he supposed to hold it for? Whom did he serve? Maximilian was no instigator. He had ideals, but unlike Juarez, being at once more limited and more kindly, more ignorant and more modest, he had not rigged himself a cause. He saw his part as carrying on where he was placed, doing perhaps a little better than expected, shedding when possible a little mild light; serving – peculiar though the form of servitude may have appeared to Juaristas – in inclination and against, a duty he had not shaped himself. Now the interests that propelled him had receded. No one wished still to mislead him; he had no more followers, only a retinue – people who were too affectionate, too loyal or too compromised to leave him at this hour.

The bottom had dropped out; the setting was still there. The ceremonial at Chapultepec Castle that Maximilian had created with a royal schoolboy's zest from the Spanish etiquette in force at the Court of Austria, his own romantic penchant for exotic parts and his notions of what was appropriate to Montezuma's Crown, was still functioning: the proper number of Creole ladies-in-waiting and Austrian ladies-in-waiting, chamberlains and adjutants and gentlemen of the bedchamber came and went at appointed hours performing appointed duties; Indian Guards changed guard; decorations were worn on occasions stated; the Levée, daily Mass, the Emperor of Austria's Birthday, precedence at the imperial table were observed – the Court went like clock-work and enhanced the unsubstantial quality of the situation. Only Maximilian himself amongst it all had become a little *débraillé*, a little lax; in the last year he had sat too much in an alpaca jacket in the shade at Cuernavaca – his beard was not always trimmed and his tunic remained unbuttoned.

The Indian servants were fond of him. He had spent much time with the gardener's family in the country. He was liked in personal contact, but he had made no public ties in Mexico. The population that had seen him, did not mind him: probably he *was* the Aztec Messiah with the fair beard who was due to arrive from across the sea some day. The people in the Juarista territory regarded him either as a vague bugbear, another false prophet landed like Cortés, or as the author of all their ills, and a focal point of hate. In more politically minded circles, he was thought of as the arch-reactionary and the sixty-two Spanish viceroys incarnate; and by the faction that had supported him, Maximilian was considered a great disappointment. He had not repealed the Reform Laws, he had not restored the Church lands, he had sympathized with the Liberals who of course would have none of him, biggest blow of all he had not been able to persuade the French to keep their soldiers in the country to hold down the Juaristas. The only thing left now was to disassociate from him as quickly as possible, poor Masimiliano, such a distinguished man, a great pity. Among the Creoles there was a certain feeling of aristocratic solidarity: a few sons would have to stay on as colonels and ADCs, and fall wherever it would be; but it was time there were an end of it. Abdication . . . One might follow into exile, Vienna was not a bad place for young men. Maximilian was not supposed to be on such good terms with his brother; though Francis-Joseph would have to do *something* . . . Of course it wasn't Paris but at least there was a proper Court, poor Eugénie, so much more chic really than the Empress Elizabeth, still one couldn't be expected to take the Bonapartes . . .

To the Emperor of Austria indeed, his brother's Mexican involvement was now an embarrassment. Trouble, expense, scandal. Francis-Joseph, always petty and not yet thirty-eight, was already a middle-aged bureaucrat and much the man who could say quite crossly forty-seven years later when they broke to him the murder of the Archduke Ferdinand at Sarajevo, '*Mir bleibt doch nichts erspart.*' Help? When it had cost so much already. Send troops? All the way to Mexico?

Napoleon's business anyway. For Heaven's sake, no abdication. The last impression one would want to give. Remind everybody of that dreadful time in '48. Max'l had much better stay where he was.

For Napoleon III, the public entrepreneur of the Mexican Empire, it was a great deal worse. He was already an ill man; things had not turned out well for the dynasty: opposition at home, Bismarck looming large, problems everywhere – money, not glory, were on the agenda, and the mood of the eve of Puebla must have seemed very remote. The Mexican campaign had become extremely unpopular with the French. The soldiers had not returned laden with gold like so many Conquistadores; instead, they had not come home at all. A comfortable occupation had turned out to be another of those trickling, draining wars in distant foreign parts. The press was rubbing it in every morning; the Chambre was a bear-garden. The soldiers' morale over there was bad: the men sold their rifles to the natives, noncoms were setting up grocery shops at Mexico City where they weighed out over the counter sugar and flour from regimental stores. And they did ask the reason why. Moreover the United States was objecting to the presence of a European army, however slovenly, at its southern border and, having meanwhile ended the Civil War, was in a position to press that objection. The whole Mexican business was becoming most compromising for France. There was no end in view. Things seemed to be slipping over there, the Republican forces gaining every year, the Monarchy showing no signs of native support. And now Maximilian was asking for reinforcements. Good money after bad . . . France could no longer be involved. Of course, there *was* the Covenant of Miramar, there *were* Napoleon's letters of promise, there *were* the guarantees of French military and

financial aid . . . Still, one might have thought that Maximilian would do *something* – in three years – or that those Paris
Mexicans knew what they were talking about. Nothing left
now but to call it off quietly. First pull out the troops . . .

Things *were* slipping over there. They had never been too
solid; and, at this moment, Maximilian had not done much
to arrest the Mexican landslide. When he arrived it had not
looked too bad. Perhaps not altogether civilized, not very
disciplined. There had been all kinds of hitches – the
reception at Vera Cruz was a little disorganized (the governor
of the port was asleep after his luncheon when the Imperial
destroyer docked); the town was a miserable slum, steaming
hot, quite empty (there had been an epidemic) and, the
sovereigns were warned, full of traitors and fever. The railway
from the coast ended on mid-precipice, and the Imperial
party was decanted into some very old carriages, '*des espèces de
diligences*', they were described in a contemporary diary,
'*peinturlurées comme des roulottes de foire, tirées par des chevaux à
demi-sauvage*'. At Puebla they were received with roses and a
Te Deum, and the entrance into the capital was formal, but
the palace was not aired and the beds were full of vermin.
The suite spent the first night on the billiard tables. The
Empress had been much upset, but Maximilian took everything with complete goodwill, with enthusiasm almost. He
was enchanted by the climate, the people, the flowers; he
fell, and remained, in love with the country. He was
extremely busy. He signed papers; he worked at his Spanish;
he spoke in public, appointed a Cabinet, distributed Orders,
he made lists. He was crowned with Carlota in the Cathedral.
He wrote a manual establishing the etiquette of the Court of

Mexico; he let it be known that he would give anyone a hearing; he was organizing himself a reign. He was brought up to it, and he knew how it was done. He moved the Court to Chapultepec and began to build. Chapultepec Castle was constructed by the 47th Viceroy, who had treated himself to a substantial fortress at the expense of the Spanish Crown, pretending to Madrid that he was building himself a summer house. It lay in a forest on a hill at the outskirts of a tough suburb. This dungeon Maximilian had transformed into a Pompeian villa, a Tuscan Pompeian villa that is, the kind he had already in mind when he decorated his Adriatic château, Miramar. The forest was cleared, the grounds terraced, a formal garden was planted; the suburb was pierced by a boulevard, now called Avenue of Reform. Maximilian sent for statuary, for furnishings, for his china collection which started a Mexican vogue for Nymphenburg; he wrote to his brother for hock and Tokay. Carlota, who was also interested in building, had trees planted in streets and donated benches, flower boxes and band stands to provincial plazas where to this day they are repainted every Patron-Saint's Day, and very popular. Mexican society took up the Empress. Her ladies were charming to her and admired her clothes, they only expressed astonishment at the Empress' wearing rubies and emeralds. Coloured stones, she was informed, were considered trash, only *plain* diamonds . . .

Something must have seemed wrong. When the Emperor became aware of the bitterness left by the Reform War, he would have liked to declare an amnesty. It was pointed out to him that the war was not over. There *was* that fighting in the north, elsewhere too – reports were always coming in of risings – not amounting to much probably, guerrillas, the worst elements in the country, though the French officers said they stuck at nothing. But it did mean that Mexico was not at peace, not entirely for the new monarchy. Then persons kept coming forward, pressing claims. They had been promised, they said, a commission, a governorship, an annuity. Promised? By whom? Well, His Majesty's agents had said . . . it had been understood . . . a reward . . . Reward for what? Why, for putting His Majesty where he was, on the throne. Maximilian and Carlota were indignant: the Emperor had no agents, nobody had *put* him anywhere. (They did not draw a connection with the presence of the French troops; those troops were there to pacify the country, after all much more savage than one would like to say in Mexico City.) The Emperor had been called to Mexico by the will of the people who dissatisfied with fifty years of republican rule had expressed their wish for a disinterested hereditary monarchy in a free plebiscite held by responsible Mexicans . . .

Yes, yes, quite. And these were the responsible Mexicans.

Maximilian did not give in, causing consternation and wounded feelings. He had no one to consult; when he mentioned the plebiscite, people became glib or embarrassed. He wanted to have the Liberals in the Cabinet. The Liberals, not liking whom he stood for, refused. The Clerico-Conservatives reminded him that he stood indeed for *them* and that he was where he was to serve their aims. Maximilian expressed the view that he had come to serve the aims of the Mexican people. The plebiscite . . . It was borne on him then that the plebiscite did not bear looking into. He wavered, but never acted on that knowledge. He was sensitive to his ambiguous position, but Carlota and considerations for the good name of his house made him regard present withdrawal as desertion, and he also began to entertain the belief, not unique in his situation, that given a chance he could still do much good to the Mexicans *malgré eux*. (The irony is that Maximilian, who was unable to deal with or see through any councillor, underling or administrative organization, and who never understood the first thing about the working and sources of political power, but who had no regard for self or faction, would have made an admirable absolute ruler could he have been wafted to that position and into direct human contact with his subjects without the intermediacy of bayonets, money, ministers and previous vested interests.) He neither quit, nor accepted to play ball with his responsible Mexicans. He was pressed, but refused to repeal the Reform Laws, and thus at once cut from under himself such Mexican support as he had, as well as the goodwill of the Vatican and much potential foreign aid, without gaining a flicker of recognition in Juarista quarters. Maximilian seems to have had a knack of walking into deadlock with a certain quixotic firmness. His stand over repeal is curious. Much in the Reform Laws must have been repellent to him; much in the Reform Laws *is* repellent. Did he feel that repeal would go against the grain of the country, that it was too late, that matters had become too tangled? Ten years are a long time. Monastries had been converted, most Church lands passed into private hands, paid for; the money had melted away. Maximilian was certainly reluctant to accept the role of the man who had been sent for to put the clock back; and both he and Carlota were open-mouthed, stout natural Catholics though they were, at the rapacious ways of the Mexican clergy, and wrote shocked accounts of them to their relatives at home. Maximilian discovered that there was no money. He was used to being told that treasury funds were low, but to this point? There appeared to be nothing. Mexico *must* have a revenue? All countries had. A number of people

turned up who offered to farm it. The Court had already
attracted a number of quacks from Europe. Maximilian
granted concessions, sold monopolies; he signed, he borrowed, he mortgaged, without knowing very much what he
was doing. When he did not understand the project, he
trusted the projector, and he often trusted the wrong person.
He and Carlota were appalled by the poverty of the people.
Was not Mexico supposed to be very rich? Silver and
minerals, and so many mines full of everything? They wished
to help. What could they do? Give the poor some land of
their own? The land belonged already to other persons.
Create employment? Many of them did not wish to work.
Raise wages? The owners said they could not afford it. Then
make the land more productive, do something to correct the
eight months' aridity? Run the mines more profitably, get
machinery? There was no money. To re-distribute the land,
to set wages, raise funds for drills and dams and reservoirs, the
Crown would have had to pass fantastic, improbable and
resented legislation, and the Crown had no support. Laws in
Mexico are seen through by civil war. The Crown might
have had power. At one moment Bazaine would have stood
by Maximilian, the troops were pledged – until counter-
order from Paris – to the Emperor's service; Bazaine may
have favoured the idea of playing a part in a strong-hand
regime. The United States might have come in, perhaps
Austria. Vistas for a soldier. Maximilian never thought of it
for one minute. In his way, he was as constitutional as Juarez.
The Emperor and Empress had gold coins distributed on their
outings, Carlota did what she could for nursing, the people
said *adiós* and went on, Maximilian withdrew his interest
from public life. Perhaps later, some day, when the country
was more quiet . . . He spent much time at the lodge in

Cuernavaca, as a private person, almost alone. Visitors described him as 'melancholy but serene', and one imagines him at once saddened by impotence, and freed. The eclipse must have been harder on the Empress. She had no taste for country life, and she was touchy about her position. Maximilian had great affection and respect for his wife – though, one gathers, not much emotional need – and he consulted her about everything; in fact Carlota was both his intimate and official adviser. She was more astute than Maximilian but her values were trashier, and she dominated his actions by the greater definiteness and strength of her desires. Carlota appears to have been a high strung woman, full of energies, with an immense appetite for glamour which, devastatingly for her, could only be realized through the intermedium of a husband's career, Maximilian proving in that respect as unsatisfactory as Charles Bovary.

The reign was still capable of gestures. To assure the succession and perpetuate the dynasty, Maximilian and Carlota, childless, adopted a small Mexican boy and had him proclaimed heir presumptive. With their strange wrong flair, they chose a grandson of that other phantom, the Emperor Augustín Iturbide. The child was invested as Crown Prince of Mexico, and painted in full regalia sitting on his new parent's lap. He looks a charming, staring, serious little boy. His mother was an American and a row was kicked up on her behalf in the US press; his aunts insisted on being created imperial princesses, thie family claimed pensions and made all kinds of embarrassing fusses, and in the end asked to annul the adoption. The boy was sent to Europe and grew up to the expected vicissitudes.

For two years things had been sliding, then suddenly everything looked quite bad. The Juaristas were taking towns,

half the provinces were risen; the families of clerico-conservatives were sailing for Europe. No fresh troops arrived from
France. Answers to frantic appeals for help came late and
vague. The Empress became alarmed: did they not *know*? She
decided to go herself and impress upon the courts of Europe
the intensity of her sense of peril. Another Te Deum was
sung at Mexico Cathedral, an escort was scraped together and
the Empress travelled to Vera Cruz and embarked for France,
carrying with her through the slow sea days the urgent vision
of the country left behind. She landed at the end of the
summer of 1866, and went on at once to Paris. A suite was
taken for her at the Grand Hotel. September was flowering
in the Tuileries Gardens, waters played, tall hats and hooped
muslins floated below the chestnuts, the rue de Rivoli was a-
click from noon till twilight with smart turn-outs. Into the
elegancies of that summer world of the late 'sixties, the
Empress of Mexico arrived like a person who has run out of
a burning house to fetch a bucket of water. The Empress
Eugénie called, held out a cheek to be kissed. You must save
my country, cried Carlota. Napoleon was not well, could not
be seen, not this week certainly; meanwhile there was
Offenbach at the opera. Carlota insisted, was fobbed off with
an official audience, called again at Saint-Cloud, opened
doors and walked into the Emperor's *cabinet de travail*. They
had an appalling scene. Later Napoleon cooled down;
Eugénie went again to the Grand; but meanwhile the worst
was out − it was no longer a question of sending help,
Napoleon planned to recall the present troops from Mexico.
Carlota whipped on to Italy; insisted on an official celebration
of the Sixteenth of September, Mexican Independence Day;
presided at the banquet; hurried on to Rome.

Maximilian was waiting. For developments, for help. For

news. In September, he heard that no more help would come; in October, that Carlota had suddenly and dramatically gone insane in the Vatican during an audience with Pius IX. This ghastly and improbable news paralysed him. It could have been the moment for departure. He thought of hurrying to Carlota, was advised against it; hesitated, set out, turned back, stayed. He waited for details; for a change, a turn, for orders. THERE WERE NO MORE ORDERS. At times he must have been assailed, even as the free traveller is assailed, by fear; by the sense of the implacable, the alien remoteness of that country. In January the French began evacuating garrison towns; on 5 February the French army marched out of Mexico City on their way to embarkation. Maximilian watched them crossing the Plaza Mayor from behind a palace window. A week later he set out for Querétaro.

The Austrian Government had a memorial chapel set up on the site where Maximilian and his two aides were shot. It is a drab little brownstone building, more like a guardhouse, standing on top of a bare, dun hill among rubble and sparse agaves. It was built in 1901 – some thirty years after the event – and now belongs to the Mexican nation, and is administered by the *Instituto Naciónal de Antropologia e Historia*, which provides a custodian, but not his shelter, who on the approach of visitors rises from under a stone to sell for the price of threepence a ticket of admission and a picture postcard of the graceless memorial. The same institution runs the collection of Maximilian miscellany, called the Political Museum, exhibited in a room at the Federal Palace of Querétaro. We wandered about the array of photographs, medals, captured banners; peered at scraps of handwriting under glass. The

275

inkstand used by the court martial . . . The stools Generals
Mejija and Miramón, the two aides that died, sat on during
the trial . . . Somebody's top boots . . . Swords . . .

The custodian was following us around. 'Accommodate
yourselves. Your Excellencies are missing the coffin.

'Please to approach again. It is the coffin of Don Masimiliano. Do not think that because it is empty, it is not the true
coffin. *La Mamacita* sent another when Don Masimiliano was
taken across the sea, but this is the true coffin of Don
Masimiliano. General Juarez came to look at Don Masimiliano in this coffin.

'Your Excellencies have not noted the bloodstain. Please
to look inside. Is it not shaped like a hand? Your Excellencies
have not noted well. Favour to use this glass. To make it
larger.'

A braided coat . . . The facsimile of the death sentence . . .
A daguerreotype of the Princess Salm-Salm on horseback . . .

'And he *could* have got away,' said E. 'It was usual. When
the Princess Salm-Salm came back from San Luís Potosí she
was so frantic that she managed to persuade him. She, and the
Belgian and Austrian Ministers, arranged it all. They bribed
everybody. It cost a fortune. A Juarista general would have
had to flee with them. When all was ready, they put a cloak
around him, and then they realized that they would have to
do something about his fair beard. No one else had a beard
like that. That must have brought it home to him: he refused
to move. Perhaps it seemed all so shabby. They argued with
him. Meanwhile, the guard had changed. The new men were
not bribed. It was too late.'

'And this is the syringe Don Masimiliano was embalmed
with. Please to look again: it is the embalming syringe of Don
Masimiliano.

'Do Your Excellencies understand? The *embalming syringe*. The syringe for embalming Don Masimiliano after he was dead.

'Please, Excellency, does the other Excellency not understand? It is of much interest. It is the embalming syringe. Favour to explain.'

Chapter Four
CUERNAVACA – ACAPULCO
– TAXCO

Et puis, et puis encore?

> *Nous avons vu des astres*
Et des flots; nous avons vu des sables aussi;
Et, malgré bien des chocs et d'imprévus désastres,
Nous nous sommes souvent ennuyés, comme ici.

THE DOMINANT of our second stay in Mexico City is irritation. Need there be all that noise? Must the trams have horns? Why have a town that size at such an altitude at all? Surely those long American motor cars can only be a nuisance in these packed streets; surely it is not rational to carry water in small earthenware vessels on the backs of women and single animals into a city of one and a half million inhabitants? There is no cohesion; no one has consulted anyone, nothing connects: the government and the governed, the goods and the consumers, the law and the practice . . .

And the baize doors do not fit tight, one is nowhere without the kitchen smells – corruption, poverty, decay, slick deals, branching interests and a sheltered foreign colony.

Every town has its addicts, inveterate cockneys who away from their native pavements expire with ennui on beach and land like chimpanzees in a northern zoo. Only here there are no natives. Everybody has just arrived. Very poor people who have lost their bearings drift in thinking of city ease; find no work (there are no industries), have no return, stay, and subsist doing odd jobs, fetching and carrying, lugging in the markets, touting, stealing — turning beggars, bandits and journeymen, spending their lives and sleep in the streets. The literate come more purposefully in the wake of the local *politicos* and foreign business concerns, ready for fat pickings, pickings and the pickings of pickings. The smallest bribe is split into seventeen unequal parts; the system is rigid and worked out down to the boy who held the blotter like a pensions list.

> '*Si l'on avait dit à Adam, le lendemain de la mort d'Abel, que dans quelques siècles il y aurait des endroits où, dans l'enceinte de quatre lieus carrées, se trouveraient réunis et amoncelés sept ou huit cent mille hommes, aurait-il cru que ces multitudes pussent jamais vivre ensemble?* Ne se scrait-il pas fait une idée encore plus affreuse *de ce qui s'y commet de crimes et de monstruosités?* C'est la réflexion qu'il faut faire pour se consoler des abus attachés à ces étonnantes réunions d'hommes.' (CHAMFORT.)

We had a busy ten days. We had to go to the bank (the Post Office people suppress letters containing cheques in the obstinate belief that there must be a way, which one day they'll find out, for them to cash those instruments themselves, and nothing will persuade them to give them up). We were after some other vanished post; we wanted to buy some books; E. had to go to the library. None of this can be accomplished without a deal of paperwork, and paperwork is not their forte. The letters B and V, for instance, are pronounced so as to be indistinguishable in sound and, to tell them apart in spelling, people call them *B Burro* and *V Vaca* respectively. So I was always careful to say at the beginning of an interview that my name was B for Donkey, yet this never prevented anyone from looking up V for Cow as well. One Sunday morning, I spent half-heartedly snooping about the Thieves' Market. We also had to begin thinking about papers, our permits were running out and as there was no provision for extending them, one was expected to travel to the border where one would be given a new permit in the time it took to write it out at the cost of five pesos and a two-thousand-mile journey. Don Otavio's brother Luís said he would arrange it for us. We had *comida* at Don Luís' house. He lived in Colonia Roma, a smart residential suburb. Outside the entrance hall sat two turkeys whom Don Luís had brought from San Pedro and was having fatted for All Saints'. We had lunch with four girls between eleven and fifteen, all dressed alike, a governess and a rather miserable younger boy; three smaller children were led in for dessert. Doña Asunçión was still recovering from her last confinement. Don Luís told us that Don Otavio was very well and had just engaged an hotel manager, an English gentleman recommended to him by friends of ours.

'How very odd,' said E. Then she told Don Luís how old Henry Ford used to run his factories.

Don Luís also took us for a drive on Chapultepec Heights at what he said used to be the fashionable hour. At our request we visited the gardens, the palace and the imperial apartments. We saw the Empress Carlota's, most luxurious, bathroom which had no window or opening other than a door leading out on to the palace grounds.

'What happened when the Empress had a bath?' we said.

'A soldier of the Indian Guard would come and, stand inside the open door,' said Don Luís. 'His back turned, of course.'

We went to see the C.s at Coyacán with traveller's tales;

and we had tea with Mrs Rawlston's daughter, Diana Wald-heim, a handsome woman with some of the charm and none of the rudeness of her mother, who spoke a concoction of Virginian English, Mexican Spanish and Bavarian German, and that concoction only; and we met Mrs Rawlston's German son-in-law who indeed for Mrs Rawlston's sins looked as much, and more, like a man-sized dachshund as it is possible for a human being to look. Mrs Waldheim's children had remained in the schoolroom.

'So you know my mother-in-law?' said Mr Waldheim, looking at us as though we were the volunteers of Balaclava. 'Will you have some brandy?'

'But I always say to Diana, it is not right for your mother to live in that big house all alone. The old lady ought to have electric light. She does not like me, but I will have it installed for her this year, as a Christmas surprise.'

'Karl is very kind to my mother,' said Mrs Waldheim; 'Mother is a little difficult sometimes.'

'Then we will all have a happy Christmas on Lake Chapala,' said her husband.

'I am sure we shall, my dear,' said his wife; and we began to admire Diana Waldheim.

Then we started for the west coast, broke the journey, and spent ten magical days near Cuernavaca. For the first time since we had left San Pedro we were in the country again, and the country at Cuernavaca is beautiful. The weather in this sheltered region is mild and luminous, and there is that miracle in Mexico, fountains in the sand: water. Springs by the road, brooks on the hillside, live water everywhere – one hears the sound at night, smells it in the fields. We were staying with a German Social-Democrat and his family, refugees. On their lawn there was a small green-tiled pool, a natural thing to have at Cuernavaca, fed by some mountain source. Here I bathed every morning. Red cigar-flowers were blooming by the edge, the sky was flawless and, swimming, one could see the snows of two volcanoes. Our friends' parents, two very old people, would come out of the house with wicker chairs and the newspaper. They had just been got out of Germany, had spent years in camps. They were very generous. '*Guten Morgen, guten Morgen,*' they cried. '*Schoenes Bad? Wuenschen viel Vergnuegen.*'

One afternoon I rattled through the valley on an empty bus. We climbed into the uplands, stopped at a village outside a sixteenth-century Dominican monastery and church, half-gutted, empty, but open to the warmth and birds. Perhaps never a great piece of architecture, but here, in the light air, above that plain, overgrown with flowers, it seemed a very moving place indeed. An Indio took me through a refectory with flaking frescoes, a chapel full of nests, into cells with a view the world might well been lost for, up to the roof where we walked on mossy stone among bell towers and hand-turned cupolas, above the slanting rays and the women hacking away in the fields. Then I returned, content, on a wooden bench, the sun in my eyes, the cool of the evening descending.

I had been rather curious about Acapulco, that Saint Moritz of the tropics where Americans fast and rich are supposed to go for big game fishing. I could not see anything being run on quite those lines here. Acapulco was once a port; and when Magellan discovered the Philippines, it became linked with the China trade, and the viceroys were able to get their silks and porcelain directly from the East. The climate was always felt to be a trial, and Philip III had Negroes imported to do the pearl-diving and thrash the sugar cane as the Indios turned out to be too frail. Acapulco is ruined now, quite monstrous, many said. But others — ah, it is still very lovely; and if one wants to see that coast at all, there is nowhere else in the nine hundred miles between there and Mazatlán where one could lay one's head. Two things I was not prepared for: that the impact of the — very great — natural beauty of the South Sea setting would be weakened by photography, impoverished by previous reels and albums of other lagoons and bays (the very opposite would have happened had one seen Tuscany or the Seine valley for the first time after the Impressionists and the Florentines); and that the man-made part of the place was a gypsy slum squeezed between the jungle and the ocean. Oh, the hotels were there, two unequal clumps of them on either side of the unpaved town. Above the mosquito belt, on a breezy cliff, stand the luxury hotels, so called because they are built of stone and provide the conveniences appropriate to the climate — air-cooling, shower-baths, electric fans — as well as such advertised attractions as nocturnal tennis courts, a sea lift and a subterranean bar. The family establishments, executed in matchboard, straggle in a line along the beach. The season is very short — *enrichissez-vous* — December to mid-January really, though the hardier native petty-rich keep on coming until Holy Week, and the rest of the year the town bakes in its own mud. Indeed, it does little else in mid-season: the cliff hotels with their hairdressers and gift-shops are self-contained and their guests lead the life of liners, while the families by the waterfront rarely heave themselves beyond beach and dining room. Imagine a major resort, imagine Cannes, consisting solely of the Carlton, the Majestic and the Martinez, some acres of churned mud and fly-blown stands, and a strip of boarding houses.

We were rather early in the year for comfort, though the prices were already high, and stayed at Los Pinguinos, a place – front on the beach, back open to leaf-hut and campfire – managed by a discouraged, young, lean and single German of a type that might have gone in with more success for a civil service career in the Silesian forestry, who kept mum about his possible political antecedents and appeared to have been unable to maintain in these parts the reputed energy of his compatriots. He was always lying down. He did have a police dog, Flora, but she seemed to be affected by the heat as much as was her master. Our fellow guests were a Mexican family and four jolly middle-aged Saxonians from Saxony, who sat in the dining room in their underwear, drinking whisky and eating plum cake through the siesta hours. They were in business in Mexico City and had not been out of the country these twenty years and thus had no political past to hide, which must have been a thorn to them for if anybody ever had occasion to use Dorothy Parker's hallucinatory sentence from the book of etiquette, 'We regret that we have come too late to accompany you upon your harp,' it was they.

The Mexican mother upset E. by wearing the kind of old-fashioned stays that brought her to the verge of public apoplexy at the end of every meal. 'Ought I not tell the poor lady to unlace herself?' she said. 'How can I put it?'

I told her that my grandmother always boasted of having worn stays throughout the hot weather in India.

'Very bad for her,' said E., undetracted. She never told the Mexican lady, and we had the same conversation every day.

We discovered what one knew but had not realized, that at daytime in the tropics, unless one has to earn a living, there is nothing for one to do, and even if one braced oneself to be about there is little that can be described as doing. One could be rowed by mulattos looking like Chinese under an awning of mats across an even bay, bathe with a straw hat in waters of topaz and pellucid green, alas warm; sit in a sweltering grove drinking the milk of freshly opened coconuts wishing that it were water and that it were cold. One could be drawn across the town by mules, and up the cliff, sit in a transparent Frigidaire above the sea, order from a list of forty-six rum cocktails, watch boys dive off a ninety-foot crag for coins, listen to Riviera voices dropping names. Three Starlit Swiz zles, please . . . *Un quinto por caridád* . . . Willy, Wally . . .

One could bathe, from our beach, only before sunrise and at brief dusk, that exquisite ten minutes when the waves stand almost black and fifty pelicans swoop plumply by one's side teaching their young to fish.

The bulk of the day one lay on one's bed, between showers, and read. The book was heavy, the paper stuck, the light through close-drawn blinds was never right. Soon one dozed. For meals, one pulled oneself up, bathed, dressed, felt bucked by the change. There was ice but it was not comestible, so the manager kept a bottle of gin on it for us, of which we drank a tumblerful diluted with a little lime-juice before lunch and dinner, enjoying a moment, but a moment only, of refreshment. Then we ate a little dull food. Every scrap of clothes began to stick — the dining room was always 95° — the jolly Saxonians sang, the Mexican mother puffed, the manager went about the tables moaning, quite truthfully, about the bad quality of everything, the soap, the plaster, the fish. So often before the pudding, one went upstairs again. Another shower, a book . . .

In this limbo we stayed rather longer than we need have

stayed. Until one day we performed the necessary actions, and got away.

This time we broke the journey at Taxco, a hill-town on the high road between Mexico City and the coast. The cool was delicious though after twenty-four hours we ceased to be aware or grateful, and here we spent three days which settled our congealing views on tourist Mexico.

Few places in this country are ill-favoured by nature. Taxco has a lovely position – houses sprawling across a slope on four levels, everywhere red-tiled roofs, archways, flowers, prospects. At every turning another portion juts into view of the cathedral, a very splendid affair, shimmering with chromatic tiles, too tall in parts, too squat in others, like a brilliant pastiche of late – very late – Hispano-American Baroque. The crafts flourish. Up and down the main street, the silversmiths squat in neat little shops tinkling away at buckles and earrings. Every white person is accosted with a string of uninflected words in debased English: stops, gapes, and buys. This street, these shops, these wares, are for the transient and the naive, just as the displays of Capri are for the Sunday Swiss and the Scandinavian Tour; the foreigners who live at Taxco take villas and stay a very long time. Some may once have thought of writing a book; a few do paint. The bars are kept by other foreigners, known by their Christian names. Two to each bar.

'Don't look,' said E. 'There are Guillermo's barons. Rosenstern . . . Don't look, they can't see us.'

But they could.

They said they were sorry they had not been able to find out more about our stolen suitcases.

We thanked them.

'We were at Guadalajara last month. That sweet American Vice-Consul gave us your address and we went out to Lake Chapala to see you. We were so sorry to hear you had left, but that divine friend of yours asked us to stay with him. We had such a good time.'

'You stayed at San Pedro?'

'We only wished you'd been there.'

The journey from Taxco to Mexico City has been described by Aldous Huxley in *Beyond the Mexique Bay*. Most accurately. The road is still as good, the drops as sheer. No parapets dull the sensations of the passengers; charabancs and limousines still race each other down the pass round hairpin bends swiping the two-seaters off the track and meet head-on with lorries.

We got into Mexico City on the eve of All Souls'. The windows of the pastry shops were displaying chocolate skulls in many sizes, inscribed with names in icing on the forehead, Juan, Manuela, Carmen, Padrecito . . . The next day all was closed in honour of the greatest holiday of the year; the cemeteries were packed with picnickers; we were presented with a mound of the Bread of the Dead and a nestful of skull-lets both by the hotel management and by Don Luís de X.'s children, and the morning after, before sunrise, we drove out of the city on our way at last to the south and the pre-Columbian ruins.

Chapter Five

OAXACA: MITLA AND
MONTE ALBÁN

Et j'ai vu quelquefois ce que l'homme a cru voir

FEBRUARY 3RD, 1544

'... I THOUGHT that having toiled in my youth, it should profit me to find rest in my old age; and so for forty years I have laboured, going sleepless, eating poorly and at times not at all, bearing armour on my back, risking my life in dangers, freely spending my means and years, all in the service of God; bringing sheep into His fold in a hemisphere far removed from ours ...

I begged Your Majesty in Madrid to be pleased to make plain his royal will to repay me for my services ...

I am old, poor and in debt in the realm to the tune of over twenty thousand ducats ... I have not left the Court for a moment, and have had three sons with me there, to say nothing of lawyers, solicitors ...

Again and again I have begged Your Majesty ... And this without delay ... I am no longer of an age to spend my time travelling from inn to inn, but must rather settle down and make up my account with God. It is a long one, and I have but short time to balance it ...

EL MARQUES DEL VALLE DE OAXACA'
(From Cortés' last letter to the Emperor Charles V)

On the back of this letter someone wrote, *Nay que Responder.* There is No Reply.

Cortés' march south from Tenochtitlán took one year. They did not know where they were going, they did not know where it would end. Return was uncertain, hope lay in reaching again some day the sea. To the south the mountains of the plateau are higher, the distance between range and range grows longer, space opens. Below the Valley of Puebla the fertile country ends, foreground ceases; the changing, bounded prospects of central Mexico, the hundred patterns of valley, hill and ridge, are abolished into a wide vast panorama of receding ranges, wave upon wave, converging on a remote horizon. Now, there is a road, built fifteen years ago; the traveller no more thinks of lacking water, risks no exposure, but the mind is still oppressed by the measureless expanse before it. Progress is not unlike flying, hour into hour, above clouds: the monotony, the isolation, the illimited confinement − space on to space and space and no exit, and the modern spirit quails after one day.

The state of Oaxaca is territory of some sixty thousand square miles inhabited by twenty-odd Indian tribes and half a million mestizos. It has mountains twelve thousand feet high, acres of unexplored tropical forest and a level sea-coast. Coffee is grown in the cold hills, vanilla and cochineal produced in the plains; there is one town of thirty thousand inhabitants and one of ten; Oaxaca is the home of the tarantula and the widow spider, the rivers are full of crocodiles, and the woods of pumas and tapirs, and there is an earthquake every spring.

Southern Mexico, not unexpectedly, is very southern. The meridional character of any country is a relative phenomenon, not consistently governed by latitude. Thus southern England is below the Highlands, but below southern England lies the grim industrial north of France. Marseilles is north of the teutonically scrubbed and honest province of Piedmont;

Boston is south of Florence; New York on the parallel of Naples; and Alabama above that Mexican outpost of northern efficiency, Monterrey. In temperate countries, the characteristics of the south are the loosening of a straighter pattern, an opening up, greater ease between man and man. Life is more immediate, the next bus not so pressing. There is leisure and it is wide awake. In the geographical south begins a rundown: laissez-faire dissolves into laisser-aller, quiescence accommodates to sloth; tolerance, bonhomie, enjoyment become habits; the lilies in the field wax a little rank. In extremer regions everything snaps tight shut again. Torpor. Indifference. There are no answers, *there are no questions*: leisure is blank and man alone, the future must bury its dead, *huis-clos*.

Southern Mexico is dour. It has the sluttish elements of the south – the flies, the dirt, the chafing harnesses on the bullock and no gaiety; no vines, no garlands, only an obdurate, sempiternal sticking in the mud.

On their march, Cortés and his men came upon the ruins of Mitla. The Spaniards were impressed. They may well have been.

Nothing is known of the ancient Zapotecs, the people who may have come from Asia across the Bering Straits, and who are believed to have built – in the ninth century, the fourth, in eleven hundred BC? – those temples at Mitla and Monte Albán. Nothing, besides fragments of the works they left. And these reveal a great deal. They are fragments only in so far as parts have not been excavated, not for any lack of durability in their construction. They are misnamed ruins: no decay has softened, no restorer's hand has touched, no wars have chipped a splinter off those monoliths, those walls, those flights of stairs. They are there; putting across what they were meant to put across. Mitla and Monte Albán are conscious works of art like Chartres carried out to create a precise atmosphere. They were not meant to please. They glorified, and induced submission to, a certain pattern. They were meant to impress, not by splendour, not by beauty, not by intimations of another vision, but with strength, with will, with inflexibility of purpose; to exclude hope, to overwhelm with power. They succeeded.

The medium is stone and space – natural space used in relation to masonry. At Monte Albán, the approaches to the sanctum are a series of stadia swept along a levelled hill-top; the courts, passages, and chambers of Mitla are so much space enclosed on a wasteland plain, conveying at once entombment and immensity. Everything is repeated, hard, grey. There is no diversionist sculpture, only a lapidary motif executed relentlessly by skilled mass labour under the whip-hand of an hierarchy. The Zapotec temples are not large, by Roman and Egyptian standards they are quite small, yet they imply crushing size. The Alley of the Columns at Mitla, that row of strange, stark, Neanderthalish pillars, is below fifteen feet high. It appears colossal. Yes, entirely successful, entirely frightening – exulting both the unimportance of the individual and the material dominance of men: the induration of the arbitrary, the organized, the State.

If the Nazis had not been so cheap, had their taste been better and their instinct for self-dramatization less Wagnerian, this is the way they would have built. They would have found in the Zapotec architecture the expression and the setting of all they stood for. They would have constructed Monte Albán at Nuremberg, and celebrated the *Heldentot* at Mitla.

Chapter Six
OAXACA: SOME AGREEABLE PEOPLE

The flesh is bruckle, and the Fiend is slee: –
Timor mortis conturbat me.

WE RETURNED from Mitla to the town of Oaxaca in an open motor lorry that happens to pass this way once a day picking up people out of nowhere along the gravelled road. A bitter wind was blowing across the cacti plains, and the passengers were shivering in their cottons. We shivered with them.

'It comes from Vera Cruz,' said our neighbour on the plank.

'It could not,' said I.

'All their ill winds do,' said E.

On the floor of the lorry stood a small, open cardboard coffin, in it decorously laid out with lace and ribbons was the body of a child.

'The little angel,' said the passengers.

'My fourth,' said the mother.

We stopped for a young Indio with a Remington Portable. He was a travelling scribe.

'Do you have much business?' we asked.

'It depends. People are very backward. I come to houses where they do not know magic from the writing machine.'

'Would it not be easier for you if you wrote by hand?'

'I do not write with my hands; I write with the writing machine. It is progress.'

'But you *can* write?'

'With the writing machine. I was taught when I was a grown man. Now, only ignorant children are taught to write with their hands.'

'And what are we stopping for now?' said E.

'The great Tree of Tule. Humboldt believed it to be the oldest living thing on earth, and the driver thinks we ought to look at it.'

'In my native country I successfully avoided seeing the Grand Canyon; I avoided the Painted Desert, my nurse did not manage to drag me to Niagara. With all respect to Alexander von Humboldt, I will not get myself off this contraption to look at a tree however interesting.'

'You need not,' said I; 'you can see it from here. This forest we are under, is *it*.'

It was a remarkable monster, a kind of cypress as large as a house and as tall as a tree.

'Good Lord,' said E., 'three thousand years in Oaxaca.'

At the time of Cortés' arrival the present capital of Oaxaca was no Tenochtitlán. There was no comfortable civilization to destroy, only an Indian fort to conquer. The Spaniards fought their way down to the Isthmus; in later years Cortés sent lieutenants, reinforcements, returned himself. The struggle with the Zapotecs was as hard as had been that with the Aztecs. When it was over, officials, friars, a bishop arrived and set out to make the place more habitable. Charles V created Cortés Marquess of the Valley of Oaxaca. The town now is rather lovely. The houses, one-storeyed against earthquake, have rustic Renaissance façades and are built of blocks of rough, greenish local stone. The plaza lies in speckled shade. On Saturdays a market spreads along every street; there is a special inn for donkeys, and a baroque church covered every foot inside from niche to vaulting with a splendid absurdity of saints and angels in gilt and painted high-relief.

Juarez came from Oaxaca, a fact commemorated by a bronze statue of the reformer, a broken crown at his feet, standing upon a concrete pedestal in an overgrown public garden.

Coffee used to be produced in the neighbourhood before partition of the land. Now that the *fincas* are divided off, the bushes are growing to seed. Coffee is a year-round business, not a household crop. One might admire the present owners' lack of interest in profit (uncertain profit, by the way: one rain in the drying season, one flutter in the New York Produce Exchange, and bang goes a year's effort), but Mexicans in towns are not pleased at having to get their coffee from Central America at three times the expense.

I went for a morning walk. Mornings in Mexico are always serene. The young blue air floats lightly upon the arid land and one is wafted along with the empyrean balloon. It is the mood of the sketches D. H. Lawrence wrote here, but it is not the dominant note of Oaxaca. It seems an odd reversal that Lawrence should have written the shrill, foreboding *Plumed Serpent* at Lake Chapala, yet strolled about the Oaxacan countryside laughing with the Indios calling to their dogs, producing the *Mornings*, one of his rare contented books. Lawrence was at Chapala in the early 'twenties at a time when the *Christero Rey* gangs used to shoot into Mrs Rawlston's garden; he is supposed to have been upset by a particularly hideous murder near the place he lived and, from his letters, he was already beginning to be fed up with living in Mexico. At Oaxaca the year before, all was still new and shiny. With Lawrence it was always one thing or another. He had layers and layers of insight into animals and people and places, but the layers did not always join. Reading him one often feels like following someone writing himself deeper and deeper into a tunnel of understanding, touch some climax of intuition, withdraw exhausted, then try another descent. Yet he could reach far. Some of the things he wrote on Mexico are amazing; certain passages, like the harping on the Aztec Mother-of-God's being a black, obsidian knife, or the rave in the *Plumed Serpent* about America as a Dead Continent, only spring into relevance here, when one is up against it, and strike with their precise significance just as so much else he wrote seems to make sense only when read *in* England. Lawrence was alive to the two intermittent keynotes of Mexico: Allegro and Panic.

At Mexico City I had been able to get hold at last of the work of a very different kind of writer. I had managed to borrow a library copy of Charles Macomb Flandrau's *Viva Mexico!*, the most enchanting, as well as extremely funny, book on Mexico. Flandrau was a Bostonian bachelor who spent the end of his life in France. He was a Harvard man, and wrote two or three other slim volumes. In 1906 he went to Mexico to keep company to a brother who was trying to raise coffee on a south-eastern slope. *Viva Mexico!* was published by Appleton, and is unfortunately out of print.* It

* Meanwhile I was pleased to hear that it *has* been republished.

is not easy to find now, particularly in Europe. I wish it were reprinted; I wish I had a copy.

This I read aloud to E. by a bad light in the evenings at Oaxaca. I transcribed one passage – accurately I hope – which I shall quote as it conveys something both of the quality of the author's temper and the atmosphere of that part of the country:

'I recalled an evening several years ago at my brother's coffee place – sixty miles from anywhere in particular. As it was in winter, or the "dry season," it had been raining, with but one or two brief intermissions, for twenty-four days. As the river was swollen and unfordable we had not been able for days to send to the village – an hour's ride away – for provisions. Meat, of course, we did not have. In a tropical and iceless country, unless one can have fresh meat every day one does not have it at all. We had run out of potatoes, we had run out of bread – we had run out of flour . . . So we dined on a tin of sardines, some chilli verde and a pile of tortillas, which are not bad when patted thin and toasted to a crisp. Probably because there were forty thousand pounds of excellent coffee piled up in sacks on the piazza, we washed down this banquet with draughts of Sir Thomas Lipton's mediocre tea. The evening was cold – as bitterly cold as it can only be in a thoroughly tropical country when the temperature drops to forty-three and a screaming wind is forcing the rain through spaces between the tiles overhead. We had also run out of petroleum and the flames of the candles on the dinner table were more often than not blue and horizontal. But somehow we dined with great gaiety and talked all the time. I remember how my brother summoned Concha the cook, and courteously attracted her attention to the fact that she had evidently dropped the teapot on the untiled kitchen floor – that the spout was clogged with mud and that it did not "wish to pour," and how he again summoned her for the purpose of declaring that the three dead wasps he had just fished out of the chilli no doubt accounted perfectly for its unusually delicious flavour. We had scarcely anything to eat, but socially the dinner was a great success. Immediately afterwards we both went to bed – each with a reading candle, a book and a hot-water bag. After half an hour's silence my brother irrelevantly exclaimed:

"What very agreeable people one runs across in queer, out-of-the-way places!"

"Who on earth are you thinking of now?" I enquired.

"Why, I was thinking of *us*!" he placidly replied, and went on with his reading.

'Perhaps we had been agreeable. At any rate we were in a queer, out-of-the-way place, that is if any place is queer and out of the way, which I am beginning rather to doubt. Since then I have often remembered that evening – how, just before it grew dark, the tattered banana trees writhed like gigantic seaweed in the wind, and the cold rain hissed from the spouts on the roof in graceful crystal tubes. Here and there the light of a brasero in a labourer's bamboo hut flared for an instant through the coffee trees. On the piazza the tired Indians, shivering in their flimsy cotton garments, had covered themselves with matting and empty coffee sacks and were trying to sleep. In the kitchen doorway a very old white-bearded man was improvising poetry – sometimes sentimental, sometimes heroic, sometimes obscene – to a huddled and enthralled audience all big hats, crimson blankets and beautiful eyes. Apart from this group, Saturnino was causing a jarana to throb in a most syncopated, minor and emotional fashion.

'During dinner we discussed, among other things, Tolstoy's *War and Peace* which we had just finished, and while agreeing that it was the greatest novel we had ever read or ever expected to read (an opinion I still possess), we did not agree about Tolstoy's characteristically cocksure remarks on the subject of predestination and freedom of the will. As neither of us had studied philosophy we were unable to command the special terminology – the specific jargon that always makes a philosophic discussion seem so profound – and our colloquial efforts to express ourselves were at times piquant. In the midst of it a tarantula slithered across the tablecloth and I squashed it with a candlestick as he was about to disappear over the table's edge. Of course we disputed as to whether or not, in the original conception of the universe, God had sketched the career of the tarantula in its relation to that of the candlestick and mine and — yes, on looking back, I feel sure we were both very agreeable.'*

Chapter Seven

PUEBLA: A GENERAL
AND A SHIP

. . . Mexicans have a genius for stringing words upon a flashing chain of shrugs and smiles — of presenting you with a verbal rosary which later you find yourself unable to tell.

CHARLES MACOMB FLANDRAU

I T IS a proposition of Mexican geographical logic that the nearest way between two points is by a distant third. The only way in fact. If one wishes to get from one place to another, one must go first somewhere else, and we had learnt the folly of attempting to demonstrate this a fallacy. Cross-country communications in England are governed by somewhat the same principle, but the scale involved is not the same. Once more, a difference in degree is a difference in kind.

At this stage we should have liked to continue to Yucatán, from Oaxaca a matter of a mere six or seven hundred miles across the swamps of Chiapas and the forests of Campeche, but it appeared that we could not. There is no road, and there is no railway. As the Indios are so fond of saying, it did not lend itself. If we wanted to get to the ruins of Uxmal and Chichen-Itzá, we should have to proceed in an opposite direction and either take an aeroplane at Mexico City or a boat at Vera Cruz. To get to either of the latter, we should have to go to Puebla.

It was a weary journey. Back again — tomorrow and

tomorrow and tomorrow – over all those mountains. The buses in the south are not at all comfortable. Every nine hours or so there would be somewhere to stop for something to eat: saucers of eggs and chilli fried in lard, clay mugs with goat milk and sugared coffee set out in a row outside a hut. There were no forks and knives, or spoons; and there was no bread. The passengers carried their own tortillas. A man gave us some of his for a present. It was the one human moment on that journey, and it was cheap to notice and sad to mind that he had produced the tortillas from inside his shirt. Hygiene has cut off man from man more than any class distinctions. Throughout it, E. read. I cannot think now how she managed it. I do not know how she stood it at all, how we both stood it. If we live to an old age, we shall tell ourselves about the thousands and thousands of miles we rocked through noons and nightfalls over the surface of Mexico in second-class motor buses, and we shall be dazzled – *Ah, que le monde est grand à la clarté des lampes.* Then we were just inured.

Nevertheless at Puebla we took a cab to the best hotel. We found it stuffed from lounge to bedroom passages with authentic Louise-Philippe commodes and looking-glasses. The French were here a long time. Like Guadalajara, Puebla *fait ville* – few Mexican towns do – and like Guadalajara it has kept its character.

There was a shipping office. '*Servidor,*' they said, 'at the disposal of Your Graces.'

But they knew little about the movements of boats to Yucatán, except that they were not always regular. 'No doubt, you will find out in Vera Cruz.'

'No doubt. Only, we don't want to go to Vera Cruz unless we are certain of getting a boat from there.'

'That is so. If you want to get a boat you must take it at Vera Cruz.'

'If there is a boat?'

'You will know in Vera Cruz.'

Unfortunately Vera Cruz did not have a good name with E.

'Twice,' she said, 'I allowed myself to be dragged to a Pacific paradise: you *will not* get me down that sierra a third time.'

'Vera Cruz is on the Atlantic,' said I, 'and nobody's ever called it a paradise.'

'There is that,' said E.

What was disclosed, from other sources, about the nature of these elusive vessels was not encouraging. One rather eccentric feature was that you were supposed to bring your own food for the voyage. I am fond of reading old P & O menus, and found this disappointing.

Our chief informant was a retired mestizo general who did not live but spent his mornings at our hotel.

'Good morning, General.'

'Good morning, madam. I kiss your feet. How are you?'

'Very well, thank you. And how are you?'

'At *your* service. And you, madam, are you well?'

'Such a lovely day, isn't it?'

'It is not worthy of you.'

'So glad that dreadful wind's died down. Do you often get it?'

'Not while you are favouring this undeserving town with your exalted presences.'

'The very elements are considerate in Mexico,' said E.

The General bowed.

'How many tons did you say that freighter had, the one that goes to Progreso?' said I.

'A number not commensurate with your merits.'

'As long as it gets there . . .'

'Ah,' said the General. The polite part of the call being now behind, he would launch into circumstantial accounts of rotten hulls, defective machinery and drunken captains.

'Drunk?' said E. 'That's bad. Our Navy and Merchant Marine are dry.'

'Worse than drunk,' said the General. 'Traitors. That Captain is conspiring with the government at Mexico. There will be a mutiny next voyage. The First Officer is an important Jesuit.'

The General, like many of his kind, had a grievance against the government. It had halved his pension. Not, he explained, that a respectable general was expected to live on his pension, or that the pension had often been paid, but it was the principle of the thing.

'I was awarded this annuity after I had the honour of placing my humble services at the disposal of President Calles,' he said. 'Now these traitors at Mexico write to me that they've cut it. If I have a valid reason against it, I should state it in writing. They expect me to write to them! The impudence. When I was young, no officer *wrote* to a government: we marched on them. Ah, times aren't what they used to be, and nor am I, or I'd show them. Pen and ink, indeed. Bullets is what they want. I tell you what's wrong these days – modern arms. Too damned expensive for poor devils like myself. Those fellows at Mexico are using machine-guns now, I dare say from aeroplanes. A government has always a way of getting hold of a bit of cash. My men had their knives, and a chap would consider himself lucky if he had a dozen rifles to a company. Some were clever at making bombs . . . never had much use for them myself, women's stuff, not soldier-like, if you know what I mean. *Of course,* when I had the privilege of serving General Villa . . .'

They were so pleasant at the shipping office that I went on seeing them in the hope of something turning up. They were getting tired of disappointing me and I could see from their faces that they were going to produce quite soon. Meanwhile, we strolled about the town. Puebla was planned four centuries ago on the lines of a modern American city: straight streets intersecting at right angles, so many houses to a block, so many flats to a house. This sobriety is offset by extreme gaudiness in everything else. The interiors of the churches are blazing forests of gold and exotic statuary, and all the fronts of all the buildings a glaze of every period, shape and colour of *mudéjar* tiles, while cornices and casements are moulded – not reticently – in white stucco. Some of the tiling is pretty, plain gold circlets on azure or deep red; some is hideous. On the whole an arty job for modern taste, but delicately managed, and the momentary effect quite charming. The tiling is not solid like so many mosques and baths, but panels are set in varying proportions in a brick façade, and this is a redeeming feature. Not much brick shows, but the occasional base or edging gives a rest and starting point to the eye.

E. stalked past it all, the way Dr Johnson must have stalked about the Hebrides.

I made the mistake of taking her to the Secret Convent. I knew it the minute we were inside and the guide tapped the wainscoting and invited us to crawl through the opening in the revolving chimney piece.

The Secret Convent of Santa Monica appears to be a respectable historical fact. It was closed by the Reform Laws in 1857; the premises were sold for secular habitation and the nuns believed to have returned to private life. In 1935, when as the result of a concordat public worship was resumed, it was found that they had not. The convent had gone underground, literally into the walls and cupboards of a block of houses in a central street of Puebla, and functioned as a religious community for seventy-eight years. During this time the nuns, being of a cloistered order, never emerged. A number of Puebla families were in it; and these helped the nuns in the comings and goings of the priest and the disposal of their dead, covered up undue amounts of ash and smoke and refuse, and guarded them from discovery by blundering tenants. They supplied them with food and – it sounds incredible – with novices. In fact, when after three-quarters of a century the convent came again into the open, the number of its actual and professed members, although all the original nuns were dead, had increased from fifty to some eighty. There were denunciations; police often searched the interested houses. Nothing was ever found. Were they taken in by the trick panelling? The families who lived in the ostensible parts of these buildings were respectable, they led public lives. Bribes may have passed; perhaps more simply, the search parties did not take their task quite seriously – they might have discovered quick enough the single priest inside the hollow chimney, but the official mind shied off when it came to looking for fifty women supposed to be living these forty years in what unaccounted space there might be in the houses of the Director of the Inter-Oceanic Railway and the Chairman of the National Credit of Puebla. With a little sang-froid, the inspector and his booted oafs breaking in upon the family breakfast could have been made to look very foolish indeed.

In the twentieth century, the rumours died down, and the discovery of the existence of the convent fifteen years ago came as a shock to the inhabitants of Puebla.

On this scene of unfathomable human faith and fortitude – surely an abstract and solitary theme – now gaping tourists and slobbering village women are made to proceed on hands and knees through double-bottomed sideboards and factitious bookcases into a kind of catacombs where they blub or giggle over immured skeletons and a conjuror's altar. This degrading sideshow is called Religious Museum.

With the best of wills it would have been hard for a person of E.'s height to get herself through these openings, and E. had no goodwill at all. Pressed onward with the tour we had got as far as a kind of concrete barrel, the Secret Chapel; the guide had finished his *peroraciónes* and was rounding up the congregation to squeeze themselves one by one through the grating in the confessional. He looked at E. and recognized the material difficulty, if no other.

'Favour to bend yourself. I will push Your Excellency.'

E. did not bend.

'Give me your hand,' a woman said. 'I will have the honour of preceding you, then I shall pull.'

'There *must* be another way out,' said E.

There was. They were obliged to open it for her. I used it too. Only it was not the exit, but the way into the Secret Refectory; and presently the members of the tour appeared, heads forward, wriggling in through a hole below a panel. When they were complete, the guide said his piece, the women touched and kissed, then he pressed a button: a trapdoor swung open from under a prie-dieu, the tour dived. E. waited. A door behind a tapestry was unlocked for her. It led into the Mother Superior's cell. And so it went on. An hour and twenty-five minutes of it, from secret cell to secret parlour, from sacristy to robing-room, whisked through a discreet door from one oppressive little stone chamber to another, waiting for the tour to catch up laboriously on their bellies, until at last through a commodious collapsible looking-glass we all emerged again into the drawing-room whence we started. E. felt outraged, the guide humiliated, the trippers cheated; the pious women whispered, *hereticas*.

'Oh, S.,' said E., 'the sights are worse than the journeys.'

After this I went to Cholula for the day. By myself. Cholula is a monument to human thoroughness. The Spanish as a matter of general policy razed every native temple in conquered territory and built a Christian church on its site. Now, Cholula at that time was not only a flourishing town, it was also something in the nature of the Aztec Rome. Quetzalcoatl in his passage on earth had spent decades teaching at Cholula. After his passing, disciples built the Great Pyramid. They also built nine minor pyramids and a temple or two on every square, at every crossing, in every street. The Spaniards counted them, 365 in all. They razed 364 temples and built 364 churches. On top of the Great Pyramid they built a Basilica. Will and labour were not lacking, even so 364 churches took a long time. They look indeed like approximate samples of the various styles of ecclesiastical architecture now represented at Rome. And they are *all* that remains of Cholula. The rest of the town, but for some four hundred inhabitants and their hovels, has disappeared. The Aztecs became impoverished, in any case the meaning of Cholula went with the temples. The Spaniards had never cared for it; instead, they founded Puebla a few miles further up where they were less hampered in their plans by the predestined locations of so many places of worship.

Now there is only one parish, but the 365 are still churches, kept consecrated by Mass being said in each of them one day a year. On the other days, the four hundred Cholulans and some country devotees potter about them at their will, adding to reliquary and decorations such items of worship as may take their unorthodox fancies. Toad gods puff their copper bellies in the tabernacles, angels sport feathers and Saint Anthony is hydra-headed. And thus, after all, the purpose of the Spaniards was defeated.

Seen from the top of the pyramid-basilica the aspect of the town is most improbable, diminished as it has in size but not in circumference. Between church and church there are only scarless rural gaps, but the distance between a central and a suburban church is still the length of a whole town. Imagine looking upon Manhattan from the Empire State and finding nothing standing except all the drug-stores in excellent repair.

The shipping office had found a boat. A freighter. Three thousand tons. Well, perhaps two. A very fine freighter. A captain *and* stewards. Cabins? Yes, cabins. And shower-baths. Food? Oh yes, much food. In fact it was a French boat, Portuguese. *From* Vera Cruz. Straight to Yucatán? Well not quite. Where to then? Such a good boat did not waste itself on Yucatán. *Where* did it go to? To Bordeaux. Bordeaux? Bordeaux-the-Other-Side-of-the-Sea.

It was a thought. The boat would leave in a month. It took five weeks, no seven. It was very inexpensive. We talked it over. Was it really necessary for me to return by way of New York? Did we really want to go to Uxmal? The great thing about this boat was that it would make no fuss about taking two small donkeys. For some time now I had been wanting to buy two Mexican baby donkeys, one grey one black, for fifteen shillings a piece. Where else in the world could one acquire two such enchanting, silk-muzzled creatures for that sum? In later life they tend to become sullen and coarse-grained, with me they would spend years of ease. I wanted to settle down, they would compel me to find a suitable rural home at once. Their influence on my choice would be good: a quiet place, some distance from a market . . . I worked it out. First I would leave them with a friend who had a cottage in Normandy – I might give one to her, I might take a third – Mme Guerinier, the farm woman who had such a way with dogs could look after them. She had never seen a donkey. E., I would put on an aeroplane that would get her to her native country before she could say San Esteban Tlaquepaque . . .

'And how do you propose to get those animals from Bordeaux to Normandy?' said E.

The shipping clerks were finding their stride. Every day more details, all splendid, were coming to light about the desirable cargo boat.

'Are you sure it exists?' said E. 'Is there such a thing as a freighter from Vera Cruz to Bordeaux?'

I reminded her of a friend of ours who had actually travelled on something of that nature.

'Ah, but Nancy commands freighters; they rise for her from the seas like Prospero's island. And nearly drown her, too.'

Meanwhile the general, tired of his gloomy tales of shipwreck and sabotage, invented a liner to Yucatán. Weekly service, female stewardesses, a band. Cabins to be had by favours of a brother officer who was at our service at Vera Cruz.

Three days later, we received two telegrams respectively offering us cabins on a boat to Bordeaux and a boat to Progreso.

'I suppose we ought to give them an answer some time,' said E.

'It says by return.'

'Yes, yes. One knows what that means. Some time. Now don't you have any of your interesting churches to look at this morning?'

Then came a letter from Don Otavio reminding us that it was a fortnight to Christmas and of our promise to spend that Feast and the winter at San Pedro, and suggesting, in five somewhat involved pages, that as I had often expressed the wish to drive a car in this country and a cousin of Doña Concepción's in Mexico was too far gone in a pregnancy to travel in hers, and her husband felt that she should not travel unaccompanied by him on the trains, and their chauffeur had said that nothing would make him go on such a journey without his master, and Doña Concepción's cousin and her husband would like to have the car at Guadalajara where they were going to spend some time, would we, could we, might we, not take amiss but consider this very irregular idea of travelling ourselves in this car from Mexico to Guadalajara? The car was not entirely uncomfortable and Doña Concepción's cousin would provide of course a *mozo* and a maid.

There were two postscripts. One said,

'I hope you are not thinking of going to Yucatán before January. The Empress Carlota, poor woman, went in the hot season and never recovered. If you must go, you can fly out to Mérida from Guadalajara.'

The other,

'The Jaime children will be down for *Noche Buena*, we are going to have suckling pig and nine *posadas*.

q. D. g.'

'Don Otavio is a very sensible man,' said E. 'Oh, good morning, General. How does one get out of Puebla?'

But the General was not ready for this yet. 'Good morning, Madams,' he said in grave rebuke. 'I kiss your feet. How have you spent the night?'

'Very well, thank you. And you?'

'At *your* service,' said the General.

Chapter Eight
TUSCUECA: THE LAST OF THE JOURNEYS

Corydon, marche davant,
Sçache où le bon vin se vend,
Fay refraischir la bouteille . . .
Achète des abricôs,
Des pompons, des artichôs
Des fraises, et de la crême:
Cerche une ombrageuse treille
Pour souz elle me coucher . . .

ONCE MORE we rose before sunrise. Once more we stumbled through pitch-black streets behind a trotting *cargador*. Puebla is a town only from 9 a.m. onwards.

'Can you send up some tea to numbers 9 and 11 at half-past four tomorrow morning?'

'Not at that hour, Señora.'

'Well, will you just have us called.'

'Not at that hour.'

'Can we get a cab?'

'No, Señora.'

'What does one do about one's bags?'

'A carrier will take them.'

'How does one get one at that hour?'

'One gets him now, Señora. We will fetch him. He will sleep outside the hotel, and tomorrow morning you must call him from your window.'

So first we woke ourselves, and then we woke the carrier. Puebla is in *Terra Fría* and it was bitter cold.

'The wind from Vera Cruz,' said E. 'It must have got it wrong about our departure.'

At the bus place, there was no bus, but an enterprising person had started a fire and was selling ladlefuls of boiling coffee for five centavos a dipping. Presently we had our shoes cleaned. It was a weird business as one could not see whoever it was that was rubbing away at one's feet by the kerb. Then someone else turned up with a tray of hard-boiled eggs. The beggars on so raw a night were late, though by and by they arrived disclosing their identity by tugging at one's garments. Then the bus was there: all lit up inside like something at a fair. For some reason it was locked, and remained so for some time.

The cold was preposterous. I had no coat. My winter clothes were at San Pedro or Anthony had taken them back to the States, but it did not matter as it was the kind of knifing wind that would have got through anything. I remember feeling neither discomfort nor impatience, everything seemed quite unreal and I had a presentiment that this would be my last journey of this kind.

Later on we saw the sun leap into the sky over the Valley of Puebla with the sudden ferocious spring that goes for sunrise in this country, and translate us from a heavy-shadowed Daumier world of walls and figures to a landscape of pure lines: frail hills, a river, paper shapes of blue-and-snow volcanoes moving in the perspective of our passage with the firm light order of the progress of a Scarlatti sonata.

'. . . *je veux*
Imiter le Chinois au coeur limpide et fin

De qui l'extase pure est de peindre la fin
Sur ses tasses de neige à la lune ravie . . .

Serein, je vais choisir un jeune paysage
Que je peindrais encore sur les tasses, distrait.
Une ligne d'azur mince et pâle serait
Un lac, parmi le ciel de porcelaine nue,
Un clair croissant perdu par une blanche nue
Trempe sa corne calme en la glace des eaux,
Non loin de trois grands cils d'émeraude, roseaux.'

All that drive we were chased by four volcanoes, like so many shifting moons, coming up as the road wound through the valley; singly, in pairs, all four, at one's right, one's left, receding, racing; suddenly still before one, near and large.

We stopped at ten thousand feet, in icy shade, on an eminence named Río Fró. There, the daydream of Acapulco, a cold caterer's buffet was spread for our refreshment. I scanned the expanse of aspic. 'There wouldn't be any soup?' I asked the attendant.

'No, Señora.'

'Anything hot at all?'

'No, Señora.'

'Is *everything* iced?'

'Everything iced. It lends itself.'

Once more we spent a week in Mexico City – mornings walking in a broiling sun in the crumbling quarters behind the Zocolá, afternoons reading in the frigid Jesuit church that had been turned into the National Library by the Revolutions. The statues of Saint Ignacio and Saint Felipe de Jesús had been tumbled from their niches, and plaster busts of Spinoza,

313

Cuvier and Descartes installed in their place. Bookshelves replaced altars. As the well-to-do classes do not patronize free institutions, and the others cannot read, this shrine of learning was delightfully peaceful. I nearly froze. We went to see the patent lawyer Don Luís was arranging with for our papers, both at his brand-new office and at the Ritz; we took our luncheons in a packed little restaurant full of dons, recommended by the C.s, near the ex-headquarters of the Inquisition and the present School of Jurisprudence. Again I tried to get a look of the inside of the cathedral, again I lost heart trying to press through a devout mob. There is a passage in Mme de la Barca that reads like something one might find quoted in *This England* and which contains mere sober truth stated with nineteenth-century unselfconsciousness.

> 'The floor is so dirty that one kneels with a feeling of horror, and an inward determination to effect as speedy a change of garments afterwards as possible. Besides many of my Indian neighbours were engaged in an occupation which I must leave to your imagination . . . I was not sorry to find myself once more in the pure air after Mass; and have since been told that, except on peculiar occasions, few ladies perform their devotions in the cathedral.'

And yet walking in these parts charmed again; I was caught by the excitement of the first time, the street cries, the look of the well-worn *palaçios*. What grand modesty to have built all those elaborate façades in local *tezontle*, a stone so soft that the most rigorous classical mouldings, the most protuberant of baroque reliefs become blurred before the century is out, what desinvolture! It makes the solid preservation of the Palazzo Strozzi look so vulgar.

We went out again to the Pyramids of the Sun and Moon. After Oaxaca, these formidable temples have an almost romantic aspect. What were those Aztecs really like? At the time of the splendours of Tenochtitlán they were already a conqueror nation, ensconced in the fairest and most prosperous portion of the world they knew, with the harshness and softnesses peculiar to established empire. We know their uncompromising sculpture; we know what they ate; we know that they were fond of gardening, smoked amber mixed with their tobacco, that they were waiting – perhaps with no great impatience – for the white Messiah from across the sea. The letters and diaries of the Conquistadores (to whom ironically we owe the description of the lyrical beauty of the city they destroyed) make us sup of the horrors of the Aztec religion and stress Aztec prowess in matters of philosophy and science, the data of which they, the Spaniards, were at such pains to burn and generally obliterate. Yet Gibbon said that the native civilizations of the Americas were 'strangely magnified' by the Conquistadores. 'There were universities in Mexico, but they were limited to droning over the scholastic philosophy in its dotage.'

Of Montezuma we know one rather wistful remark. Cortés, who somewhat leaned on the Aztec tradition of the White Messiah, had a theological conversation with the King in which he must have tried to establish the common origin of their discrepant creeds. Montezuma replied mildly that they were not natives of the land but had come to it a long time ago and therefore were well prepared to believe that they had erred somewhat from the true faith during the long time they had left their native land.

We rang up Mrs Rawlston's daughter, Mrs Waldheim that was, but learned that she and the children had already left for

Lake Chapala. Mr Waldheim was on the telephone and told us that he was flying out on the 24th with a case of eggnog and a side of wild boar.

'She will like that, the old lady? Do you think? Yes? She can cook *das Wildschwein* on the new electric stove I am giving her. Is it not a beautiful Christmas thought?'

I said it was.

'My mother-in-law will appreciate it? Perhaps she will let Willi and Hansi go to the German school again? Well, we shall see you there. You must come and have some eggnog. Merry Christmas.'

Then one fine morning at a civilized hour we set out ourselves. The car, what advertisements call one of the better makes of American automobile, was not at all uncomfortable. We had managed to eliminate the maid; about the *mozo* everybody had been adamant. He sat, a large hat strapped on to his chin, a handkerchief tied over his mouth, bolt upright in the back, impervious to human intercourse. First we tried to talk to him, then he made us nervous, later we forgot about him. The day was flawless, the road clear. It was the third month of the dry season, and the colours of the earth and fields had changed to sand and fawn and terracotta; the hills, bare of the lush Rousseau growths of August, revealed the contours of Italian paintings. Sometimes a black pig, glossy like a seal, would walk deliberately across our path. Towns appeared, spread across the plains, as Lawrence put it, as though they had been brought and unfolded from a napkin. We enjoyed ourselves.

At Toluca we stopped among the bustle of a midday market to give the *mozo* a chance to buy something.

'¿*Tamales*? Hot *tamales*? Wouldn't you like some?'

'*Quesadillas*, look. They are frying *quesadillas*.'

'And there are *empanadas* just out of the oven.'

'Do you want some *enchiladas*? *Gorditas*? *Garbanzas*? *Chimole*? Or do you want some *guacamole*? Do you want a nice *requeson*? Do you want some maize-cakes? Fish-cakes? Cheese-cakes? Meat-cakes? Honey-cakes? Curd-cakes?'

He shook his head.

'Oh my God,' said E., 'what *does* he eat?'

We had been given instructions as to the *mozo*'s maintenance. He was to sleep on or by the car but not *in* the car. He was to get his own food for which he was to be given a peso a day. A number of pesos had been pressed upon us, one to be doled out every morning or the *mozo* would spend the entire amount at once on tequila and bottled orangeade. An excess of these were apt to give the *mozo* a melancholy, and when he had a melancholy he was unreliable.

The *mozo*, on the other hand, had the money for our oil and petrol. It had been considered unheard of that we might pay for these ourselves, and not seemly that there should be accounts, except for the simple arithmetic of the *mozo*'s pesos, between us and the cousins of Doña Concepción. The *mozo* would spend his own money as he wished, but would never touch his master's or a sum so far beyond his computations. Thus, we had been entrusted with the money for the *mozo*'s food, and the *mozo* with the money for our petrol.

All had a difficult time of it. The *mozo* would not eat, and we could find no petrol. Such pumps as there are, at Toluca, at San José Purúa, were closed.

'*No hay.*'

'But why?'

'*No hay.*'

We were carrying a reserve. I put the thought out of my mind.

We had meant to lunch at San José, a Lourdes-and-Spa for the rheumatic, but found the place taken over by the newly shod. A jukebox was playing tangos from a ghastly new hostelry. So instead we ate a picnic in a mulberry grove in the valley of Zitacuaro. As soon as we had turned our backs the *mozo* untied the handkerchief from over his mouth, produced tortillas and red pepper, and ate.

In the afternoon we did some serious climbing. Then we descended into a region of small lakes. It was not inhabited.

E. looked up from her book. 'You know, I think there hasn't been a single car on this road all day. Perhaps there just is no gas.'

There came after all a village. I stopped to make some sleeveless enquiries and while I stopped the *mozo* flicked an eyelid. A woman came forward from a stand with a bottle of orangeade. Another economic gesture and the *mozo* was provided with a measure of tequila and a pinch of salt. Again he untied his handkerchief. First he licked the salt, then he gulped the tequila, then slowly but in one pull he drank down the orangeade. Then he held out his peso note, keeping his palm flat until he had got the copper change.

The next place was large and the inhabitants had heard of *gasolina*. It was to be had in a near remoteness. The *mozo* made an auction-room gesture and repeated his performance. There was still some change.

'Better not stop again,' said E.

'Much better.'

'Are we all right for gas?'

'I suppose so.'

We were. And so once more at nightfall we arrived at Morelia. It was a warm, dry December evening and my thoughts were mainly on petrol.

Some inter-politico squeeze was going on and half the motored population of the Republic was stuck at Morelia on their way to Christmas celebrations in the central west. There was a three day old queue, two miles of Buick behind bus behind Buick stretching from the bean fields to the garage plaza. I took E. and bags to the hotel, drove back, put the car at the end of the queue and, beginning to understand his uses, left the *mozo*. I returned on foot.

Morelia was of course full up to the last square cot. Families were sleeping on pallets in hotel corridors. The only people who were comfortable were ourselves – Don Luís having booked for us in advance at a small place we had not noticed half a year ago, where we were well looked after and rather undercharged – and a troupe of actors from California who were some weeks gone with a film and had taken over a floor of the Hotel Virrey de Mendoza.

I saw the stars, jingling in Mexican riding costumes, emerge from the Mendoza Bar. A crowd of youths and women was hanging about the entrance.

'*¡Un quinto! ¡Por amor de Dios un quinto!*'

The stars drew fountain-pens.

'*¡Por caridad de la Madre de Dios un QUINTO!*'

The pens wavered. The outstretched hands were bare. Two sets of blank stares met.

The crowd fled. The stars looked much put out.

★

On the morning of the second day petrol had come in. By noon the hotel *mozo* received a communication – I never knew in what way – from our *mozo* that it was time for me to come out to move the car. This I did three times that day. By teatime, I had got as far as the actual town. Then the garage closed.

'Well, you can't expect them to work late,' said the hotel manager, 'not after a heavy day like this. They've been making much money today, I shouldn't wonder if they stayed closed now for the rest of the week.'

They did not, however, and by next evening the petrol had run out again.

The car was now well advanced into the town. It stood in the main street of Morelia, the *mozo* sitting inside hat and all, and the sight was one not easy to avoid. Whenever I saw him he was in that position; I did not go into the question of his sleeping one at all. Every morning I took him a peso, but he continued to nourish himself exclusively from a stock of tortillas and red pepper. Once E. bought him a meat-cake. He appeared not to see it, so E. left it by him on the seat and next time we went it was gone. After this we would leave fruit and sandwiches in the car. Sometimes they disappeared, sometimes not. We would bring a bag of sweet buns, saying 'for your dinner', and find them untouched two hours later. We learnt that he took food only when it was not wrapped, in small quantities and placed quite near him. It made us feel very uncomfortable.

Every night, warming over dinner, I would tell E. what I was going to say to the *mozo*, how I would beg him to communicate, implore him to speak. Every morning it seemed unattemptable.

More petrol arrived and I spent an afternoon moving the

car a few feet every ten minutes. At closing time, it was opposite the Virrey de Mendoza where it was much admired. The handsomest car we've had in the queue yet, they said.

Next morning it was moved on again towards more humble quarters. Then the garage shut for the weekend.

Don Otavio sent an anxious telegram. Reassured him with the reason for our delay. On Monday morning we received a second:

ASK FOR ONE JOSE MARIA ARTEGAS AND MENTION ENRIQUEZ NAME

'Indeed,' said the manager, 'José María Artegas. He is well known. At present he is working with the film artists at the Mendoza. He is their local confidence man. I shall send him to you at once.'

José María Artegas said that he had the honour of being our and Don Enriquez' servant. He said his poor house and humble person and meagre services were at our disposal though at present it was petrol people were most after. He said that as it happened he was managing certain international stores which, though not exactly for liquidation, were in excess of computed consumption to the extent of a disposable surplus. At the door he said not to bring the car but to bring a *mozo* and a barrel.

I did. The *mozo* paid. There was no change.

'What *I* should like to know,' said E., 'is whether we are instrumental in rooking Hollywood, or whether Hollywood is in with Señor José María Artegas.'

★

Don Otavio had had the considerate idea to save us a change of car and break of journey at Guadalajara, as well as the long boat trip from Chapala. We were not to go by either of these places but continue west in the state of Michoacán, take the Colima road and, at the point from which we would see Lake Chapala, leave the car and proceed to a village on the south shore, named Tuscueca, from where a boat would take us across the narrow part to San Pedro in less than forty minutes. The car would be fetched and driven back again to the Guadalajara highway – a matter of a mere hundred miles – by Doña Concepción's cousins and their chauffeur. Don Otavio wrote that this was the way his father used to travel when arriving from Mexico; nobody had tried it for some years, but Mr Middleton had said that he saw no reason why it should not work. I looked at the map and saw that he might be right.

'*My* father,' said E., 'told me never to trust a short cut.'

'Well, I shouldn't call it that.'

We had a hard time finding Tuscueca as the lake could be seen from many points, and villages from none.

The south shore of Lake Chapala, so pleasantly divined from the other side, is reedy, bare and windy. After taking several wrong cactus fields, we got at last to Tuscueca and found it darkest mud-hut.

There was no boat.

The inhabitants lay doggo. There was nowhere to sit down. We felt somewhat conspicuous. 'What if there is no boat?' said E.

'There will be a boat.'

'What if they mixed up the day? What if they didn't get our telegram? S., I had a bad feeling the moment I heard that Mr Middleton was in on this.'

'I think I can see a sail.'

'*I am not* going to stand here like Madame Butterfly.'

'We could go back to the car, *if* we can find it. We could sleep in the car. Like the *mozo*. You know, I believe he did all the time.'

It was not a sail.

'Oh, for an honest train,' said E. 'This teaches us for trying to travel like nineteenth-century satraps.'

Then there was the sound of an engine. Don Enriquez' launch slid through the waters. In the prow stood Domingo and Andreas holding blankets, shouting, waving.

'*¡Adiós, adiós!* Doña E., Doña Sibilla, *adiós!*'

And in the stern, gleaming, stood a large tea-basket.

E. and I looked at each other: 'It is not possible. It cannot be. All as before?'

'All as before.'

Part Four

THE END OF A VISIT

Chapter One
RETURN TO SAN PEDRO

Pervixi: neque enim fortuna malignor unquam
eripiet nobis quod prior hora dedit.

HOW DESCRIBE that slow winter, so leisured in unfold-ing, so brief in passage, that was a radiant summer? How record the long lull, the safe sequence, the seamless span of equal days . . .

Tâche donc, instrument des fuites, Ô maligne
Syrinx, de refleurir aux lacs où tu m'attends!

. . . .

Ainsi, quand des raisins j'ai sucé la clarté
Pour bannir un regret par ma feinte écarté
Rieur, j'élève au ciel d'été la grappe vide
Et, soufflant dans les peaux lumineuses, avide
D'ivresse, jusqu'au soir je regarde au travers.
O nymphes, regonflons des souvenirs divers.

We were then each working on a book and had reached midstream, that prosperous passage between the struggle of the beginning and the obsession of the end, when the book moves with its own existence and has not yet absorbed one's own, and the daily quarrying is an anchor rather than a burden, a secret discipline at once attaching and detaching, muffling and heightening the rest of living. Within these shafts we strayed at will between two dreams, the life of our books, and the life of the hacienda.

Every day we wore linen clothes, every day we bathed. We had never been so free. Letters were lost or late, everything else in abeyance among those birds and fruit and flowers – anxiety, money, love; the vicissitudes of friends, the miseries of politics, ourselves perhaps.

Christmas was celebrated with barbarity and opulence.

At midnight on Christmas Eve, a harassed wanderer was reported at the gates, requesting the loan of a mule, a *mozo* and a lantern. Don Otavio went out to see.

It was Mr Waldheim. 'He was much upset, poor man. He would not come in.'

'What is he doing with your mule and lantern at this time of night?'

'He said he was going to Ajijíc to spend Christmas with the witch from Germany. I hope there is nothing wrong.'

'I hope not.'

Next morning early, Mrs Waldheim rode over and had a talk with Don Otavio. Diana Rawlston was supposed to have been madly in love with Don Otavio fifteen years ago, with the mothers all against it; though Mr Middleton said that there was never anything in it, and one's own impression was that she adored her dachshund husband. Mrs Rawlston, it appeared, had turned him out of the house last night for singing a German song. Just as Karl was sitting down at the piano, with the tree lit up too . . . Karl had cried.

'Diana is miserable, and Mrs Rawlston won't have him back,' said Don Otavio. 'Diana says it will break his heart if he has to spend Christmas without her and the children. We must try to do something.'

'What *was* the German song?' said E.

'A Christmas song. "Holy Night".'

'Oh dear,' said E., 'those Germans.'

'Would it do any good if you talked to Mrs Rawlston?' said Don Otavio.

'No,' said E.

'Otavio, what if you asked them all to your *tertulia* tonight?' said I. 'Mrs Rawlston could scarcely . . . though of course she could. Perhaps it isn't such a good idea.'

'What if Mr Waldheim feels like singing "Stille Nacht" here?' Said E.

'It is not a good idea at all. Mr Middleton is coming. Do you not remember, or had you left when Mrs Rawlston called Mr Middleton a nigger-lover? He has been very angry ever since. He says he will see anyone he pleases in his house. Poor Blanche says that now he wants to ask a Negro friend to stay, only Mr Middleton does not know any Negroes and he does not like anyone to stay with him.'

'He might draw Mrs Rawlston's thunder tonight. Mr Middleton is made of sterner stuff than poor Waldheim seems to be.'

'I cannot ask Mrs Rawlston having asked Mr Middleton first and knowing how he feels about her,' said Don Otavio. 'It is unthinkable.'

'I don't see,' said E., 'why Mrs Waldheim and the Waldheim children cannot all have a nice Christmas with the homoepathic lady from Magdeburg, which I understand is the place she originally came from?'

'That would not be respectful to Diana's mother,' said

Don Otavio, 'the way Mrs Rawlston feels about the Germans, poor people.'

'It did not prevent her from marrying one.'

'I suppose in the circumstances Mr Middleton would be delighted to have the Waldheims to Christmas dinner,' said I.

'Diana would not wish to leave her mother all alone,' said Don Otavio.

'Mrs Rawlston can hardly be sharing her son-in-law's sentiments about that festival,' said E.

'Besides we could ask her here,' said I.

'You *forget* Mr Middleton,' said Don Otavio.

'Mr Middleton is having the Waldheims at *his* house.'

'He cannot,' said Don Otavio. 'He is dining with me. That is a previous engagement.'

'You would be relieved.'

'That is not the point,' said Don Otavio.

'Well, what are we to do? The Waldheims cannot be separated; Mr Waldheim and Mrs Rawlston, and Mrs Rawlston and Mr Middleton must be separated; Mr Waldheim is not allowed in Mrs Rawlston's house, Mrs Waldheim may not go to the German witch's, Mr Middleton may not ask anyone to his and Mrs Rawlston cannot be asked here. We need more houses.'

'There is Peter Saunders and his sister at San Antonio,' said Don Otavio. 'They keep more to themselves, but Peter is a great friend of Diana's and Mrs Rawlston likes Peter. You must take the boat and call at their place now and explain it all to them. You did meet them once, did you not?'

'*It is unthinkable,*' said I.

'Impasse,' said E. 'I've never seen such a lot of people with so many different susceptibilities. I will go after all and *speak* to my countrywoman, these southerners needn't think they own the world.'

But it was no good. Mr Waldheim would have to spend the evening at the witch's harmonium, drinking herb tea; and Mrs Waldheim would sit with her mother under the blazing new electric light, trying to make it nice for the children, pulling crackers . . .

Don Otavio's housekeeping was at high pitch that day. In the afternoon I went for a long walk. It was warm and such Indios as I passed were carried by their donkeys. In a mango grove I met another figure evidently abroad for exercise. It was an old friend. The last time I saw him was in Paris in the spring of 1939, he was studying I think, with Lhôte; the last I heard of him was from Singapore in '42.

'Jack,' I said, 'this isn't possible.'

'I've been doing portraits of the provincial Governor's wife and sisters, and their jewels. Now I'm staying with a friend of mine down the lake.'

'I always thought you wouldn't stick to painting.'

'Come back to Peter's place with me and have some tea. It's only a mile or so. You know Peter Saunders and his sister, don't you?'

'I don't think so.'

'They are charming.'

He was right. In the next months we saw the Saunders constantly; we became great friends; we still are. Peter's sister lives in England and if Peter ever leaves Mexico, he and I have an engagement to motor in the French Pyrenees. Yet during all that time, they never touched a card in my presence

or mentioned that afternoon at Mrs Rawlston's house. I often
wanted to, but never brought myself to the point.

That Christmas Day, Jack D. and I walked into their patio.

'How do you do,' they said.

'How do you do,' said I.

Later Peter showed me over the house he had slowly built
with, and sometimes against, the advice offered by Mr
Middleton. 'The worst of it is,' he said, 'that the old boy is
generally right.'

Presently Peter said, 'What is all this about Diana's husband
being turned out in the middle of the night? Do you know
anything about it? Do tell us.'

'Oh, it is too bad. Mrs Rawlston *is* naughty. Poor Diana.
We must try to do something.'

So Mrs Rawlston dined with the Saunders at San Antonio,
and the Waldheims came to Don Otavio's party at San Pedro.
They brought the wild boar, half cooked, and Domingo and
Andreas handed it round, hair and all, after the ninth *posada*
just before the nesselrode pudding and the marzipan camel.
Mr Middleton enjoyed himself like one o'clock with Doña
Anna; Doña Anna's band never ceased the *mañanitas* and Mr
Waldheim sat good and quiet with his wife and children.

Chapter Two
CLOUDS

A MONG THE servants all was *regular*: Guadalupe nursed
the fowls, the cook cooked, the laundress washed,
Jesús gardened. 'What has happened to all of them?' I said to
Guadalupe, 'Angelita is sober, Carmelita isn't being beaten,
Andreas doesn't eat the sugar and say it was the horses. What
is going on?'

'It is the priest,' said Guadalupe. 'When Jesús started
beating his wife again, we sent for him. He frightened them
very much.'

'Good Lord,' I said, 'of course Jesús *is* back. Wasn't he off
to make his fortune in Texas?'

'He did not go to Texas, *niña*; he drank his mother's cow.'

Preparations for the hotel were going on in a leisurely way.
Things arrived from Guadalajara and Don Otavio was having
them polished and put away in cupboards. Don Enriquez had
won a big case for a big *politico* – 'I believe it was settled what
they call out of court,' said Don Otavio – and he and Doña
Victoria had gone to Paris. Doña Concepción was expecting
a baby and did not come out so often now, so it was I who
sat with Don Otavio and Don Otavio's Juan over lists and
plans, and rowed with them in the cool of the evening to
Tarrascan villages to order rugs and glass. The current
products of those local manufacturers were usually hideous

but they were able to copy the decent older designs, often their own, Don Otavio asked them to reproduce. Don Otavio loved to shop. His difficulty lay in getting anyone to make or sell him more than six of anything, which was perhaps just as well as at the time there wasn't too much money. There *was* the capital his aunt had put up, Don Otavio explained, but she was not letting him have that all at once. Doña Isabella-María had a new confessor who was interesting her in a grotto in the valley of Zapopan where a boy had seen a blue light that spoke. When the boy recovered, his goitre had gone. It was all very pious and important, Don Otavio said, his aunt and the Bishop of Guadalajara were looking into it, there were more cures of goitres, but just at the moment the grotto did rather hold up the hotel. They had meant to open for Holy Week, at the latest for the rains, now what with Enriquez away too, one did not know. Also there was the question of the clientele.

'Enriquez says the way to get one is to advertise. In foreign newspapers. But all kinds of people read them nowadays . . . It is a little delicate.'

'Otavio,' I said, 'do you really want this hotel?'

'Naturally. People all the time, and dinner parties. We may get quite rich. Why do you ask in that way?'

'Oh I don't know. Only, if I had a place like San Pedro I couldn't bear the thought.'

'Ah *niña*, it is well for you to talk . . . You would not know that times have changed. Here we are all ruined and have to make our money. Enriquez says we must be realists.

'But do not worry yourself. I will have a manager to see to all that. A gentleman-manager, not a businessman from Mexico who would run the hotel like a ministry. An English gentleman gentleman-manager. I do hope we can get the one your friends said they would write to, the one they said you knew.'

'Oh, Otavio, I told you they aren't friends. And I can't think of a single gentleman-manager I know. Though it *was* kind of you to put them up.'

'They were two very charming gentlemen,' said Don Otavio, and I let it go at that.

Chapter Three

A TRIP IN THE JUNGLE:
MR MIDDLETON WINS

'YOU ARE RIGHT, I cannot stand Acapulco,' said Peter Saunders. 'And I have no wish to see that other place. All the same the Pacific Coast must be lovely. If only one could get to the parts one cannot get to. And now I know one can. There is a place below here, an Indian fishing port with one clean inn on a cool beach. No mosquitoes. The Middletons have been going every January, sly-boots. That's the one time of year you're supposed to be able to get a car through the Colima jungle. I wish we'd all go. There aren't many places like that left, you know; in a few years it'll be an airline and bungalows. Do come. You can go to Yucatán in February. It won't take us long. A day or two down to Autlán, that's the last place one can stay in before the jungle. One day each way for that. One's *got* to get through in one go. It's heavenly, full of orchids and dwarf parrots. *If only* I knew the way.'

'Don Otavio might. They used to own half of Colima.'

'I don't think Don Otavio can read a map,' said Jack D.

'It wouldn't be on a map,' said Peter, 'it's that kind of trail. Two trails. Richard Middleton says one must on no account take the other one.'

'It *would* mean asking Mr Middleton.'

'I shan't,' said Peter. 'Not after the way he was right about my chimney.'

I did ask Mr Middleton. He was much pleased. He said it

was not difficult but a question of choosing the right trail according to the weather. He drew a chart. He made a list of equipment. He told what to wear; he worked out a timetable. The great thing, he said, was to get to Autlán good and early on the day before crossing the jungle so as to have a clear six hours of daylight for doing any little thing that needed seeing to. He said we had much better wait a week or two, then he could come along and arrange everything. He could not get away at present because of the cucumber frames, besides it was still early for the journey, there was bound to be water in the arroyos.

The next day he called to discuss a spare dynamo, first-aid and vaccination. In the evening he sent a message asking us to weigh our prospective kit so that he might work out a rational way of disposing it between two cars. Then he sent a *mozo* over to San Antonio for the measurements of Peter's dickey. For the water-filter, the *mozo* explained; it was very large.

Peter was furious. A simple serious rage. He was not going to keep Birmingham hours in the jungle, he said, and the only way out for us now was to go at once. 'We'll say you didn't have the time to wait until the end of the month.'

'Very well. Only Mr Middleton hasn't said yet *which* trail to take in *which* weather.'

'If he's worked it out by himself, I don't see why we can't. We aren't morons. Have you ever travelled with Richard Middleton? I have. We go now, or we don't go at all.'

We went next morning, before lunch that is, Peter, Jack and I and Peter's two cocker spaniels. 'Richard Middleton always leaves his with the American vet at Guadalajara,' said Peter. 'I shall take mine.' Peter's sister was on her way back to England, and E., in so many words, had refused to come.

Between us we brought – two thermos flasks, one of them not very well insulated, a pint of rum, a Woolworth bottle of insect repellent, a box Kodak, Mr Middleton's chart, a medal lent by Don Otavio, some books and the dog's baskets. Jack also had a penknife. We lunched at Chapala, where Peter kept his car, and we did not get to Autlán that day.

We found a waterfall. We bathed, and Peter washed the dogs. 'Mountain water, so good for their coats,' he said. 'Do you mind if I give them some of your insect oil?' Presently we picked some limes and mixed the tea from one thermos with the ice in the other and the rum from the bottle. After nightfall we got to a village that was having a fiesta. It was a creepy fiesta – a crocodile of youths walking around the plaza in one direction, and one of girls in another; men bent over silent, sticky games of chance at acetylene-lit booths. We thought of Mr Middleton and enjoyed everything. We liked the watermelon, and Jack lost five pesos in coppers trying to learn to understand the lotto. He and Peter had drinks in a cantina where I was not allowed; we bought some stew and garbanzas at a stall and ate our dinner in the street. For the dogs we got a piece of grilled meat and fed them tactfully in the car. Then we saw a bitch with the mange. We gave her some food and she looked at us.

'Oh, what good is that going to be tomorrow,' said Peter. 'They're everywhere. Let's get out of this place. I wish we hadn't stopped.'

'When I tell your *mozos* that dogs have to eat the same as they do,' said Jack, 'they giggle. Can't their priests do something?'

'*They* could, but they don't.'

After that, we stopped for the night at the first possible place.

But in the morning the sun was bright. Again we dawdled. Peter bought some tiles, and Jack bought hats in markets. We stopped to look at pretty village churches, intimations of baroque traced in pink sand by a child's finger, already sinking. The road was steep. Below three thousand feet, the fields began to look dried up and we to feel the heat of the low country.

'Not much chance of the arroyos being flooded,' said Peter.

We reached Autlán at dusk with a flat tyre.

Peter said there must be a torch somewhere, but when we found it the battery had given out.

'Never mind. We'll get the damned thing changed tomorrow morning.'

The inn at Autlán proved to provide the necessities of life. We were served with an ample supper of fried eggs, tough beef steak, maize cakes and chilli in an unkempt patio. There was tepid bottled beer and we were told that we could certainly have boiled water tomorrow. The *Padrona* was rather immersed in a sheaf of sewing machine catalogues, but brightened when she found out that we could read.

Spanish advertisements are rich in metaphor and very long. The catalogues rumbled on like seventeenth-century funeral orations.

The *Padrona* thanked us.

'Now have you made up your mind which one you want?' said Peter.

'I do not want a sewing-machine. I have three.'

'Then why bother with all those catalogues?'

'I like the explanations. They are more beautiful than the pictures.'

'The literary life,' said Jack. 'We must tell E.'

We were lit to our sleeping quarters with a candle. They were two vast attics, one for men, one for women. There were no other female travellers at Autlán so I was alone in mine. The beds were planks, solid wooden planks, with clean sheets. I chose one.

'Like girls at a fashionable school,' I said next morning. 'To keep their backs straight. You know it's no worse than lying on the floor, as long as one doesn't try to turn. How impossible of me to have slept on a plank for the first time in my life, and made a thing of it, and thought of girls' schools, when so many people had to.'

'I had to,' said Jack, 'I dare say so has Peter. That doesn't make it any the less uncomfortable now and I'd *much* rather think of girls' schools.'

'I say,' said Peter, 'do you think we ought to have that tyre mended before we start? My spare *is* in rather poor shape.'

Mr Middleton had spoken of six new tyres, extra inners and a patent lubrication to spray the rubber with every half-hour in the heat. I knew better than to mention this.

'We might as well,' said Jack.

There was no one in Autlán able to perform this feat. Jack said *he* could, there was nothing to it.

'So like my grandfather's motoring days,' said Peter.

Then Jack said that Peter didn't have at all the right things for mending a tyre, and this was not the way he'd been taught to in the army.

Peter said not to be such a fusspot, they might as well have Mr Middleton, and everyone knew American mechanics mended everything with a bit of string and a hairpin.

Jack said he wished he had a hairpin; and anyway what about air?

'Oh, for Christ's sake, one thing at a time,' said Peter.

I left the scene. Driving to the coast was not well thought of at Autlán. In fact it was not thought of at all. It did not lend itself. Were they sure now? Quite sure. From Navidad perhaps, yes, from Navidad the oxen went down one, two, three times a month to the coast. From Navidad, not from Autlán.

I told this to Peter. 'Nonsense,' he said, 'half the time they don't know what they are talking about. Richard Middleton, damn him, no one mentioned Navidad before. Where is it?'

'I don't know.'

'There you are.'

Jack had mended the tyre and found a boy and a bicycle pump. 'I'm filthy,' he said, 'before I do anything I must have a bath.'

So they lit a brazier at the inn, heated three buckets of water and carried them upstairs.

The pump boy vanished at once.

Jack came out in white flannels, smelling of bay-rum. 'That tyre's still half down.'

'Did you give him any money?'

'Fifty centavos.'

'I shouldn't have done that.'

'You might have told me, Peter.'

'Oh, I can't think of everything. I wish we'd get out of this bloody place soon.'

'It *would* be nice to get to the sea,' said I.

'Better have something to eat first, though.'

'Here?' said Jack. 'Not again?'

'There isn't anywhere else. You can save your steak for the dogs.'

At breakfast there had been eggs, beef steak, maize cakes, beans and chilli. 'What's for lunch?'

341

'Let me see,' said the *Padrona*. 'I can give you some eggs. Fried eggs. And a nice beef steak. And some beans.'

'Aren't there any vegetables?'

'Yes, beans.'

'Fresh vegetables?'

'*No hay.*'

'No tomatoes? Any fruit?'

'*No hay.*'

'There must be fruit. We saw it on the trees.'

'*No hay.*'

After this meal, Jack produced another boy. Peter sent him away.

'You must find the first one,' he said. 'He was paid and he's got to finish the job. It's a matter of principle. They mustn't think they can get away with everything. You don't want to spoil the place.'

Jack said considering the amount of time he intended to spend at Autlán he could not care less.

'That's frightfully irresponsible,' said Peter.

'I can't bear to think of anything happening to Mr Middleton,' said I, 'I believe Peter is only waiting to step into his shoes.'

'Don't see why he should have it *all* his own way. And Jack, there's your boy. Or is it?'

'I wouldn't know.'

'Oh, hell, let them both pump. And then let's be off. It'll be dark soon.'

'That's what I've been thinking,' said Jack.

'How far is it, exactly?' said I.

'Oh, about thirty miles as the crow flies. One can't tell about those trails. Perhaps more.'

'*Do* we go as the crow flies?'

'Do you both *want* to spend another night at Autlán?' said Peter.

'Not if we can get to the coast.'

'Can one get through in the dark, Peter?'

'I shouldn't think so.'

'Is one supposed to sleep in the jungle?'

'Three people and two dogs in one car,' said I.

So as it happened we did find ourselves at Autlán with several clear hours of daylight in front of us. I took Jack aside. 'I am sorry to sound like *The Boy's Own Paper*, but oughtn't we to have an axe or something to hack our way through the vegetation?'

'I thought of that. And it's the one thing we'll be able to find here.'

So we went and bought a machete.

Later we played nursery dominoes. We dined off eggs, beef steak, maize cakes, beans and chilli, and went to bed at ten. We were down again at quite an early hour. We had breakfast, then Peter said he had better give the dogs a good walk before we got to the really hot parts; so what with that and Jack's bath and Jack's packing and waiting for a dinner to be put up to take for the dogs, we started at a quarter to eleven.

First there were about ten miles of abrupt descent and these we did in just under two hours. It was blazing hot.

'We'll be in the shade soon,' said Peter. 'Wait till we get into the orchid forests.'

Then the dirt-road stopped and a trail began. We got out Mr Middleton's chart. Nothing looked in the least like it.

'Well, there's only one trail as far as I can see,' said Peter; 'that's a mercy.'

We plodded through a stretch of sand and conifers. It was

343

heavy going and we had to change down into first. The engine was heating fast.

'What oil are you using, Peter?'

'Oh, I don't know, the one the man at Chapala puts in.'

It was tricky progress. Every now and then we got stuck. Each time it was a business getting off again. The dogs would hurl themselves out of the car and had to be urged back in; the wheels turned *in statu quo* churning up the sand. We spread a mackintosh, two of us pushed, the third accelerated, and we all hated the noise made by the engine at these moments. Afterwards the ones who'd pushed had to scramble on to the car again without arresting its precarious motion. At the best of times, these would have been exertions; in that temperature, they took on the nature of an improbable subhuman tussle, something that had already taken place in a remembered tale of stokers.

Then undergrowth began, first straggly then thickening, and suddenly we were in a steaming tunnel of fat leaves. But the trail continued sandy and the attention of all three of us remained riveted on the driving. Then there was a clearing, and once more we were among thin pines.

'Was that the jungle, Peter?'

'Look, people!' There was indeed a coconut-fibre hut.

'*This* is what we want,' said Jack, leaping out of the car, 'that mackintosh is in shreds.'

He returned with the roof. 'Nice bit of matting. They said they'd make themselves another one for tonight.'

Presently we came to the first arroyo. It was full of water. 'It can't,' said Peter. 'Not with everything else bone dry. It's not the season.'

It was not deep, our battery was high – in one terrific splash Peter drove across. We held our breaths: the engine

344

went on running. Soon the greenery closed in again; the sand became clogged with damp and we got stuck almost at once. The fibre matting proved a help.

'I believe I've been stung,' said Jack when we were going again.

'So do I.'

'Biting insects, sucking insects. What else do you expect?' said Peter.

'I think I saw a green-and-pink wing.'

'It *is* all rather beautiful, or isn't it?'

'I think it's more what we used to call bogus,' said Jack.

The dogs did not like it at all. They were miserable – ears sticking to their heads, tongues lolling out; they shook, they whimpered, they would not come out any more at the stops but moistly clung to us. We gave them the water in the thermos.

There was another clearing and, soon, another arroyo. It was dry.

'You see,' said Peter.

The radiator was boiling; the gears stuck. 'Better stop for a bit. Give it a chance to cool down.'

'Cool,' said Jack.

We waited, watching the steam hiss from under the bonnet. Jack smoked, Peter and I pressed a warm, quivering spaniel to our sides.

The next arroyo was flooded. We got through, but once on the other side the engine sputtered out. 'Sparkplugs got a bit wet. Nothing to it. Soon be dry in this weather.'

'What time is it?' said Jack.

In the next arroyo we got stuck. The water was half-way up the engine, the spark plugs did not dry. 'If there was one hut, there must be others,' said Peter. 'Let's look in different directions, but one of us must stay with these poor dogs.'

Jack and Peter went off, I stayed in the car in mid-arroyo. It was impossible to read or doze and I was frantically bored.

After a time, a man passed with an ox. They were most obliging; and when Jack and Peter returned very cross, they were gone and the car the other side of the arroyo, all dry.

'How very clever of you,' they said.

Presently the trail forked into four. We took the second on our right. After half a mile it fizzled out in a lot of sand. We had a hard time turning the car. 'Well, that eliminates one road,' said Peter.

'Do you think it is *wise* to go on?' said Jack.

'Not particularly,' said Peter. 'But I'll be damned before I let Richard Know-All Middleton tell me he told me so. We've got to get to the coast.'

'And I do want to see the seaside,' said I.

The outside-left trail led into thick growth. We turned up the windows, and the car charged and crashed like an inexperienced elephant.

'This must be the real jungle,' said Peter.

Later we came again on to open ground, the trail hardened but began to climb sharply. 'How very odd,' said Peter.

We were never out of first now, the radiator had not been off the boil for two hours. There was another arroyo, with very rapid water, we just cleared it.

'You know that you're murdering your car, Peter?' said Jack.

'It's my car, isn't it?'

'We all know that. Stop being an ass.'

'We may be only a few miles from the coast.'

'Or we may not.'

'My dear Jack, you don't think we *can* get back . . .'

'Very likely not. But it's worth trying while we still have an engine running and some daylight.'

'I do have rather a frightful headache, Peter,' said I.

'Take an aspirin. I must say you two are difficult people to travel with.'

It was settled by the next arroyo which was deep, wide and swift. We plunged a stick: the water came above battery level. 'Oh, very well then,' said Peter, 'have it your own way.'

From then on, we only strained to keep going. There was not much we could do, having neither tools nor time, but we exercised a kind of faith-healer's intensity on keeping the car together. It smoked, it steamed, it spat oil; two valves gave out, the clutch and self-starter jammed, every joint, spring and piston shrieked and wheezed in a reproachful death-rattle. We got stuck; we lost the trail; we heaved, we cranked, we fanned, we pushed and propped. We prayed. Jack did wonders without a hairpin. We dared not think of the two bad arroyos to be recrossed, we dared not look at the oil or the petrol gauge; above all we dared not look at the time. If we spoke it was only to reassure the dogs. We had a blow-out and put on the threadbare spare. The nuts were red-hot, the jack slipped, and in spite of complete concentration the change consumed twenty-five minutes.

At a quarter of an hour before dark we reached the clearing with the coconut-fibre hut.

The owners asked us in. They tried to give us some maize cakes, beans and chilli. We drank a little coconut milk and bowl after bowl of arroyo water. Jack and I could not understand a word anyone said. Peter later told us that it must have been one of the Otomian dialects. It was clear, however,

A VISIT TO DON OTAVIO

that we were to spend the night. The hut was full of people and our open-handed hosts had neglected to replace the roof they had given to Jack earlier in the day. The consequent exposure might have added greatly to our discomforts had we been in a more receptive state, and this pursued me as an intensely significant parable throughout a near delirious night. As I lay on the ground between an Indio woman and a spaniel (there had been no room for bringing in their baskets and moreover the dogs were frightened by the presence of some pigs), I came near fitting the answer to the question of the brotherhood of man. It was a beautiful piece of joinery, though hard to hold, and it had to be slid into the opening of a large square box, an exacting and elusive task, and whenever I had the box complete, it came to pieces in my hands.

Next morning we were ourselves.

'I am sure Richard Middleton would have antagonized our hosts at once,' said Peter; 'they'd never have asked him to dinner and put him up. That's one for us.'

We actually started at dawn. As our engine could now only be expected to make intermittent efforts, we reached the dirtroad in the early afternoon and got ready for the climb to Autlán.

'We *will* be there for dinner,' said Peter.

'Oh,' said I. 'And to think we'll all be able to get a bath.'

'You haven't been gone a week,' said Don Otavio, 'did you not like the coast?'

'It is always a pleasure to get back to San Pedro.'

'You are too kind.'

★

'Never mind about not getting there,' said E., 'I dare say you would have found one of those resorts. But I'm glad for you to have had the journey. You always seem to have to do so much when *we* travel, having those two nice young men with you must have been such a change. As our mothers used to say, travelling with a man makes all the difference.'

'Don Otavio wishes to know,' said Juan, 'whether you would like anything special for dinner tonight, or whether you would prefer Soledad to take you up a tray?'

'A tray, please,' said I, 'if I may.'

Chapter Four
LOCAL MEDICINE

The next day I felt quite ill. Mr Middleton hurried to my bedside like a Christian gentleman.

'You did take the quinine in the doses I wrote down for you?'

It was the moment for pure truth. 'There wasn't any,' said I.

'What? Ran out of quinine? I've never heard of such a thing.'

I said nothing, allowing truth to be stained.

'I wonder whether my doses were large enough. Hard to tell with some people.'

Then he said, 'That's no malaria. Temperature's all wrong for one thing. That's nothing I would know anything about. If I were you I'd get myself into Guadalajara as fast as I can. One or two good men there, though I dare say they won't have the laboratory equipment for dealing with this kind of thing. They'll be wanting to make some tests. Interesting sort of germs you pick up in those places. Always something new. You're sure you took all the precautions I told you? Peter look after you properly?'

'Not all the precautions.'

'Ah well, everyone's bound to slip up over something. Even experienced people do.'

'You see,' said I. 'I don't think I can face the journey to Guadalajara. I know I cannot.'

'You are in rather poor shape. All the same, you know . . .'

'There must be someone?'

'Local man drinks as you probably heard, and what you want is a specialist.'

'A specialist for *what*?'

'Oh, quite. They'll have a hard time diagnosing this.'

I did not budge. At that time I would rather have died than moved, and I knew I was not dying. 'It's no worse than some peculiar kind of influenza,' I told E., 'the only thing to do is to keep quiet.'

Don Otavio, who did not share E.'s prejudices in favour of qualified attendance, abetted me. 'All these doctors will make her very ill,' he said.

'She is ill,' said E.

'Too ill to leave San Pedro.'

All the same Don Otavio thought I ought to see someone. The servants would expect it. We compromised on the witch from Germany.

'It is an inflammation,' she said; 'it will go. I have exactly the right remedies for you only I do not have them any more.' She grabbed among a bagful of phials with minute white pellets. 'Soon I shall be able to get them again from Germany.'

Meanwhile I was to drink an infusion of oat straw and rest. E. waylaid her and they had a talk.

I did not get better. One, two weeks passed; Don Otavio was an angel of kindness. There was nothing he did not do. He would have read to me had I asked him to. One day, when I was low, the cook sent up a candle and a spoon. Every bone in my face was aching horribly and I was never without an ice compress. I lit the candle, heated the spoon in the flame, and pressed it against my cheeks and forehead. The heat was grateful. After an hour of this treatment I began to feel some slight relief.

Guadalupe came in. 'What are you doing?' she said. 'Don't you know what a candle and spoon are for? You are not so ignorant. You must wait until you are alone and then you must light the candle and hold the spoon and say your prayers backwards. It is not something one does often, but at times it helps.'

A few days later came a message that the doctor was ready to see me. It was his sober week. 'You must go, *niña*,' said Don Otavio, 'Soledad, Juan and Domingo and I will take you in the boat.'

'You must go,' said E.

'Can't he come here?'

'Only for childbirth.'

The doctor saw me in his mother-in-law's chemist shop. He was an avuncular, middle-aged man, neither very Indian nor very white, in a spotty brown lounge suit. His manner to me was kind. We sat in two wicker chairs and conversed while the business of the pharmacy, chiefly sweets and purgatives, went on around us. Then the doctor took me out into the street where the light was better, and while I stood against the shop front looked into my throat and nose. He prescribed some drops and Cachets-Midi, an anti-grippe preparation I remembered from my childhood and which I daresay had been popular with Bazaine's men, and himself helped his mother-in-law to hunt for the cachets on the shelves.

That evening my temperature went up to 106°. It did not come down next day. Dr Gomez had relapsed into a tequila coma and could not be appealed to. Don Otavio took over.

He sent for penicillin; he sent the boat for the telephone operator at Chapala who had learned to give injections. For twenty-four hours the telephone service remained closed. Later on the operator was taken to and fro every few hours to deal both with the injections and the trunk calls. In one day the temperature went down, on the second I was out of pain, on the third I was up. In a week I was well.

Dr Gomez, sober once more, wished to have particulars of the cure. Once more he examined me outside the chemist shop. 'All your symptoms are gone, *niña*; it was a very wonderful idea. You must have twelve more doses to prevent recurrence,' he said; and behind the counter gave me the most painful inter-muscular injection I ever had.

I completed the course in the switchboard cell at the Chapala Post Office.

'But whatever made you think of it, Otavio?' I said.

'We do not have many medicines. Only Cachets-Midi and Asperina and these new things. You had tried Cachets-Midi.'

'It might have gone wrong,' said E.

'No, no. My aunt's nuns use penicillin all the time. It is very harmless.'

Later on, I happened to mention this to a doctor in New York. 'What you had sounds like this new kind of anthrax infection,' he said, 'it's getting quite common on the eastern seaboard. I wonder where you got it. Did you say you spent the summer before in Connecticut? Well, that's it. It takes some time to develop; I guess the heat or something brought it out in Mexico. Good thing for you it did. Penicillin? That's interesting, now. We've been thinking of that. Of course, we're still at the experimental stage.'

Chapter Five
THE BEST OF ALL
POSSIBLE WORLDS

I WAS SHOCKED to find how much time had passed.
February was almost out, and it was now too late in the
year for Yucatán.

'Now you must stay,' said Don Otavio.

'We shall have to go some day. We must begin to think of
that.'

'Do not think of it. Not for a long time. No, not Easter.
You cannot leave before the Rains. Then everything will look
again like last year. You must stay at least until the Rains.'

We did not think of it; not for an extra gift of months.
Every day was itself, but I knew that time was up. Though I
was well again, my illness had left me with a kind of nervous
acuteness that made everything come to me edged and over-
exposed. Above all I craved slow pace, and I seldom left San
Pedro. I would take a canoe out on to the lake or ride with
Don Otavio in the afternoon, but I did not like to be away
for more than a few hours at a time. E. had taken to seeing
people at Chapala and to spending every now and then a day
or two at Guadalajara with Jack and Peter, and she also kept
up a fighting acquaintance with Mrs Rawlston. It was a dry
Dry Season, the price of maize had gone up and there were
pistolleros in the hills. Don Otavio did not like us to go out
after dark without Andreas or Domingo with a musket. E.
had demurred at appearing at a house for dinner like something out of Fra Diavolo.

354

'I never carried a gun on Park Avenue during Prohibition,' she told Don Otavio.

But Don Otavio did not twig at all, and E. soon became unconscious of her bodyguard. I made the *pistolleros* an excuse for not going out for dinner.

E. used to come back elated from Mrs Rawlston's. 'Such a set-to about the Dixiecrats,' she said; 'and I must say the old girl does do one well – pity you didn't go – we had some very wonderful red wine, something quite rare I should think. Her son-in-law gave it to her, she told us. Didn't make a crack at him, civil as civil, Mrs Rawlston must be mellowing.'

'Soledad has accepted Domingo,' said Don Otavio.

'*Not* Domingo.'

'He has been asking her a very long time. He is a good boy, with not much ill-temper. They will both live here.'

'How can she marry a clod-hopper?'

'It is suitable. Who knows, one day they may even get married in church. We must give them a nice party for their first wedding.'

'Bottom in the woods of Athens,' said E.

More and bigger crates arrived and a set of little enamelled disks with numbers which enchanted Don Otavio and mystified the servants.

Andreas took hammer and nails, Juan carried the box, Don Otavio and I followed, and we set out to do the numbering of the bedrooms. We paused outside a door. Juan proffered his box, Don Otavio pulled out a disk as though he were drawing the lottery. 'Shall we put this one here?'

'Oughtn't there be a system,' said I.

'That is a good idea. Let us think of one.'

We came to Don Otavio's father's room, now occupied by E. and her stack of note-books. 'We will make this one No. 1, do you not think so?'

Andreas hammered the disk above the door.

'That looks very nice. It looks – businesslike?'

'I do not like it at all,' said I.

'Niña, you are in a very strange mood.'

A few days later he said, 'I think you were right. I should not have had the numbers put on before the alterations. Enriquez writes that some of these big rooms will have to be divided up. And there are too many loggias. He says you can buy houses now all ready built, and he may bring some to put up on the lawn. He and the manager will see to all that. You know the manager is coming, the one your friends are sending. I have engaged him. My aunt is much pleased. She is sending him his fare from New York.'

'What did you say his name was?'

'Bill. Bill Something. I am not good at English names.'

'And what is this English gentleman doing in New York?' said E.

'Managing an hotel. The letter says he is an experienced manager.'

March and April passed without major disturbances. I received one or two letters that required an answer, the servants all got exceedingly drunk during Holy Week, the weather became almost hot and the level of the lake sank. The American Consul at Guadalajara gave a large party and Mr Middleton organized an excursion to one of the lake's unexplored islands. E. went to the first, I went to neither. Then the President of the Republic arrived on a goodwill tour of the Province. There was a dance at the gubernatorial palace, which proved publicity for Jack's portraits; the President gave a banquet at Guadalajara for some three hundred of his more presentable supporters, and a bucolic spread at Chapala for the rank and file. Diaz' daughter's villa was opened for the occasion, and we all went over to see the food and drink arrive for two thousand persons.

E. was delighted. 'Exactly like the political barbecues in the West,' she said. 'Liquor and roast animals.'

'Do ladies go to political functions in your country?' said Don Otavio.

The presidential train from Mexico was so late that the ball, the banquet and the picnic had each to be put a day forward, a fact which much increased the popularity of the visit.

'Now everything must be paid for twice,' explained Don Otavio.

We watched the arrival of the presidential party from the balcony of a house in Chapala. First there were some motorcyclists with guns. These must have somewhat out-distanced the body, because after them there came nothing. Ten minutes later the motorcyclists sped by from the opposite direction, and after another while reappeared from their original one. There was another pause, and then came a dozen open cars jamful with ruffians in large hats, covered with firearms. Another pause and another line of cars similarly occupied.

'What a lot of bodyguard,' said E.

'These are the guests,' said Don Otavio. 'Look, this is the Judge of the Western District Division. And here is the Mayor of Zapopan.'

'And where is the President?'

'He does not eat with them. He will come later.'

Indeed after some hours a fast limousine sped by revealing behind closed windows a man with a sallow complexion and a top hat. All that time, fireworks never ceased. Guadalajaran firms, the inn at Chapala, petitioners, villages, private persons from about the lake, all had sent contributions – rockets, handmade crackers, set-pieces sparkling *Viva Mexico* or *Remember the Poor of San Tomás Poxcuoco*, flying beetles sporting the President's initials. The witch from Germany had sent a large balloon bearing in phosphorescent lettering the legend,

GEDENKET DES VOLKES DER DICHTER UND DENKER

It was well made and stayed aloft a long time. For weeks we would see it floating through the night past the San Pedro shore. It frightened many drunks, and gave her much prestige.

'You seem sad, *niña*, is there anything I can do for you?'

'Oh, Otavio . . . You've done everything.'

'No, no. Is there anything that would put you in spirits? We have been quiet lately. Would you like to go to Doña Anna's? Would you like Guadalupe to kill a chicken? Would you like some champagne?'

'Otavio.'

'Yes?'

'I hardly like to say it. You know those Lafites and Margaux ageing away in your cellar . . . One does think about them. You said you and your brothers didn't like them, otherwise I wouldn't mention it, well to me, you see, the thought of having a glass of claret of that kind . . . Oh, do stop me.'

'Those French red wines? I gave them to Mr Waldheim.'

'Otavio!'

'He asked me for them. He went to the cellar with me at Christmas, you remember.'

'Oh.'

'I did not quite like giving them to him as I do not like them myself. It seemed so discourteous. I insisted on his taking at least a bottle of Cointreau. He really seemed to want to have those wines, poor man.'

'All of them?'

'Yes, I believe so. He came himself with the *mozo*. There were just a few dozen. You could have had them all.'

The date of Soledad's wedding was settled for the third week in May.

In the same week, the new manager was to arrive and Don Enriquez return from Europe. Transformations were to begin immediately afterwards. The Blessing of the Animals was on the 24th, the Fiesta of Tlayacán the next day. Our own departure was to take place at the end of the month.

At the end of April, Jack left for San Salvador to do the presidential family in oils, and on May 1st Doña Concepción had her baby. Don Otavio went to Guadalajara and stayed away a week. During his absence a young Mexican arrived by hired boat from Chapala and asked to see the boss. It was Guillermo.

We expressed mutual surprise.

'You are staying at the hotel?' said Guillermo.

'What hotel?'

'Don Otavio de X.'s hotel. I am the new manager.'

We packed him off to Guadalajara to interview Don Otavio.

'I thought this was a resort,' said Guillermo.

'*Not yet*,' said E.

'You know that I did most of the running of that place? You will say so?'

'A Thirty-third Street rooming house?' said E.

'It was an experience.'

'No doubt,' said E.

'Weren't you expected weeks later?' said I.

'You see, it was not quite convenient for me to stay on in New York just now.'

'I see,' said E.

'Poor Guillermo,' I said later, 'we must have been a shock – that is one thing Rosencrantz and Guildenstern mismanaged, they could hardly be expected to foresee my falling ill in the jungle and our spending our old age with Don Otavio – and you were not kind.'

'Ought we to warn Otavio?'

'I suppose he can see for himself.'

'I wonder.'

'See what, anyway?'

'Yes, that's it. What do we really know *against* Guillermo?'

'Nothing.'

'Exactly. It is only the unfortunate impression he makes. That is really so above board of him.'

'It will be fair warning.'

Don Otavio returned from Guadalajara in low spirits. His aunt had been difficult. There was no pronouncement yet on the grotto.

'She is getting impatient, poor woman. She said if they are

not going to make up their minds soon she will turn to something else. She says that Rome is getting very stuffy these days. They were pleased enough with any little miracle when we were keeping the Faith alive under the Reform Laws, but nowadays, it's all witnessed testimonials in triplicate. It is not enough for them to know that the goitres are gone, they want proof that the people *had* goitres. As if it could be a cure if they were not gone. Like a lot of tax-collecting clerks. Aunt Isabella-María says she does not like that kind of attitude, it is unbecoming to a great church.'

Don Otavio had come back without Guillermo. He had sent him to Mexico, there was nothing for him to do here and Guillermo had expressed alacrity to go. There were a number of things to be bought that could not be had at Guadalajara, and Guillermo was taking some papers for Don Luís to sign.

'The post is so unreliable,' said Don Otavio.

Domingo had been sent with Guillermo. 'Bill is now our manager, it is suitable for him to have a *mozo* and there will be much to wrap up. We are going to have new vases everywhere. Domingo wanted to see Mexico, now that he is going to be married he will not be able to travel so much.'

It grew warmer. Every day the lake sank a little lower, there were no signs of rain. Soledad sewed, Guadalupe fattened some turkeys, Doña Anna was asked and arranged for lending the band, Don Otavio deliberated whether he should give Domingo a bicycle. Don Jaime came out to remove his things from the hacienda, and we were getting ready to move across to the villa the day after the wedding. Workmen had already dumped a mess of plaster in the back patio. Proofs arrived of advertisements appearing in the travel sections of the *New York* and *Chicago Tribunes* and the *Los Angeles Examiner*. Don Otavio pasted them in a scrapbook – started for the occasion – and forwarded to Don Enriquez the first letter of inquiry that came from Pittsburgh and demanded particulars as to sports, recreation facilities and rates. E. paced the ex-governor's bedroom and tried to finish a chapter.

Three days before Soledad's wedding we received word that Guillermo had been arrested at Mexico City.

Don Otavio started at once for Guadalajara. He returned two days later, very quiet. He came up to the west loggia and sat down. 'Poor Bill is going to be all right. Enriquez is getting him out, and Luís is looking after him. There is no kitchen in his prison. I do not think it is poor Bill's fault. It is something about his papers and their not believing that he is a foreigner. It is not unusual. Enriquez says they did not like the place they arrested Bill in, and they did not like his hotel, and that there is also something about a debt. But it is all quite sad and unfortunate. My aunt is very angry. You see, Bill used our name. Enriquez is angry, too. And Jaime. And now I must go and speak to Juan. *¿Con su permiso?*'

'Can you make out what happened?' I said to E.

'Only that Guillermo made his unfortunate impression on the police.'

In the evening Don Otavio said, 'There has been a general disgust and now there will be no hotel.

'Oh, it is not only poor Bill. The Vatican has decided against the grotto, we just heard. You see, Aunt Isabella-María had already put in quite a lot of money. She is very much upset, poor woman. She has sacked her confessor. She says in candles alone it was a fortune and what good is the land to her now. She says it makes one understand why there are so many heresies. And Enriquez, too, has taken against the hotel. He says that now that politics are again more open to us, he is not going to waste his time making up weekly bills and that *I* am no good, and in any case Americans with money go to Europe again now, and he's seen what people want and it is not San Pedro. He says San Pedro is hopeless. You would have to spend millions and pull down every stone and pillar to get something that looked more like San José Purúa, and then where would you be? At Tlayacán with no road. The money has just been spent again on the President's Ball. And a motor boat, Enriquez says, is all very well but people want to use their cars, and such tourists future as the Republic might have was all on the Taxco Highway, and he has heard of a nice piece of land, right on the road, not all cluttered up with old houses, and he might think of developing that. You couldn't even sell San Pedro, he says. Nowadays the only thing to do with a place like that was to live in it, that was all it was good for.'

'So the workmen will *not* start in the day after Soledad's wedding?'

'There will be no wedding. They took Domingo.'

'What do you mean?'

'The military. When the police went for poor Bill, they arrested Domingo too. It is usual. They let him go, but they found out that he had not done his service – he would have been called up last year but Enriquez got him off, only it does not count outside the province. So they sent him straight into barracks at Uxpan.'

'For how long?'

'A few years. It depends.'

'Poor Domingo.'

'No, no. Domingo always said he wanted to be a soldier. He was so disappointed last year. Enriquez didn't know, he naturally arranges exemption for our servants – something with a list in the War Office – and then it was too late.'

'And what does Soledad say?'

'Soledad is pleased. She says she would like to stay on as she is. She did not want to get married to anyone very much. Domingo pressed her so. That reminds me I must tell Guadalupe to take those turkeys off milk.'

A few days later Don Otavio said, 'Now poor Domingo will not have his wedding present. He did want a bicycle so. Perhaps I could send it to him just the same. Where he is now, he will even be able to use it. They have a road.'

'Otavio,' said I, 'do you mind very much?'

'About the hotel? It would have been nice to get rich and have charming people to stay all the time. But Enriquez says they would not always be charming and we might get poorer. Perhaps it would have been a little difficult. We had so many disgusts over it already. Who knows, perhaps Enriquez is right and I might not have been very good at business. Now there will be more room for my nieces and nephews, and E. can have my father's suite whenever she comes. Perhaps it is better so?'

Our tickets arrived. We were flying to New York straight from Guadalajara.

'You know I shall rather mind leaving here,' said E. 'I

seem to feel no elation at the thought of returning to my native country. I am afraid Otavio will be right: we shall be quite uncomfortable and not at all happy.'

Three days later we all went to Chapala for the Blessing of the Animals. Every beast from round the lake, in festive garb, had been taken to receive this annual benediction. I still felt uneasy in large gatherings, and the crush, the noise, the smells, were overwhelming. A crowd of mules and bullocks in garlands and fine hats was pressing in the square outside the church. The smaller animals had a difficult time of it. There were new-born calves carried on donkey's backs, pigs clasped to bosoms, chickens clutched by clumsy children, canaries in cages, a huge, angry parrot on a stick, guinea-pigs in apron pockets, ducks in baskets, cats immune on roofs, mongrel puppies led by strings, Don Otavio's Maltese terrier and Doña Anna's griffon carried in the arms of chauffeurs, and smelly rabbits carried by their ears; between them wandered straying geese, shuddering horses and a superb white angora goat who was made way for by the bullocks. The church bells went like mad, the priest held up the sacrament, outlined a blessing, people knelt in the dust raising their screeching beasts towards the holy monstrance – *Mamacita del cielo, Madrecita María, Virgen,* howling, braying, yelping, cackling, squeaking . . .

'Such a kind letter from Luís,' said Don Otavio in the evening. 'He does not seem to mind the trouble we gave him at all. He likes Bill. He says he is very nice and useful and if he can manage to arrange poor Bill's papers so that he can stay, he will make him his secretary. Luís says Bill is just what he always wanted, and Bill likes to be at Mexico. He would have been wasted at San Pedro.'

The next day the Enriquezes and the Jaimes came down for the Fiesta of Tlayacán. Doña Concepción looked ravishing; Doña Victoria was in a good mood.

'You may as well keep Mama's silver, *chiquito*,' she said to Don Otavio. 'It belongs to San Pedro.'

We sat over a long *comida*, and only started for Tlayacán in time for the bull-baiting. As we entered the pleasure grounds, the grandstand, a scaffolding of sticks and strings, collapsed and two hundred people in gay clothes, very drunk, slowly, slowly fell into the trees below.

'I think I shall go now,' I said. 'I don't think the fiesta can do any better than this.'

'I will go too,' said Doña Concepción; 'I still feel the heat rather.'

We went back to San Pedro, accompanied by Andreas. At the gates we sent him back to the fiesta. The other servants had gone, the house was still. 'Let us sit on the west loggia,' said Doña Concepción, 'I like it at this hour.'

Presently she said, 'You are leaving tomorrow, are you not? For long?'

I did not answer.

'How lonely it will be for Tavio. You heard our news? The Enriquezes are going to live at Mexico. Enriquez says Guadalajara has had it; and my husband will have to go quite often. So the children and I shall spend more time at San Pedro. Jaime wants the new baby to be brought up in the country. He says it is time for us to learn to live again like gentlemen.'

'That will be nice for Otavio,' said I.

'Yes, I think it will. I was so sorry for him at first about the hotel. Now, I am not sure. They all turned on him and said it was his fault, and what with Enriquez having these new ideas and Aunt Isabella-María being so put out at having lost all that money and saying she was tired with dealing with confessors and managers and people like that, it was very sad for poor Otavio. But now Aunt Isabella-María has had such a charming letter from Monsignore saying that, privately speaking, everybody in Rome liked the idea of Aunt Isabella-María's grotto so much, and that the miracles sounded splendid, but perhaps just at present it was not wise to develop another grotto, having so many on their hands, one had to be so careful these days when there are communists to think of as well as Protestants. After all, if the grotto was what they all hoped it was, it was sure to triumph in the end, and Aunt Isabella-María was too faithful a daughter not to understand that it did not matter in the least whether it remained unrecognized for another hundred years or two. Aunt Isabella-María was to think of the lives of the Saints, and perhaps something could be arranged for buying back some of the candles. Meanwhile if there was any little personal favour she would like to ask, Monsignore was almost certain to be able to assure her that someone who had laboured so devotedly and so long in the Good Field would not find an unsympathetic ear.

'So now, you see, Aunt Isabella-María and Monsignore are going to make poor Tavio into a kind of titular lay *abbé*. I do not quite know what that is; Monsignore is working at it. There was Tavio still wondering about his vocation, and not being able to be a priest because he hasn't studied for the examinations, and not wanting to go away and be a monk somewhere. And now he is going to be made into an honorary *abbé* and live at San Pedro. He will be here *and* in the Church, and it will be so nice for him to have ecclesiastical status. No one can tease him any more for not being married. He can have us to stay with him, and all his friends. Aunt Isabella-María will leave him money to stay at San Pedro just as he is. She always said she was going to leave her money to the Church but did not like the idea of leaving it away from the family, but now of course Tavio will be in the Church in a way, so it would be leaving the money to the Church and keeping it in the family too, would it not? Perhaps it is a good thing after all about the hotel, because San Pedro will be Tavio's retreat, and Monsignore could not have made him into that kind of an *abbé* if Tavio were running an hotel. Perhaps it was not meant to be. Perhaps Tavio can find out now whether he really has a vocation. Or perhaps this is his vocation? Belonging to the Church, living at San Pedro? Who knows, Doña Sibilla, it may be all for the best?'

'It all is for the best,' said I.

TITLES IN SERIES

For a complete list of titles, visit www.nyrb.com or write to:
Catalog Requests, NYRB, 435 Hudson Street, New York, NY 10014

J.R. ACKERLEY Hindoo Holiday*
J.R. ACKERLEY My Dog Tulip*
J.R. ACKERLEY My Father and Myself*
J.R. ACKERLEY We Think the World of You*
HENRY ADAMS The Jeffersonian Transformation
RENATA ADLER Pitch Dark*
RENATA ADLER Speedboat*
AESCHYLUS Prometheus Bound; translated by Joel Agee*
CÉLESTE ALBARET Monsieur Proust
DANTE ALIGHIERI The Inferno
DANTE ALIGHIERI The New Life
KINGSLEY AMIS The Alteration*
KINGSLEY AMIS Dear Illusion: Collected Stories*
KINGSLEY AMIS Ending Up*
KINGSLEY AMIS Girl, 20*
KINGSLEY AMIS The Green Man*
KINGSLEY AMIS Lucky Jim*
KINGSLEY AMIS The Old Devils*
KINGSLEY AMIS One Fat Englishman*
KINGSLEY AMIS Take a Girl Like You*
ROBERTO ARLT The Seven Madmen*
WILLIAM ATTAWAY Blood on the Forge
W.H. AUDEN (EDITOR) The Living Thoughts of Kierkegaard
W.H. AUDEN W.H. Auden's Book of Light Verse
ERICH AUERBACH Dante: Poet of the Secular World
DOROTHY BAKER Cassandra at the Wedding*
DOROTHY BAKER Young Man with a Horn*
J.A. BAKER The Peregrine
S. JOSEPHINE BAKER Fighting for Life*
HONORÉ DE BALZAC The Human Comedy: Selected Stories*
HONORÉ DE BALZAC The Unknown Masterpiece *and* Gambara*
VICKI BAUM Grand Hotel*
SYBILLE BEDFORD A Legacy*
SYBILLE BEDFORD A Visit to Don Otavio: A Mexican Journey*
MAX BEERBOHM The Prince of Minor Writers: The Selected Essays of Max Beerbohm*
MAX BEERBOHM Seven Men
STEPHEN BENATAR Wish Her Safe at Home*
FRANS G. BENGTSSON The Long Ships*
ALEXANDER BERKMAN Prison Memoirs of an Anarchist
GEORGES BERNANOS Mouchette
MIRON BIAŁOSZEWSKI A Memoir of the Warsaw Uprising*
ADOLFO BIOY CASARES Asleep in the Sun
ADOLFO BIOY CASARES The Invention of Morel
EVE BABITZ Eve's Hollywood*
CAROLINE BLACKWOOD Corrigan*
CAROLINE BLACKWOOD Great Granny Webster*
RONALD BLYTHE Akenfield: Portrait of an English Village*

* *Also available as an electronic book.*

NICOLAS BOUVIER The Way of the World

EMMANUEL BOVE Henri Duchemin and His Shadows*

MALCOLM BRALY On the Yard*

MILLEN BRAND The Outward Room*

SIR THOMAS BROWNE Religio Medici and Urne-Buriall*

JOHN HORNE BURNS The Gallery

ROBERT BURTON The Anatomy of Melancholy

CAMARA LAYE The Radiance of the King

GIROLAMO CARDANO The Book of My Life

DON CARPENTER Hard Rain Falling*

J.L. CARR A Month in the Country*

BLAISE CENDRARS Moravagine

EILEEN CHANG Love in a Fallen City

EILEEN CHANG Naked Earth*

JOAN CHASE During the Reign of the Queen of Persia*

ELLIOTT CHAZE Black Wings Has My Angel*

UPAMANYU CHATTERJEE English, August: An Indian Story

NIRAD C. CHAUDHURI The Autobiography of an Unknown Indian

ANTON CHEKHOV Peasants and Other Stories

ANTON CHEKHOV The Prank: The Best of Young Chekhov*

GABRIEL CHEVALLIER Fear: A Novel of World War I*

JEAN-PAUL CLÉBERT Paris Vagabond*

RICHARD COBB Paris and Elsewhere

COLETTE The Pure and the Impure

JOHN COLLIER Fancies and Goodnights

CARLO COLLODI The Adventures of Pinocchio*

IVY COMPTON-BURNETT A House and Its Head

IVY COMPTON-BURNETT Manservant and Maidservant

BARBARA COMYNS The Vet's Daughter

BARBARA COMYNS Our Spoons Came from Woolworths*

ALBERT COSSERY The Jokers*

ALBERT COSSERY Proud Beggars*

HAROLD CRUSE The Crisis of the Negro Intellectual

ASTOLPHE DE CUSTINE Letters from Russia*

LORENZO DA PONTE Memoirs

ELIZABETH DAVID A Book of Mediterranean Food

ELIZABETH DAVID Summer Cooking

L.J. DAVIS A Meaningful Life*

AGNES DE MILLE Dance to the Piper*

VIVANT DENON No Tomorrow/Point de lendemain

MARIA DERMOÛT The Ten Thousand Things

DER NISTER The Family Mashber

TIBOR DÉRY Niki: The Story of a Dog

JEAN D'ORMESSON The Glory of the Empire: A Novel, A History*

ARTHUR CONAN DOYLE The Exploits and Adventures of Brigadier Gerard

CHARLES DUFF A Handbook on Hanging

BRUCE DUFFY The World As I Found It*

DAPHNE DU MAURIER Don't Look Now: Stories

ELAINE DUNDY The Dud Avocado*

ELAINE DUNDY The Old Man and Me*

G.B. EDWARDS The Book of Ebenezer Le Page*

JOHN EHLE The Land Breakers*

MARCELLUS EMANTS A Posthumous Confession

EURIPIDES Grief Lessons: Four Plays; translated by Anne Carson
J.G. FARRELL Troubles*
J.G. FARRELL The Siege of Krishnapur*
J.G. FARRELL The Singapore Grip*
ELIZA FAY Original Letters from India
KENNETH FEARING The Big Clock
KENNETH FEARING Clark Gifford's Body
FÉLIX FÉNÉON Novels in Three Lines*
M.I. FINLEY The World of Odysseus
THOMAS FLANAGAN The Year of the French*
BENJAMIN FONDANE Existential Monday: Philosophical Essays*
SANFORD FRIEDMAN Conversations with Beethoven*
SANFORD FRIEDMAN Totempole*
MASANOBU FUKUOKA The One-Straw Revolution*
MARC FUMAROLI When the World Spoke French
CARLO EMILIO GADDA That Awful Mess on the Via Merulana
BENITO PÉREZ GÁLDOS Tristana*
MAVIS GALLANT The Cost of Living: Early and Uncollected Stories*
MAVIS GALLANT Paris Stories*
MAVIS GALLANT A Fairly Good Time *with* Green Water, Green Sky*
MAVIS GALLANT Varieties of Exile*
GABRIEL GARCÍA MÁRQUEZ Clandestine in Chile: The Adventures of Miguel Littín
LEONARD GARDNER Fat City*
ALAN GARNER Red Shift*
WILLIAM H. GASS In the Heart of the Heart of the Country: And Other Stories*
WILLIAM H. GASS On Being Blue: A Philosophical Inquiry*
THÉOPHILE GAUTIER My Fantoms
JEAN GENET Prisoner of Love
ÉLISABETH GILLE The Mirador: Dreamed Memories of Irène Némirovsky by Her Daughter*
JEAN GIONO Hill*
JOHN GLASSCO Memoirs of Montparnasse*
P.V. GLOB The Bog People: Iron-Age Man Preserved
NIKOLAI GOGOL Dead Souls*
EDMOND AND JULES DE GONCOURT Pages from the Goncourt Journals
PAUL GOODMAN Growing Up Absurd: Problems of Youth in the Organized Society*
EDWARD GOREY (EDITOR) The Haunted Looking Glass
JEREMIAS GOTTHELF The Black Spider*
A.C. GRAHAM Poems of the Late T'ang
WILLIAM LINDSAY GRESHAM Nightmare Alley*
EMMETT GROGAN Ringolevio: A Life Played for Keeps
VASILY GROSSMAN An Armenian Sketchbook*
VASILY GROSSMAN Everything Flows*
VASILY GROSSMAN Life and Fate*
VASILY GROSSMAN The Road*
OAKLEY HALL Warlock
PATRICK HAMILTON The Slaves of Solitude*
PATRICK HAMILTON Twenty Thousand Streets Under the Sky*
PETER HANDKE Short Letter, Long Farewell
PETER HANDKE Slow Homecoming
ELIZABETH HARDWICK The New York Stories of Elizabeth Hardwick*
ELIZABETH HARDWICK Seduction and Betrayal*
ELIZABETH HARDWICK Sleepless Nights*
L.P. HARTLEY Eustace and Hilda: A Trilogy*

L.P. HARTLEY The Go-Between*

NATHANIEL HAWTHORNE Twenty Days with Julian & Little Bunny by Papa

ALFRED HAYES In Love*

ALFRED HAYES My Face for the World to See*

PAUL HAZARD The Crisis of the European Mind: 1680–1715*

GILBERT HIGHET Poets in a Landscape

RUSSELL HOBAN Turtle Diary*

JANET HOBHOUSE The Furies

HUGO VON HOFMANNSTHAL The Lord Chandos Letter*

JAMES HOGG The Private Memoirs and Confessions of a Justified Sinner

RICHARD HOLMES Shelley: The Pursuit*

ALISTAIR HORNE A Savage War of Peace: Algeria 1954–1962*

GEOFFREY HOUSEHOLD Rogue Male*

WILLIAM DEAN HOWELLS Indian Summer

BOHUMIL HRABAL Dancing Lessons for the Advanced in Age*

BOHUMIL HRABAL The Little Town Where Time Stood Still*

DOROTHY B. HUGHES The Expendable Man*

RICHARD HUGHES A High Wind in Jamaica*

RICHARD HUGHES In Hazard*

RICHARD HUGHES The Fox in the Attic (The Human Predicament, Vol. 1)*

RICHARD HUGHES The Wooden Shepherdess (The Human Predicament, Vol. 2)*

INTIZAR HUSAIN Basti*

MAUDE HUTCHINS Victorine

YASUSHI INOUE Tun-huang*

HENRY JAMES The Ivory Tower

HENRY JAMES The New York Stories of Henry James*

HENRY JAMES The Other House

HENRY JAMES The Outcry

TOVE JANSSON Fair Play *

TOVE JANSSON The Summer Book*

TOVE JANSSON The True Deceiver*

TOVE JANSSON The Woman Who Borrowed Memories: Selected Stories*

RANDALL JARRELL (EDITOR) Randall Jarrell's Book of Stories

DAVID JONES In Parenthesis

JOSEPH JOUBERT The Notebooks of Joseph Joubert; translated by Paul Auster

KABIR Songs of Kabir; translated by Arvind Krishna Mehrotra*

FRIGYES KARINTHY A Journey Round My Skull

ERICH KÄSTNER Going to the Dogs: The Story of a Moralist*

HELEN KELLER The World I Live In

YASHAR KEMAL Memed, My Hawk

YASHAR KEMAL They Burn the Thistles

MURRAY KEMPTON Part of Our Time: Some Ruins and Monuments of the Thirties*

RAYMOND KENNEDY Ride a Cockhorse*

DAVID KIDD Peking Story*

ROBERT KIRK The Secret Commonwealth of Elves, Fauns, and Fairies

ARUN KOLATKAR Jejuri

DEZSŐ KOSZTOLÁNYI Skylark*

TÉTÉ-MICHEL KPOMASSIE An African in Greenland

GYULA KRÚDY The Adventures of Sindbad*

GYULA KRÚDY Sunflower*

SIGIZMUND KRZHIZHANOVSKY Autobiography of a Corpse*

SIGIZMUND KRZHIZHANOVSKY The Letter Killers Club*

SIGIZMUND KRZHIZHANOVSKY Memories of the Future

K'UNG SHANG-JEN The Peach Blossom Fan*

GIUSEPPE TOMASI DI LAMPEDUSA The Professor and the Siren

GERT LEDIG The Stalin Front*

MARGARET LEECH Reveille in Washington: 1860–1865*

PATRICK LEIGH FERMOR Between the Woods and the Water*

PATRICK LEIGH FERMOR The Broken Road*

PATRICK LEIGH FERMOR Mani: Travels in the Southern Peloponnese*

PATRICK LEIGH FERMOR Roumeli: Travels in Northern Greece*

PATRICK LEIGH FERMOR A Time of Gifts*

PATRICK LEIGH FERMOR A Time to Keep Silence*

PATRICK LEIGH FERMOR The Traveller's Tree*

D.B. WYNDHAM LEWIS AND CHARLES LEE (EDITORS) The Stuffed Owl

SIMON LEYS The Death of Napoleon*

SIMON LEYS The Hall of Uselessness: Collected Essays*

GEORG CHRISTOPH LICHTENBERG The Waste Books

JAKOV LIND Soul of Wood and Other Stories

H.P. LOVECRAFT AND OTHERS Shadows of Carcosa: Tales of Cosmic Horror*

DWIGHT MACDONALD Masscult and Midcult: Essays Against the American Grain*

CURZIO MALAPARTE Kaputt

CURZIO MALAPARTE The Skin

JANET MALCOLM In the Freud Archives

JEAN-PATRICK MANCHETTE Fatale*

JEAN-PATRICK MANCHETTE The Mad and the Bad*

OSIP MANDELSTAM The Selected Poems of Osip Mandelstam

OLIVIA MANNING Fortunes of War: The Balkan Trilogy*

OLIVIA MANNING Fortunes of War: The Levant Trilogy*

OLIVIA MANNING School for Love*

JAMES VANCE MARSHALL Walkabout*

GUY DE MAUPASSANT Afloat

GUY DE MAUPASSANT Alien Hearts*

JAMES McCOURT Mawrdew Czgowchwz*

WILLIAM McPHERSON Testing the Current*

MEZZ MEZZROW AND BERNARD WOLFE Really the Blues*

HENRI MICHAUX Miserable Miracle

JESSICA MITFORD Hons and Rebels

JESSICA MITFORD Poison Penmanship*

NANCY MITFORD Frederick the Great*

NANCY MITFORD Madame de Pompadour*

NANCY MITFORD The Sun King*

NANCY MITFORD Voltaire in Love*

PATRICK MODIANO In the Café of Lost Youth*

PATRICK MODIANO Young Once*

MICHEL DE MONTAIGNE Shakespeare's Montaigne; translated by John Florio*

HENRY DE MONTHERLANT Chaos and Night

BRIAN MOORE The Lonely Passion of Judith Hearne*

BRIAN MOORE The Mangan Inheritance*

ALBERTO MORAVIA Agostino*

ALBERTO MORAVIA Boredom*

ALBERTO MORAVIA Contempt*

JAN MORRIS Conundrum*

JAN MORRIS Hav*

PENELOPE MORTIMER The Pumpkin Eater*

ÁLVARO MUTIS The Adventures and Misadventures of Maqroll

L.H. MYERS The Root and the Flower*
NESCIO Amsterdam Stories*
DARCY O'BRIEN A Way of Life, Like Any Other
SILVINA OCAMPO Thus Were Their Faces*
YURI OLESHA Envy*
IONA AND PETER OPIE The Lore and Language of Schoolchildren
IRIS OWENS After Claude*
RUSSELL PAGE The Education of a Gardener
ALEXANDROS PAPADIAMANTIS The Murderess
BORIS PASTERNAK, MARINA TSVETAYEVA, AND RAINER MARIA RILKE Letters, Summer 1926
CESARE PAVESE The Moon and the Bonfires
CESARE PAVESE The Selected Works of Cesare Pavese
BORISLAV PEKIĆ Houses*
ELEANOR PERÉNYI More Was Lost: A Memoir*
LUIGI PIRANDELLO The Late Mattia Pascal
JOSEP PLA The Gray Notebook
ANDREY PLATONOV The Foundation Pit
ANDREY PLATONOV Happy Moscow
ANDREY PLATONOV Soul and Other Stories
J.F. POWERS Morte d'Urban*
J.F. POWERS The Stories of J.F. Powers*
J.F. POWERS Wheat That Springeth Green*
CHRISTOPHER PRIEST Inverted World*
BOLESŁAW PRUS The Doll*
GEORGE PSYCHOUNDAKIS The Cretan Runner: His Story of the German Occupation*
ALEXANDER PUSHKIN The Captain's Daughter*
QIU MIAOJIN Last Words from Montmartre*
RAYMOND QUENEAU We Always Treat Women Too Well
RAYMOND QUENEAU Witch Grass
RAYMOND RADIGUET Count d'Orgel's Ball
FRIEDRICH RECK Diary of a Man in Despair*
JULES RENARD Nature Stories*
JEAN RENOIR Renoir, My Father
GREGOR VON REZZORI An Ermine in Czernopol*
GREGOR VON REZZORI Memoirs of an Anti-Semite*
GREGOR VON REZZORI The Snows of Yesteryear: Portraits for an Autobiography*
TIM ROBINSON Stones of Aran: Labyrinth
TIM ROBINSON Stones of Aran: Pilgrimage
MILTON ROKEACH The Three Christs of Ypsilanti*
FR. ROLFE Hadrian the Seventh
GILLIAN ROSE Love's Work
LINDA ROSENKRANTZ Talk*
WILLIAM ROUGHEAD Classic Crimes
CONSTANCE ROURKE American Humor: A Study of the National Character
SAKI The Unrest-Cure and Other Stories; illustrated by Edward Gorey
TAYEB SALIH Season of Migration to the North
TAYEB SALIH The Wedding of Zein*
JEAN-PAUL SARTRE We Have Only This Life to Live: Selected Essays. 1939–1975
GERSHOM SCHOLEM Walter Benjamin: The Story of a Friendship*
DANIEL PAUL SCHREBER Memoirs of My Nervous Illness
JAMES SCHUYLER Alfred and Guinevere
JAMES SCHUYLER What's for Dinner?*
SIMONE SCHWARZ-BART The Bridge of Beyond*

LEONARDO SCIASCIA The Day of the Owl
LEONARDO SCIASCIA Equal Danger
LEONARDO SCIASCIA The Moro Affair
LEONARDO SCIASCIA To Each His Own
LEONARDO SCIASCIA The Wine-Dark Sea
VICTOR SEGALEN René Leys*
ANNA SEGHERS Transit*
PHILIPE-PAUL DE SÉGUR Defeat: Napoleon's Russian Campaign
GILBERT SELDES The Stammering Century*
VICTOR SERGE The Case of Comrade Tulayev*
VICTOR SERGE Conquered City*
VICTOR SERGE Memoirs of a Revolutionary
VICTOR SERGE Midnight in the Century*
VICTOR SERGE Unforgiving Years
SHCHEDRIN The Golovlyov Family
ROBERT SHECKLEY The Store of the Worlds: The Stories of Robert Sheckley*
GEORGES SIMENON Act of Passion*
GEORGES SIMENON Dirty Snow*
GEORGES SIMENON Monsieur Monde Vanishes*
GEORGES SIMENON Pedigree*
GEORGES SIMENON Three Bedrooms in Manhattan*
GEORGES SIMENON Tropic Moon*
GEORGES SIMENON The Widow*
CHARLES SIMIC Dime-Store Alchemy: The Art of Joseph Cornell
MAY SINCLAIR Mary Olivier: A Life*
WILLIAM SLOANE The Rim of Morning: Two Tales of Cosmic Horror*
SASHA SOKOLOV A School for Fools*
VLADIMIR SOROKIN Ice Trilogy*
VLADIMIR SOROKIN The Queue
NATSUME SŌSEKI The Gate*
DAVID STACTON The Judges of the Secret Court*
JEAN STAFFORD The Mountain Lion
CHRISTINA STEAD Letty Fox: Her Luck
GEORGE R. STEWART Names on the Land
STENDHAL The Life of Henry Brulard
ADALBERT STIFTER Rock Crystal*
THEODOR STORM The Rider on the White Horse
JEAN STROUSE Alice James: A Biography*
HOWARD STURGIS Belchamber
ITALO SVEVO As a Man Grows Older
HARVEY SWADOS Nights in the Gardens of Brooklyn
A.J.A. SYMONS The Quest for Corvo
MAGDA SZABÓ The Door*
ANTAL SZERB Journey by Moonlight*
ELIZABETH TAYLOR Angel*
ELIZABETH TAYLOR A Game of Hide and Seek*
ELIZABETH TAYLOR A View of the Harbour*
ELIZABETH TAYLOR You'll Enjoy It When You Get There: The Stories of Elizabeth Taylor*
TEFFI Memories: From Moscow to the Black Sea*
TEFFI Tolstoy, Rasputin, Others, and Me: The Best of Teffi*
HENRY DAVID THOREAU The Journal: 1837–1861*
ALEKSANDAR TIŠMA The Book of Blam*
ALEKSANDAR TIŠMA The Use of Man*

TATYANA TOLSTAYA The Slynx
TATYANA TOLSTAYA White Walls: Collected Stories
EDWARD JOHN TRELAWNY Records of Shelley, Byron, and the Author
LIONEL TRILLING The Liberal Imagination*
LIONEL TRILLING The Middle of the Journey*
THOMAS TRYON The Other*
IVAN TURGENEV Virgin Soil
JULES VALLÈS The Child
RAMÓN DEL VALLE-INCLÁN Tyrant Banderas*
MARK VAN DOREN Shakespeare
CARL VAN VECHTEN The Tiger in the House
ELIZABETH VON ARNIM The Enchanted April*
EDWARD LEWIS WALLANT The Tenants of Moonbloom
ROBERT WALSER Berlin Stories*
ROBERT WALSER Jakob von Gunten
ROBERT WALSER A Schoolboy's Diary and Other Stories*
REX WARNER Men and Gods
SYLVIA TOWNSEND WARNER Lolly Willowes*
SYLVIA TOWNSEND WARNER Mr. Fortune*
SYLVIA TOWNSEND WARNER Summer Will Show*
JAKOB WASSERMANN My Marriage*
ALEKSANDER WAT My Century*
C.V. WEDGWOOD The Thirty Years War
SIMONE WEIL On the Abolition of All Political Parties*
SIMONE WEIL AND RACHEL BESPALOFF War and the Iliad
GLENWAY WESCOTT Apartment in Athens*
GLENWAY WESCOTT The Pilgrim Hawk*
REBECCA WEST The Fountain Overflows
EDITH WHARTON The New York Stories of Edith Wharton*
KATHARINE S. WHITE Onward and Upward in the Garden*
PATRICK WHITE Riders in the Chariot
T.H. WHITE The Goshawk*
JOHN WILLIAMS Augustus*
JOHN WILLIAMS Butcher's Crossing*
JOHN WILLIAMS (EDITOR) English Renaissance Poetry: A Collection of Shorter Poems*
JOHN WILLIAMS Stoner*
ANGUS WILSON Anglo-Saxon Attitudes
EDMUND WILSON Memoirs of Hecate County
RUDOLF AND MARGARET WITTKOWER Born Under Saturn
GEOFFREY WOLFF Black Sun*
FRANCIS WYNDHAM The Complete Fiction
JOHN WYNDHAM Chocky
JOHN WYNDHAM The Chrysalids
BÉLA ZOMBORY-MOLDOVÁN The Burning of the World: A Memoir of 1914*
STEFAN ZWEIG Beware of Pity*
STEFAN ZWEIG Chess Story*
STEFAN ZWEIG Confusion*
STEFAN ZWEIG Journey Into the Past*
STEFAN ZWEIG The Post-Office Girl*